The Twentieth-Century Russian Novel

An Introduction

David Gillespie

BERG

Oxford • Washington, D.C.

First published in 1996 by
Berg Publishers Limited
Editorial offices:
150 Cowley Road, Oxford, OX4 1JJ, UK
13950 Park Center Road, Herndon, VA 22071, USA

Library of Congress Cataloging-in-Publication Data

A catalogue record for this book is available from the Library of Congress

British Library Cataloguing-in-Publication Data

A catalogue record for this book is available from the British Library.

ISBN 1 85973 078 7 (Cloth)
1 85973 083 3 (Paper)

Printed in the United Kingdom by WBC Bookbinders, Bridgend,
Mid Glamorgan.

Contents

Preface   vii

Introduction   1

1   Evgenii Zamiatin (1884–1937), *We* (*Мы*)   7

2   Isaak Babel' (1894–1940), *Red Cavalry* (*Конармия*)   24

3   Iurii Olesha (1899–1960), *Envy* (*Зависть*)   43

4   Nikolai Ostrovskii (1904–36), *How the Steel was Tempered* (*Как закалялась сталь*)   62

5   Mikhail Bulgakov (1891–40), *The Master and Margarita* (*Мастер и Маргарита*)   81

6   Boris Pasternak (1890–1960), *Doctor Zhivago* (*Доктор Живаго*)   102

7   Alexander Solzhenitsyn (b. 1918), *Cancer Ward* (*Раковый корпус*)   132

8   Andrei Bitov (b. 1937), *Pushkin House* (*Пушкинский дом*)   152

Select Bibliography   171

Index   178

Preface

This book has come about as a result of teaching a course on the twentieth-century Russian novel to final year students, and the merging realization of a need to provide up-to-date secondary materials for such a course. This textbook, therefore, is a response to what I see as the desirability of combining analyses of many of the novels studied in universities in one volume. It is aimed at students, and not only of Russian; it is to be hoped that the general reader interested in Russian culture will also find something of value and interest.

Each chapter concentrates on a particular novel, and I have endeavoured to structure each study in a certain way. Thus, the introduction to a novel will discuss briefly the career of its author and the reception of that work on its publication. Sometimes, when discussing a work that was banned in the Soviet Union, this introduction will touch on this work's reception in the West and then in Russia. Subsections include 'Plot', 'Theme', 'Characterization', 'Style' and 'Imagery', with a 'Conclusion' to bring each chapter to an end. In other words, the chapters offer an attempt to crystallize what I see as the main tasks of formal aesthetic criticism, and so to enable students to come to a clear understanding of the significance of a literary work. Conclusions or judgments may not be astoundingly new, but this study is not meant as a radical re-interpretation of the twentieth-century Russian literary experience.

In transliterating titles and names from Cyrillic, I have followed the American Library of Congress system. Work on it has been carried out in the libraries of the universities of Bath, Bristol, the Free University of Berlin and the Russian State Library in Moscow (formerly the Lenin State Library), and I am eternally grateful for the help given to me by the staff of these institutions. Because the book has been inspired by the work of my students, it is to them that I dedicate it, past, present and future.

Introduction

This book is not meant as a detailed historical guide to the development of the novel in Russia in the twentieth century, although generic questions are touched upon. Rather, I have chosen eight novels, seven of which are well-known in translation in English, in order to offer the kind of detailed analysis that I believe students of Russian literature require. Furthermore, no such study, explicitly geared towards students' needs, exists in English, although such guides are common in Russia itself. The novels have not been chosen arbitrarily, but with an eye to the texts most frequently studied in undergraduate courses. Some readers will no doubt quibble at the choice of novels offered, and I will be reproached for not including, for instance, novels by Andrei Platonov or Vasilii Grossman. In choosing eight novels, I have been selective, but I believe that these eight novels are studied frequently in undergraduate courses exactly because they strive to link past and present, provide graphic illustrations of Russia's twentieth-century experience, and attempt also, in their vastly different ways, to proffer a treatise on Russia's future.

The reader will find that all the quotations are in English translation followed by the Russian original; page numbers are given for both editions. This is to help both students and general readers unfamiliar with Russian but who may be reading a particular work as part of a course in comparative literature, or indeed out of informed general interest. The translation in most cases is taken from the standard published version, except for references to Ostrovskii's *How the Steel Was Tempered* (*Как закалялась сталь*), where the translations are all my own.

The novels chosen are not all part of what used to be known as Soviet literature, as those by Zamiatin, Pasternak and Bitov were originally published abroad and made their way into print in their homeland only during the years of *glasnost'*. This is not to say that these are the best novels written in Russia; rather, questions of what is 'good' or 'bad' in a literary text are more often than not based on subjective value judgments and are usually frowned upon in modern literary criticism. Rather, I have endeavoured in my approach to highlight the poetics of a work in terms of themes and style, including imagery, in order to guide the specialized and general reader around the terrain commonly known as literary analysis. Each novel is introduced with a brief outline of its creator's career and its own reception, especially but not exclusively in Russia. I have tried to avoid such issues as the 'civic-mindedness' of a given work, that is, its social importance, and have tried to steer clear of ideological questions of a novel's worth. Such questions, it seems to me, seem now rather anachronistic in the post-Soviet period, as the perception of Russian literature at last moves away from civic positions and the writer ceases to be a moral guide or teacher to his oppressed and often tyrannized people.

Nevertheless, it is possible to sketch the history of Russian literature in the twentieth century through these works. Zamiatin's *We* (*Мы*) is one of the first novels written in Soviet Russia, although it was one of the last to be published in that country before its demise on 31 December 1991. The first modernist novel in Russia (although it cannot be called the first Soviet modernist novel as it was published in the USSR only under Gorbachev in 1988), it is set in a future society run on mathematical principles where man's reason and logic are dominant. God is dead, and everyone, on pain of death, must conform in every way to the norms and rules of this society, the Single State. But the relentless rationalism of this society is offset by Zamiatin's introduction of modernist motifs such as dreams, the proliferation of vivid, often clashing colours, and highly stylized imagery. Babel''s *Red Cavalry* (*Конармия*) has a similarly modernist approach, with ornate imagery and vivid colours often contrasting with the horrors and casual brutalities of the Russian Civil War. Babel' shows his Red Cossacks creating a new world through blood and violence, yet they are simple, elemental creatures unable to comprehend the precise nature of this new world. Most of the novel, arranged as a set of short stories united through their setting and the recurrence of characters, is narrated from the viewpoint of an outsider, Liutov, a Jewish intellectual for whom the Cossacks are a natural foe. Amid the carnage and violence, there are moments of beauty and inspiration. Babel' reflects on Russia's links with the cultural heritage of Europe, the relationship of Christianity and Judaism, and, fundamentally, on the role of the artist within a collective.

This latter theme lies at the heart of Olesha's *Envy* (*Зависть*), also written in the early years of the Soviet regime and also blessed with a blaze of extravagant imagery. This short novel differs from those hitherto studied in that it concentrates more fully on modes of perception and seeing, so that what the characters see, or think they see, is not necessarily what actually is. The plot revolves around the conflict of the old world and the new world as represented by opposing sets of characters, amid fears, shared by the author himself, that the new world, rather like Zamiatin's Single State, is doing away with emotion and individualism.

When one reads Nikolai Ostrovskii's novel *How the Steel Was Tempered*, it is possible to believe that the aim of the new world built by the Bolsheviks in the aftermath of the ruinous Civil War denied any place to the individual. Here the collective is all, and through the personal trials and torments of the central character the reader is meant to learn the true meaning of devotion to the cause, self-abnegation and the triumph of the will. Despite huge odds placed before him by both human enemies and the forces of nature, Pavel Korchagin, though physically debilitated, becomes inwardly strong and totally committed – a personification of pure will.

Ostrovskii's novel is a perfect example of socialist realism in practice. This 'artistic method' was meant to replace the diffuse and individualistic literary strivings of the early Soviet years, as under Stalin, literature and the arts were required to fall into line in much the same way as had agriculture and the urban workforce during collectivization and industrialization of the late 1920s and early 1930s. Nevertheless, its champions saw it a continuation of the Russian literary tradition, rooted in a social realism but now reinforced with a defiant and, as they saw it, infallible ideological underpinning. The 'method' has been well defined by Neil Cornwell:

> Some argue that socialist realism is a logical inheritance of the nineteenth-century Russian tradition of utilitarian aesthetics in literary criticism (stemming from Belinsky and Chernyshevsky). It can very plausibly be seen, however, as a hasty and haphazard formula (concocted probably by Gorky and Zhdanov, in consultation with Stalin) hurriedly imposed from above, a crude attempt to direct and finally control the rich and varied literature which had flourished in a more revolutionary environment. Its shaky Marxist basis was given a dubious veneer of Leninist legitimacy by invoking Lenin's article 'On Party Organization and Party Literature' of 1905, which was almost certainly intended to apply only to political and publicistic writing emanating from the Party.[1]

Bulgakov's novel *The Master and Margarita* (*Мастер и Маргарита*) offers a deliberate and occasionally hilarious debunking of the socialist realist myth, as the author interweaves a plot about a frustrated and desperate writer struggling with his Muse and the woman he loves, demons on the loose causing havoc in Moscow (not least to the institutions of Bulgakov's hated Writers' Union), and Jesus Christ and Pontius Pilate. All of these narrative levels are united by the theme of moral cowardice, the necessity to be true to oneself. But more fundamentally, the novel is about the power of truth and the written word in an age of tyranny, whether this be Stalin's Russia or the Holy Land under Roman occupation. The same can be said about Pasternak's *Doctor Zhivago* (*Доктор Живаго*), with its emphasis on the truth of Christ in human history and the creativity of the poet as a guarantee of immortality. Both novels have an epic sweep; they cover large areas of human history and stand as impressive monuments to individual integrity amid the pressures and dangers of living and working in a totalitarian state.

This is even more applicable to Solzhenitsyn's *Cancer Ward* (*Раковый корпус*), which directly addresses the most catastrophic feature of Russia's twentieth-century history, the Gulag. Both the novels by Pasternak and Bulgakov, as well as Solzhenitsyn's, defy socialist realist strictures, but they also reject the experimental modernist forms of the 1920s. Rather, their point of reference is the Russian cultural tradition as represented by the century preceding 1917, and they are purposefully set in the genre of the epic novel. *Cancer Ward* differs from *The Master and Margarita* and *Doctor Zhivago* not only in its choice of grim subject matter, but also in its treatment of Soviet society and history. Solzhenitsyn attempts a bold cross-section of Soviet society, and reserves his ire mostly for the new aristocracy which attains success and surrounds itself with wealth, having built careers literally over the dead bodies of others. Here too, however, there is much symbolism, on a par with the works of the 1920s, and the moral theme is ever-present: whether in the Gulag or the cancer clinic, it is not enough simply to survive physically. In order to remain a man, one has to remain morally intact as well.

With our final novel, Bitov's *Pushkin House* (*Пушкинский дом*), we enter the post-modernist realms of fractured narrative and multiple narrative possibilities, reflections not only on the Russian literary heritage and the contemporary Soviet literary process but also on the nature of fictional discourse itself. The relationship of literature to life itself is at stake, as Bitov sets out to affirm the relevance of the pre–1917 Russian literary heritage and to denounce the betrayal of that heritage by the generation of 'the fathers' of the 'sons' that represent Bitov's generation.

In generic terms, then, we have moved from modernism to socialist realism, progressed to the rejection of this and the rediscovery of the nineteenth-century novel emphasizing moral accountability and the possibility of spiritual rebirth, and finally reached the post-modernist narrative of continuities through seeming disconnections and unity through dislocation. In thematic terms these novels, for all their obvious disparateness, have a common theme: the role (and fate) of the writer in the modern age. All the central characters are, to a greater or lesser extent, writer figures, or (in Solzhenistyn's case) figures who represent the writer's consciousness. In the introduction to his comprehensive study of Russian literature since 1917, Edward J. Brown has noted that 'the most pervasive and characteristic concern of Russian literature since the Revolution has been the paramount political problem: the fate of the individual human being in a mass society'.[2] But it is more than this: it is about the fate of the writer as the representative and the guardian of Russian culture, a rich, varied and beloved culture that provides the only source, given the paucity of political or social institutions, of national identity in the post-Communist age.

It is on this last note that I bring to an end this introduction. This is not the place for political prediction, but given the cataclysmic nature of Russian history in the twentieth century, of which the Russian novel has tried to comprehend and make sense, certain strictures would seem to be called for. Russia since the fall of the Communist regime is undergoing tremendous cultural, social and political change, and looks set to continue doing so for some time. Literature too is at a crossroads, for the traditional civic role of the writer has now all but vanished. As society democratizes, the gulf between the rulers and the ruled narrows, and so the place the writer occupies in that gulf – an alternative government, as Solzhenitsyn memorably put it – becomes increasingly invalid. Perhaps we are witnessing the normalization of literature, with its division as in other market-led societies into low-brow, middle-brow and high-brow categories.

It is not the purpose of this book to mark or indeed lament the changes in the Russian social or cultural consciousness, but rather to help the student and the general reader through some of the novels that have by and large characterized the development of the Russian literary consciousness in the twentieth century. It is to be hoped that along the way the reader will gain some insights into how some of these writers, through their faith in the truth of the written word, helped bring about the end of the tyranny that dominated, and in some cases destroyed, their lives and careers.

Notes

1. Neil Cornwell, 'Through the Clouds of Soviet Literature', *The Crane Bag*, vol. 7, no. 1 (1983), p. 18. Vissarion Belinskii (1811–48) was a radical literary critic whose work emphasised the social context and

significance of literature; Nikolai Chernyshevskii (1828–89) also belonged to the radical intelligentsia, and his novel *What Is To Be Done?* (*Что делать?*, 1863) is a landmark in utilitarian and didactic literature in Russia. In the twentieth century, Maksim Gorky (pseudonym of Aleksei Maksimovich Peshkov, 1868–1936) was an eminent pre-revolutionary writer who romanticized the struggles of the lower classes and painted scathing portraits of the bourgeoisie and aristocracy. He became known as the father of Soviet literature, as his novel *Mother* (*Мать*, 1906) was praised as the first socialist realist novel. Andrei Zhdanov (1896–1948) was Stalin's cultural spokesman for most of the 1930s and 1940s, and his report in 1946 on the literary journals *Zvezda* ('The Star') and *Leningrad* occasioned the most rigorous and repressive cultural policy that has ever existed in Russia, which lasted until Stalin's death in 1953.

2. Edward J. Brown, *Russian Literature since the Revolution*, revised and enlarged edition, Cambridge, MA, 1982, p. 1.

−1−

Evgenii Zamiatin (1884–1937), *We* (*Мы*)

Introduction and Background

Evgenii Ivanovich Zamiatin was born in 1884 in Tambov province, the son of a schoolteacher. His mother was a musician, and in his autobiography Zamiatin admits to growing up 'under the piano'. He completed his schooling in Voronezh, and enroled in the St. Petersburg Polytechnic Institute as a naval engineer. During his studies he travelled to several major ports and cities, including Helsingfors, Odessa, Alexandria, Salonika and Jerusalem. While still a student, he held pro-Bolshevik sympathies, was a political activist and even had a printing press in his room. He graduated in 1908, and in that year began writing. He only began writing seriously, however, in 1911, and before the Revolution he managed to publish several short works that attracted the attention of literary critics. In 1916 he travelled to Tyneside in England to work on the construction of Russian ice-breakers, and, as a result of this experience, wrote the novella *Islanders* (*Островитяне*), a satire on English morals and hypocrisy.

On returning to Russia in September 1917 he began working as a full-time writer and teacher. In Petrograd, as St Petersburg was known from 1914–24, when it changed its name to Leningrad (since 1991 it has once again become St Petersburg), Zamiatin became a leading member of the literary intelligentsia. He did editorial work on several literary journals, worked on translations of H. G. Wells, Jack London, Rolland Romain and others into Russian, and gave many lectures on literary techniques. He was also writing creatively at this time, and continued to do so until about 1921. His major work, *We*, was written in 1920–1 and published abroad in translation in 1925. Reviled by communists in the USSR, the novel was published in Russia only under Gorbachev, in 1988. Zamiatin's creative literary output may have dwindled as the 1920s progressed, but he continued with his editorial work, writing essays and articles. He wrote screenplays for the emerging Soviet cinema, and his plays *The Flea* (*Блоха*) and *The Society of Honorary Bellringers* (*Общество Почетных Звонарей*) were performed in Moscow and Leningrad in the mid–1920s.[1]

Throughout this time Zamiatin, a former Bolshevik who had even suffered exile and imprisonment for his beliefs under the Tsar, published anti-Bolshevik articles in the periodical press, criticizing the dictatorship of the proletariat, the Communist Party's monopoly of power and the banality of the 'new' proletarian literature. Communist-minded critics had been criticizing Zamiatin for his opposition to the Revolution since 1922, but after 1929 he, along with his fellow writer Boris Pil'niak, was persistently attacked by critics from RAPP (Russian Association of Proletarian Writers), a dogmatic organization that saw itself as the watchdog of proletarian values in literature. After 1929, and until it was disbanded in 1932 along with all other literary groupings to make way for the monolithic Soviet Writers' Union, RAPP was the most powerful literary organization in the USSR. It saw its mission as the promotion of 'proletarian' values, and sought to root out the enemies of the Revolution. Along with Pil'niak, Zamiatin was denounced and reviled, his books were removed from the shelves of public libraries, his plays taken from theatre repertories, and the publication of his works and books was stopped. By 1931 his position had become intolerable. It was the sheer 'hopelessness' of his situation, this 'death sentence pronounced on me as a writer', as he expressed it, that spurred him in June 1931 to write a letter to Stalin, asking for permission for himself and his wife to go abroad. Surprisingly, he was allowed to leave. He and his wife left Russia in September of the same year, settling in Paris, where Zamiatin died in 1937. His last work remains the unfinished novel *The Scourge of God* (*Бич божий*).

For over half a century Zamiatin remained unpublished in his own country, unknown to a new post-war generation, his name omitted from Soviet histories of literature or glibly dismissed as a 'reactionary' writer who 'truly took an inglorious and shameful path, to the ranks of the obscurantists who strive ... to remove man from art'.[2] His literary rehabilitation in the USSR began in 1986, with the publication of a book of his works in Voronezh.[3] In the post-*glasnost'* and post-USSR period Zamiatin's *oeuvre* has returned to Russia in its entirety, and his name has been rightfully restored to its place in Russian literary history of the twentieth century.

Theme and Characterization

We is an anti-utopian satire (a dystopia) that succeeds not only in expressing Zamiatin's fears for man's soul in the technological age, but also in attacking political and cultural dogma in Russia at the time it was written. Zamiatin may be writing about a fictional society many centuries in the future, but he includes in his text many references to modern society (of which more later). The novel has often been compared to other anti-utopias, such as George Orwell's *Nineteen Eighty-Four* and Aldous Huxley's *Brave New World*, but there is one distinctive difference. According to Andrew Barratt:

> Put in the most general terms, Zamyatin's theme in *We* is tyranny. His particular approach to this theme, however, differs radically from that of Orwell in *1984*, or of Huxley in *Brave New World*, to cite the novels with which *We* is most commonly compared. Orwell's treatment of the theme is essentially political and illustrates his belief that any monopoly of political power leads inevitably to corruption and acute social inequality. Huxley, on the other hand, develops the Dostoevskian investigation into the idea of benign dictatorship and its implications for individual freedom. Zamyatin differs from both Orwell and Huxley in that his investigation of tyranny centres not so much on the political or the philosophical issues involved, but rather on the *psychology* of tyranny.[4]

The plot of *We* is set a thousand years in the future, after the Single State has been established on earth in the aftermath of a society shattered by the Two Hundred Years War. This war 'between the town and the country' left only 0.2% of the earth's population alive. Individuals are now referred to as 'numbers', and the Single State is run on the lines of rationality and mathematical verisimilitude. Indeed, people as individuals no longer exist, as each 'number' is required to subordinate his or her individuality to the needs of the collective, and the State does not flinch from coercion to achieve this. Hunger no longer is a problem, as all food is synthetic. Everyone has a number, the 'numbers' walk in unison to work, dress alike and live in glass houses so that everyone knows everything about everyone else, and no one is allowed to have secrets (the only privacy they have is the right to put up curtains on so-called 'sexual days'). The Table of Hourly Commandments (Часовая Скрижаль) regulates daily lives, including leisure and work time and the times when people must go to sleep and get up. Personal choice is no longer possible, as each 'number' is assigned a sexual partner, and people have the right to have children only if they conform to the Paternal and Maternal Norms. Microphones on streets pick up conversations which are listened to by the Guardians (Хранители), ruthless enforcers of conformity.

This society is ruled by the Benefactor (Благодетель), and all dissidence or non-conformity is punished by death in the State Machine (sometimes preceded by torture in the Gas Bell). Other institutions include the State Newspaper, the central Square of the Cube on which the Holiday of Justice is held, the Guardians' Bureau, the Day of Unanimity, and the Institute of State Poets and Writers (a perceptive premonition of the actual Writers' Union set up in the USSR in 1932). A Green Wall separates the Single State from the 'wild' world of nature beyond, and none of the 'numbers' are allowed to venture beyond this wall.

We learn all this from the words of D–503, an engineer entrusted with working on the Integral, a spaceship designed to conquer distant planets and bring mathematically-based happiness to the universe. The narrative is entirely in the form of 'notes' or 'entries' into his diary, and these notes relate the plot development and constitute the structure of the novel. Aspects of this society are given to us in the first few pages of the novel. In particular, the contemporary Soviet relevance is evident in the use of such slogans as 'long live the Benefactor' ('Да здравствует Благодетель'), 'the great historic hour' ('великий исторический час'), and 'the glorious deed' ('славный подвиг'), all easily recognizable phrases from Bolshevik propaganda. But there are also other set phrases particular to this futuristic society, such as the need 'to subjugate unknown creatures to the beneficent yoke of reason' ('благодетельному игу разума подчинить неведомые существа'), 'mathematically infallible happiness' ('математически-безошибочное счастье'), 'the savage state of freedom' ('дикое состояние счастья'), 'integrating the endless equalization of the universe' ('проинтегрировать бесконечное вселенское уравнение'), and 'the great, divine, exact, wise straight line' ('великая, божественная, точная, мудрая прямая'). All this is part of the 'the mathematically perfect life of the Single State' ('математически совершенная жизнь Единого Государства'). We learn from D–503's second note of the State's philosophy and ideological rationale: nature as perceived beyond the Wall is 'wild', contrasted to logic and thought, and he himself is unable to understand why the 'ancients' were inspired by such things as clouds. He prefers a clear sky, sterile and 'impeccable', like the Green Wall. D–503 is enraptured by the movement of machines, and he does not appreciate the sense of wonder aroused in his mate 0–90 by the coming of spring.

In his third note D–503 explains the movement of human history, and how it has come to settle at this point:

> For this much is clear: all human history, in so far as we have any knowledge of it, is a history of the transition from nomadic forms to ever more sedentary ones. Does it not follow from this, then, that the most sedentary form of life (ours) is at the same time the most perfect one (ours, again)? If men did dash about from one end of the earth to the other, why, it was only in the prehistoric times, when there were such things as nations, wars, trafficking, discoveries of sundry Americas. But who needs all that nowadays, and what for?

(Ведь ясно: вся человеческая история, сколько мы ее знаем, это
история перехода от кочевых форм к все более оседлым. Разве не
следует отсюда, что наиболее оседлая форма жизни (наша) – есть
вместе с тем и наиболее совершенная (наша). Если люди метались
по земле из конца в конец, так это только во времена
доисторические, когда были нации, торговли, открытия разных
америк. Но зачем, кому это теперь нужно?)[5]

The influence of Dostoevskii on Zamiatin's thought is apparent. It is
as if the Grand Inquisitor from *The Brothers Karamazov* had ultimately
been triumphant. In this society individual 'freedom' has been
sacrificed for universal 'happiness', and the glass dome that surrounds
the city resembles the Crystal Palace so abhorred by Dostoevskii. The
Underground Man's hatred of 'two times two' recurs in the poem
glorifying the multiplication table:

Eternal lovers are these Two-Times-Two,
Forever blent in a passionate Four
No others can so ardently adore
As these inseparable Two-Times-Two! (p. 76)

(Вечно влюбленные дважды два,
Вечно слитые в страстном четыре,
Самые жаркие любовники в мире –
Неотрывающиеся дважды два . . .) (p. 50)

Indeed, it has been noted that D–503's final meeting with the
Benefactor bears a resemblance to the meeting of Christ and the Grand
Inquisitor in *The Brothers Karamazov*.[6]

The underlying concept of this society is uniformity. Time is
regulated by the Table, so that everyone gets up, eats, goes to work and
goes to bed at the same time; the hours 1600–1700 and 2100–2200 are
'personal hours'. In other words, everyone lives for the common good
and must subordinate personal needs and feelings to the collective
good. Freedom, therefore, is 'unorganized' and 'wild', morality is
'mathematical', ethics are 'scientific' and sexuality is controlled in the
form of the permitted 'sexual days'. The Sexual Bureau analyses
everyone's hormone level to determine their level of sexual activity.
Even the past, as in the above quotation, is subjected to the relentless
argument of logic, the 'straight line'. Now there are no longer jealousies
or tragedies of passion: 'the great force of logic cleanses everything it
may come into contact with' (p. 38) ('великая сила логики очищает
все', p. 22).

The State's reliance on mathematical certainty and pure reason
brings us to the underlying philosophy of the novel: the struggle in

human history between 'entropy' and 'energy'. The rebellious I–330 puts this in simple terms to a disbelieving D–503:

> Look: there are two forces in this world – entropy and energy. The first leads to beatific quietism, to a happy equilibrium; the other, to the destruction of equilibrium, to excruciatingly perpetual motion. It was entropy which our – or rather your – ancestors, the Christians, worshipped as a god. But we are anti-Christians, we – (p. 161).

> (Вот: две силы в мире – энтропия и энергия. Одна – к бдаженному покою, счастливому равновесию, другая – к разрушению равновесия, к мучительно-бесконечному движению, энтропии – наши, или вернее – ваши предки, христиане, поклонялись, как Богу. А мы, анти-христиане, мы . . .) (p. 112)

In a long debate between the two we see the fundamental theme of the novel, and of Zamiatin's own fears of a Bolshevik regime and a Marxist-Leninist ideology that proclaimed itself as the culmination of human strivings in history. For I–330, history is never-ending and mankind moves forward all the time through his ideas and his imagination. Motion, variety and plurality are keys to human history, she asserts, thereby also expressing Zamiatin's own faith in mathematical infinity, onward movement and the absence of finality. D–503 tries to persuade her that 'the Benefactor is a disinfection, brought to the utmost pinnacle of perfection and indispensable to humanity' (p. 163) ('необходимая для человечества усовершенствованнейшая дезинфекция', p. 113), but I–330 has the final word:

> There it is, that very same entropy. To you, a mathematician – isn't it clear to you that it is only in differences – differences! – in temperature, only in thermal contrasts, that life lies? But if everywhere, throughout the universe, there are only equally warm – or equally cool – bodies, they must be thrust out of the way, so that there may be fire, an explosion, Gehenna. (p. 170)

> (Вот тут она самая и есть – энтропия, психологическая знтропия. Тебе, математику – разве не ясно, что только разности – температур, только тепловые контрасты – только в них жизнь. А если всюду, по всей вселенной, одинаково-теплые – или одинаково-прохладные, тела . . . Их надо столкнуть, чтобы огонь, взрыв, геенна.) (p. 118)

D–503 falls in love with I–330 and becomes, like her, a dissident. Furthermore, he also actively helps the MEFIs, a revolutionary group to which I–330 belongs, in their subversive activities. The MEFIs are dedicated to the restoration of human emotion and feeling.

However, D–503 rebels against the State not only because of his attraction to I–330. He also doubts the regime's own mathematically-based rationale. In particular, even as a schoolboy he feared the equation $\sqrt{-1}$, as its very insolubility was irrational: there should be no unanswered problems in the Single State. He consistently denies the beauty of the natural world, likens men to machines and the workings of the human body to those of a mechanism, and, conversely, gives the Integral human features. He prefers triangles, squares and circles in society and people. The Single State itself is a huge, enclosed space, surrounded by a wall, with buildings and public squares constructed according to strict geometrical principles. D–503 praises walls, obstacles and barriers, but breaks out of this enclosed space when he ventures beyond the Green Wall into the forest. Symbolically, he breaks out of his own spiritual prison by getting O–90, his assigned sexual partner, pregnant and by helping the MEFIs steal the Integral.

I–330 takes him to the Ancient House, where artifacts from the twentieth century are preserved and where there is a secret tunnel that leads beyond the Wall. She also introduces him to old music, alcohol (which is banned) and old forms of dress. Indeed, D–503 falls in love with her, thus coming under the influence of his irrational and impulsive nature. In short, he discovers his soul; he has dreams (considered unhealthy) and joins the rebels who attempt (unsuccessfully) to seize the Integral on its maiden flight. However, as others in the Single State also discover the power of their imagination, and civil unrest spreads throughout the city culminating in the destruction of the Green Wall, D–503 is captured by the Guardians and succumbs to the Great Operation, designed to cut out the power of imagination and fantasy. After the operation D–503 meets with the Benefactor and informs on I–330, who is captured, tortured and executed. However, there is hope for humanity: O–90, illegally pregnant with his child (she is ten centimetres shorter than the Maternal Norm), escapes beyond the Wall. The novel nevertheless ends with the triumph of rationality and D–503's optimistic reaffirmation of faith: 'And I hope that we will conquer. More than that: I am certain that we shall. For rationality must conquer' (p. 221) ('И я надеюсь – мы победим. Больше – я уверен – мы победим. Потому что разум должен победить', p. 154).

In the Single State the greatest book of antiquity is not, as we might expect, the Bible or works by Shakespeare, Pushkin or Dostoevskii, but something rather more prosaic and strictly rational: a Railway Timetable. The State Poet R–13 affirms that the role of literature is now different: 'Fortunately, the antediluvian times of all those Shakespeares and Dostoevskys – or whatever they called them – are over' (p. 56) ('К счастью, допотопные времена всевозможных Шекспиров и Достоевских – или как их там прошли', p. 35). By way of illustration, D–503 delights in the poem glorifying the multiplication table. Literature is no longer based on irrational or spontaneous emotions or feelings, nor does it celebrate the elemental or the wild aspects of life; rather, it is cerebral, organized and, above all, useful, totally devoted to the service of the State:

> How could it have come about (I was thinking) that the ancients had not been struck by the whole preponderousness of their literature and poetry? The most enormous, magnificent force of the artistic words was expanded by them utterly in vain. It is simply laughable: each one wrote about whatever happened to pop into his head – just as laughable and preposterous as the fact that the ancients permitted the sea to pound doltishly against the shore around the clock, while the millions of kilogrammetres imprisoned in the waves were utilized merely to warm up the emotions of enamoured couples. Out of the enamoured susuration of the waves we have obtained electricity; from a feral beast spattering foam we have made a domestic animal – and in precisely the same way we have gentled and saddled that once wild element of poesy. Nowadays poesy is no longer the unpardonable shrill clamour of a nightingale – poesy is service to the State, poesy is utility. (p. 77)

> (Я думал: как могло случиться, что древним не бросалось в глаза вся нелепость их литературы и поэзии. Огромнейшая великолепная сила художественного слова – тратилась совершенно зря. Просто смешно: всякий писал – о чем ему вздумается. Так же смешно и нелепо, как то, что море у древних круглые сутки туго билось о берег и заключенные в волнах миллионы килограммометров – уходили только на подогревание чувств у влюбленных. Мы из влюбленного шепота волн – добыли электричество, из брызжущего бешеной пеной зверя – мы сделали домашнее животное; и точно так же у нас приручена и оседлана, когда-то дикая, стихия поэзии. Теперь поэзия – уже не беспардонный соловьиный свист: поэзия – государственная служба, поэзия – полезность.) (p. 51)

Music is also composed according to mathematical principles. D–503 listens to the 'incongruous, fussy chatters of strings under percussion' (p. 34) ('нелепую, суетливую трескотню струн', p. 20) of twentieth-century music (Skriabin), and is relieved then to hear the music of modernity:

> With what delight I listened next to our contemporary music! (It was played towards the conclusion of the talk, to demonstrate the contrast.) Crystalline chromatic scales converging and diverging in endless series – and the summarizing chords of the formulae of Taylor, of MacLauren; the full-toned, squarely-massive passages of the Pythagorean theorem; the pensive melodies of an expiringly oscillatory movement; vivid cadences, alternating with the pauses of Frauenhofer's lines – the spectral analysis of planets . . .

What grandeur! What irrevocable regularity! And how self-willed the music of the ancients, restrained by nothing save wild fantasies . . . (pp. 34–5)

(С каким наслаждением я слушал затем нашу теперешнюю музыку. (Она продемонстрирована была в конце – для контраста.) Хрустальные хроматические ступени сходящихся и расходящихся бесконечных рядов – и суммирующие аккорды формул Тейлора, Маклорена; целотонные, квадратно-грузные ходы Пифагоровых штанов; грустные мелодии затухающе-колебательного движения; переменяющиеся фраунгоферовыми линиями пауз яркие такты – спектральный анализ планет . . . Какое величие! Какая незыблемая закономерность! И как жалка своевольная, ничем – кроме диких фантазий – не ограниченная музыка древних . . .) (p. 20)

It is interesting to note the harsh consonantal sounds in the Russian, and how the translator has tried to render them. They suggest a soulless, robotic music designed and organized for unthinking and unfeeling automata.[7]

The main characters of the novel, apart from D–503, are his illicit lover I–330, his official partner 0–90, the State poet R–13 (who is also one of I–330's lovers, and who dies in the unrest), the Guardian S–4711, a secret member of the MEFIs and also a lover of I–330, the receptionist at D–503's house Iu, who finds his notes and, coming under the spell of the irrational side of her nature, falls in love with him, and the Benefactor, whom D–503 meets twice. All of them are characterized through reference to physical attributes: with O–90 it is her pink lips and blue eyes, S–4711 is seen as a snake through the shape of the letter that forms his name, the poet R–13 has large lips and frequently sprays his interlocutor with spittle, D–503 is ashamed of his shaggy 'paws', and I–330's smile seems to 'bite'. However, none of these characters apart from D–503 is developed to any degree and, because the novel is narrated in the form of D–503's notes-cum-diary, we learn nothing about their thoughts or feelings. Rather, the psychological investigation in the novel is devoted exclusively to the workings of D–503's mind.

However, the two female characters deserve further comment. Both rebel against their male-dominated society, both are explicit in their celebration of their own sexuality, both are stronger than the male (here D–503), as Boris Lanin has stated:

In the male civilization of the Single State the women are unhappy but not helpless. They still have the right to rebellion, and this rebellion is above all connected with their female nature: if the selfless love of I–330 becomes a feat in itself, then for O–90, the folds on whose wrists are admired voluptuously, and whose admiration is then recorded in documentary manner by the hero, the cause for rebellion is her exclusion from child-bearing.[8]

Significantly, both women are betrayed by D–503 but both remain faithful to him. They thus join a long list of female characters in Russian literature who are inwardly stronger than the male, but who suffer through him.

Style and Imagery

As a psychological study, the novel has both subtlety and variety. On the one hand, D–503's notes show a mind in ferment: ostensibly a loyal and unquestioning citizen, entrusted with the grandiose task of constructing the Integral, he is smitten with love and desire for I–330. This new feeling causes him to do things his rational mind knows are unsound, such as helping in the abduction of the Integral and going beyond the Wall. In short, we see the struggle of the irrational side with the rational, the emerging of the unconscious through layers of consciously repressed rationalism. Moreover, before the 'fantasectomy' operation, D–503 is aware of his own duality in the form of his hairy arms, which he describes disparagingly as 'paws'. Only after the operation does he succeed in destroying his other, natural, self.

Furthermore, by presenting aspects of this society through the viewpoint of such a loyal citizen, Zamiatin creates a distance between what is depicted and the reader's perception of it. There is no doubt, therefore, that such aspects of the Single State as the all-pervasive Guardians, microphones on the street to pick up conversations, the Wall that serves not to keep enemies out but rather to keep the population in, glass houses where no-one has any privacy and the requirement to inform on others, by being depicted through the initially positive and unquestioning viewpoint of D–503, arouse in the reader a critical and negative response. Zamiatin thus proves himself to be not only a stylist of some virtuosity, but also adept at handling the psychological expectations of both his main character and his reader.

There is in D–503's writings a constant struggle between the human and the inhuman. D–503's conscious imagery revolves around his use of mechanical and impersonal imagery: 'we are one mighty, million-celled organism' (p. 138) ('мы единый, могучий миллионноклеточный организм', p. 94), he asserts, and further delights in the uniformity of society:

> The Table of Hourly Commandments, however, really does transform each one of us into the six-wheeled steel hero of a great poem. Each morning, with six-wheeled precision, at the very same minute and the very same second we, in our millions, arise as one. At the very same hour we mono-millionedly begin work, and, when we finish it, we do so mono-millionedly. And, merging into but one body with multi-millioned hands, at the very

second designated by the Tables of Hourly Commandments we bring our spoons up to our mouths; at the very same second, likewise, we set out for a walk, or go to an auditorium, or the Hall of Taylor Exercises, or retire to sleep. (pp. 28–29)

(Но Часовая Скрижаль – каждого из нас наяву превращает в стального шестиколесного героя великой поэмы. Каждое утро, с шестиколесной точностью, в один и тот же час и в одну и ту же минуту, – мы, миллионы, встаем, как один. В один и тот же час мы единомиллионно, начинаем работу – единомиллионно кончаем. И сливаясь в единое, миллионнорукое тело, в одну и ту же, назначенную Скрижалью секунду, – мы подносим ложки ко рту, – выходим на прогулку и идем в аудиторium, в зал Тейлоровских экзерсисов, отходим ко сну . . .) (p. 16)

D–503 consistently likens human actions to those of machines: he notes the 'cast-iron' hands of the Benefactor, human limbs are 'springs', voices are 'metallic' and the body, under the stress of conflicting emotions, has to fight to regain control of its reason. Fundamental aspects of human life – love and death, for instance – are reduced to mathematical formulae, and he routinely reflects on his chances of being in the same auditorium as I–330 in terms of probability theory:

First of all, I actually was assigned to Auditorium 112, just as she had told me I would be. Even though the probability of such an assignment was

$$\frac{1,500}{10,000,000} = \frac{3}{20,000}$$

(1,500 represents the auditoria, and there are 10,000,000 of us numbers). (p. 32)

(Первое: я, действительно, получил наряд быть именно в аудиториуме 112, как она мне и говорила. Хотя вероятность была –

$$\frac{1500}{10,000,000} = \frac{3}{20,000}$$

(1500 – это число аудиториумов, 10,000,000 – нумеров).) (p. 18)

However, Zamiatin subverts D–503's discourse of initially unquestioning conformity from the outset, as his character has continually to correct himself from saying 'I' by replacing it with 'we'. Also, despite D–503's assertions, emotions are still powerful forces in the individual. Jealousy does still exist, as O–90 is hurt by his liaison with I–330 and he himself is anxious at the prospect of I–330 having other lovers.

The novel does contain many references to Christian motifs and themes. The Benefactor, as he descends from the sky to address the multitude, has a God-like status, and the Guardians are referred to as 'guardian angels'. There is no higher spiritual authority than materialism and the power of logic. The poets have come down to earth, as have the gods: 'the gods have become even as we; *ergo*, we have become even as the gods' (p. 78) ('Боги стали, как мы: эрго – мы стали, как боги', p. 52). As if to exemplify this statement, D–503 consistently utters the oath 'ради Благодетеля' – for the Benefactor's sake – thus showing how far this society has moved from 'ancient' times when men said 'ради Бога' – for God's sake.

Despite the avowed materialist rationality of the Single State, it nevertheless needs a religious aspect to its rituals and philosophy. It rationalizes its own collective ethos in starkly religious terms:

> We walked along, a single million-headed body, and within each of us was that meek joyfulness which, probably, constitutes the life of molecules, atoms and phagocytes. In the world of antiquity this was understood by the Christians, our only (even though very far from perfect) predecessors: meekness is a virtue, while pride is a vice; they also understood that We is from God, while I is from the Devil. (pp 129–30)

> (Мы идем – одно миллионноголовое тело, и в каждом из нас – та смиренная радость, какою, вероятно, живут молекулы, атомы, фагоциты. В древнем мире – это понимали христиане, единственные наши (хотя и очень несовершенные) предшественники: смирение – добродетель, а гордыня – порок, и что «Мы» – от Бога, а «Я» – от диавола.) (р. 89)

Furthermore, the public holiday Day of Unanimity coincides with Easter, and D–503 describes the Single State as 'a single Church'. I–330's tempting of D–503 with alcohol is a parody of Eve's tempting of Adam in the Garden of Eden, and indeed there are several suggestions that in this earthly paradise D–503 is Adam and his lover is Eve. The Guardian S–4711 is several times described as a snake, especially given that he is also a spy, thus suggesting his role as the serpent, the agent of the Devil.[9]

One of the fundamental images in the novel is that of something enclosed or encased, like the 'numbers' in the Single State, struggling to break free.[10] The struggle is between form and content, the outer casing and the life surging under the surface to assert itself. This can be said of D–503's irrational impulses, fighting their way to the surface through layers of rationality and logic; it can also be seen in the child in O–90's womb, the symbol of the future life. Thus also, 'numbers' such as I–330 become free when they remove their uniforms to reveal human beauty and arouse sexual desire. When the unrest begins, people copulate in their glass dwellings in full view of others, without feeling shame or embarrassment, in a carnivalesque celebration of unfettered sensuality.

D–503's notes are preoccupied with colour imagery, thus expressing his irrational but vivid powers of imagination. The most important colour in the novel is yellow, as it is the colour of the sun, representing fire and light, and thus also comes to represent passion and the desire for freedom. I–330 seduces D–503 wearing a yellow dress, flowers beyond the Wall are seen by the yellow of their pollen and D–503 sees an animal with yellow eyes beyond the Wall. In other words, yellow is associated with passion and the life-giving force of nature. Other vivid colours such as black (I–330 dresses in black for the concert of ancient music, elsewhere she puts on black stockings and hat and has black eyebrows, the piano she plays is black, the birds that enter the city once the Wall is blown up are described as a black swarm) and red (the colour of the Ancient House) are also strongly associated with the world beyond the Wall, the world of freedom, irrationality and humanity.

Vivid colours also express the sheer variety and vitality of the life of the past. When D–503 awakes on the other side of the Wall, he finds himself immersed in a blaze of colour, surrounded by unfamiliar images and concepts:

On the meadow a crowd of three or four hundred . . . people (let *people* stand: I find it difficult to use another word) were making a lot of noise around a bare rock that looked like a skull. Just as out of the sum total of faces of those filling the rostra you would at first flush perceive only those familiar to you, so in this instance I at first saw only our grey-blue unifs. But another second passed – and among the unifs I distinguished, perfectly clearly and starkly, dark-coloured, rufous, gold-tinted, dark-bay, roan, white people – *people*, apparently. They were all unclothed and all were grown over with short, glossy pelage, somewhat like that of the stuffed *horse* which anyone may see in the Prehistoric Museum. The faces of the females were, however, exactly the same – yes, yes, *exactly* the same – as those of our women, delicately rosy and not overgrown with hair; their breasts – large, firm, of splendidly beautiful geometrical forms – were likewise free of hair. Among the males only a part of the face was not hirsute, much the same as with our ancestors. (p. 153)

(На поляне, вокруг голого, похожего на череп, камня – шумела толпа в триста-четыреста . . . человек, – пусть «человек», мне трудно говорить иначе. Как на трибунах из общей суммы в первый момент воспринимаете только знакомых, так и здесь я сперва увидел только наши серо-голубые юнифы. А затем – секунда – и среди юниф, совершенно отчетливо и просто: вороные, рыжие, золотистые, караковые, чалые, белые люди, – по-видимому, люди. Все они были без одежд, и все были покрыты короткой блестящей шерстью – вроде той, какую каждый может видеть на лошадином чучеле в Доисторическом Музее. Но у самок – были лица точно такие – да, да, точно такие же, – как и у наших женщин: нежно розовые и не заросшие волосами, и у них свободны от волос были также груди – крупные, крепкие, прекрасной геометрической формы. У самцов без шерсти была только часть лица – как у наших предков.) (pp. 105–6)

The Single State is associated primarily with blue and grey, the colours associated with metal and glass: the uniforms of the masses are blue, buildings are blue, even the sun is blue when perceived from inside the city, all suggesting sterility and deadness. Other colours, however, are used to characterize both the Single State and the world beyond the Wall. Pink is the colour of the ticket entitling a 'number' to sexual activity, but it is also the colour of O–90's lips. Skin is white, as is the electrical beam used to execute offenders. Gold is the colour of the badges the 'numbers' have to wear, but it is also positive when it is the colour of the sun's rays. The wall separating man from nature is green, but the world beyond that wall is green with natural life. The use of colour in the novel has aroused comment:

> Zamjatin uses color to bring out fundamental differences between the modern world and the world of the past. Color is not utilized the same way in portraying the world of the ancients as it is in portraying the world of the moderns. In presentations of the ancient world color conveys strong, primitive emotions – emotions absent from the world of the One State.[11]

Conclusion

Zamiatin's view of the future of human civilization is far from optimistic, although there are hopeful signs amid the gloom. He is attacking the philosophy of a society that feels it no longer needs to evolve or go forward, that regards uniformity and stasis – entropy – as the ideal culmination of human activity. There are unmistakeable signs that he saw in Bolshevik propaganda at the time of writing the idea that society no longer needed to develop because it had now reached its highest stage.[12] There is also an element of criticism of the 'freedom fighters', the MEFIs, for they too see their ideas as leading to the perfect society. Their apparent defeat shows that society keeps moving and developing according to the mathematical rules of infinity: there is no end, no final number, no ultimate stage of development.

Zamiatin's compelling vision achieves its narrative power through its mode of narration, through the notes of D–503, so that we get an exclusively one-sided picture. But, through the author's skillful narration, the reader's view of the Single State, initially sceptical, becomes increasingly critical. Furthermore, with its abundance of colour imagery subverting the rationalistic images and symbols of the Single State, the author affirms the power of the irrational, the soul, the side of man that cannot be reduced to mathematical equations. *We* remains a book of its time, warning against the materialism of a State that killed God in order to create its own spiritual symbols, but it has proved to be prophetic in its anticipation of the Stalinist nightmare, where individual identity became subsumed in the collective identity, and where millions of individual deaths could be rationalized as necessary for the collective good.[13]

Notes

1. This biographical sketch of Zamiatin is culled from several sources: the writer's own 'autobiographies', written in 1924 and 1929 and published, respectively, in Evgenii Zamiatin, *Сочинения* ('Works'), Moscow, 1988, pp. 475–6, and Evgenii Zamiatin, *Сочинения* ('Works'), Munich, vol. I, 1970, pp. 25–32. There is a very detailed account of this period of Zamiatin's life in Alex M. Shane, *The Life and Works of Evgenij Zamjatin*, Berkeley, CA, 1968, pp. 3–54.
2. M. N. Kuznetsov, *Советский роман: очерки (The Soviet Novel: Essays)*, Moscow, 1963, p. 136, as quoted in Gary Kern (ed. and trans.), *Zamyatin's "We": A Collection of Critical Essays*, Ann Arbor, MI, 1988, p. 55. For a detailed account of Zamiatin's troubles in the 1920s, see Shane, *The Life and Works of Evgenij Zamjatin*, pp. 55–81.
3. Evgenii Zamiatin, *Повести. Рассказы (Novellas. Stories)*, introduced by O. Mikhailov, Voronezh, 1986.
4. Andrew Barratt, 'The First Entry of *We*: An Explication', in J. Andrew (ed.), *The Structural Analysis of Russian Narrative Fiction*, Keele, no date, p. 110.
5. Evgenii Zamiatin, *We*, trans. Bernard Guilbert Guerney, Harmondsworth, 1972, pp. 27–8; *Сочинения*, Moscow, 1988, p. 15. All further references to the novel will be taken from these editions, with relevant page numbers incorporated into the text.

6. See for example Richard A. Gregg, 'Two Adams and Eve in the Crystal Palace: Dostoevsky, the Bible, and *We*', in Kern (ed.), *Zamyatin's "We"*, p. 66.
7. Colin MacLauren (1698–1746) was an eminent mathematician, who developed Sir Isaac Newton's work on gravitation, geometry and calculus; F. W. Taylor (1856–1915) became famous for his book *The Principles of Scientific Management*, published in New York in 1919. It is also possible that Zamiatin had in mind the mathematician Brook Taylor (1685–1731), noted for his work on developing calculus. M. A. Hersh notes:

> It is likely that Zamyatin chose the name Taylor for the ideologue of the Single State and its timetable as a result of the, for him fortunate, coincidence, of it being the name of both the originator of Taylor's theorem and the original efficiency scientist. The name 'Taylor' then encapsulates both the idea of increasing happiness through precise specification of the way in which all activities are to be performed and the mass state in which individualism is not permitted, since *my ot boga, ya ot diavola.* [. . .] However, it is highly unlikely that he is criticising technologically developed societies *per se*. His criticism is directed rather at the fossilisation or stasis resulting from continuous development of one idea *ad absurdum*, as well as all states which abuse or misunderstand particular theories or ideologies whether deliberately or otherwise and use this misunderstanding to place restrictions on their citizens.

See M. A. Hersh, 'Zamyatin's "We": A Mathematical Model Society', *Rusistika*, 8, 1993, pp. 22–3.
8. Boris Lanin, 'Images of Women in Russian Anti-utopian Literature', *Slavonic and East European Review*, vol. 71, no. 4, 1993, p. 646.
9. Richard A. Gregg also argues that D–503 can be seen as a Christ-like figure: 'And the hero, whose forty days of temptation in the wilderness of doubt (there are forty entries in the journal) and thirty-two years of age at his "death" are obvious allusions to his Christlike role, feels a solitude akin to that of Jesus before His crucifixion. [. . .] D–503's ultimate decision is, of course, the opposite of Christ's. Instead of dying so that men may be free, he lives so that they will remain slaves' (Gregg, 'Two Adams And Eve', pp. 66–7).
10. Carl R. Proffer comments:

> Logic keeps the form hard and compact, but irrationality (human feelings and emotions) melts the metal, transforming it into a formless molten mass.
> With the removal of fancy this irrational human spirit, inner fire of life is quenched. But Zamyatin believes that the human mind and body must

struggle free from the cold artificial shell of logic in which they are imprisoned by such a society. There can be no freedom for a man when he is thus immured, shielded from life by uniforms, glass, habit, and strict regimentation.

See Carl R. Proffer, 'Notes on the Imagery in Zamyatin's *We*', in Kern (ed.), *Zamyatin's "We"*, p. 97.

11. Sona S. Hoisington and Lynn Imbery, 'Zamjatin's Modernist Palette: Colors and their Function in *We*', *Slavic and East European Journal*, vol. 36, no. 2, 1992, p. 163.

12. Alan Myers, however, has shown that Zamiatin may well have been influenced by his experiences supervising the construction of Russian ice-breakers on Tyneside, and that many aspects of his time in England are reflected in the novel. For instance, the huge glazed sheds used for protection against the elements when building the ships became coloured green by the elements, and the numbers of the main characters are the numbers of the ships being constructed. Furthermore, clocking-on cards for employees – both male and female – in the shipward were pink! See Alan Myers, 'Evgenii Zamiatin in Newcastle', *Slavonic and East European Review*, vol. 68, no. 1, 1990, pp. 91–9, and the same author, 'Zamiatin in Newcastle: The Green Wall and the Pink Ticket', *Slavonic and East European Review*, vol. 71, no. 3, 1993, pp. 416–27.

13. Compare the words of Nadezhda Mandel'shtam, a survivor of the Stalin years:

The loss of 'self' leads either to self-effacement (as in my case) or to blatant individualism with its extremes of egocentrism and self-assertiveness. The outward signs may differ, but it is the same sickness: the atrophy of true personality. And the cause is the same in both cases, namely, the severing of all social bonds. The question is: how did it happen? We saw it come about in front of our very eyes. All intermediate links, such as the family, one's circle of friends, class, society itself – each abruptly disappeared, leaving every one of us to stand alone before the mysterious force embodied in the State, with its powers of life and death. In ordinary parlance this was summed up in the word 'Lubianka'.

See Nadezhda Mandel'shtam, *Hope Abandoned: A Memoir*, trans. Max Hayward, Harmondsworth, 1976, pp. 18–19. The Lubianka was the headquarters of the NKVD, Stalin's dreaded secret police.

Isaak Babel' (1894–1940), *Red Cavalry* (*Конармия*)

Introduction and Background

Isaak Babel' was born in Odessa, the son of a respectable and pious Jewish businessman. Odessa at the turn of the century was a cosmopolitan city with colonies of Greeks, English, Poles, French and Germans, a port on the Black Sea regularly visited by ships from Europe and America. Moreover, it was the second busiest port of the Russian empire. More importantly for Babel''s art, Odessa was one of the major European centres of Jewish culture; Jews made up about one third of the entire half-million population of the city. When he was a child Babel''s parents moved from Odessa to Nikolaev, a small port nearby, but returned to Odessa in 1905.

In that year Babel' entered the Odessa Commercial School, where he studied for the next six years. It was here that he began reading French literature, and began to move away from Jewish culture. As Milton Ehre notes: 'Babel' had taken his first step into the mainstream of European literature, bypassing the lively but provincial springs of Yiddish literature.'[1] From 1911–16 he studied at the Kiev Institute of Finance and Commerce (in 1914 the institute was moved to Saratov). He then moved to St Petersburg (Petrograd as it was then called), where he worked on the newspaper *Novaia zhizn'* ('New Life'), run by Maksim Gor'kii, until it was closed down in the summer of 1918. From then until 1924 Babel' worked in various capacities, in the army on the Rumanian front, in the Cheka, as a food requisitioner, in the Commissariat for Education and as a frontline journalist. It was this latter circumstance which is most important for an understanding of *Red Cavalry*.

In 1920 Babel' was assigned as war correspondent to the mounted cavalry led by Semen Budennyi, which was fighting against Polish and other anti-Soviet forces in Belorussia, Ukraine and Lithuania. In his 1920 diary, published only in 1989, Babel' shows the Cossacks in the same brutal light as in his subsequent fiction, and likewise gives a far from romantic picture of the Civil War. This diary is also important for the light it throws on Babel''s own response to the atrocities he witnessed (rape, torture of prisoners, the widespread syphilis amongst the Red Army soldiers) and which he describes dispassionately in *Red Cavalry*, and for the details, events and characters that were to feature in the novel.[2] In the diary there is no room for stylistic niceties, but there is an unmistakeable sympathy for the suffering of the Jews and a sure sense of his own alienation from them.

Based on his notes and diaries, the series of short stories and sketches written 1923–5 that came to be called *Red Cavalry* were published in book form in 1926, translated into all the other major European languages, and made Babel' an overnight success.[3] Budennyi, however, in articles published in 1924 and 1928, took great exception to the negative portrayal of the Red Army, defended the actions of his men, and accused Babel' himself of really being interested only in sex and slander. However, Babel' was defended by his benefactor Gor'kii. In 1924 he settled in Moscow, where he lived until his arrest during the Great Terror in 1939. The date of Babel''s death in the Gulag has previously been given as 17 March 1941, although the researcher Vitalii Shentalinskii has recently shown that Babel' was executed in a Moscow prison on 26 January 1940.[4] He was posthumously rehabilitated in March 1954.

Plot, Theme and Characterization

Although *Red Cavalry* is composed of thirty-six short stories, the work is unified by its consistency of theme, imagery, characters and religious motifs. Each of the stories is entirely self-contained and can be read separately, but the work can only be appreciated fully as an integrated whole; Babel' conceived the work as a whole, and the arrangement of the stories within the cycle is his own. With its highly stylized imagery, fragmented narration and presentation of violent and irrational acts, and its concentration on an alienated, dispassionate consciousness, *Red Cavalry* lays claim to being the first Soviet modernist novel. It is in sharp contrast to other works that deal with the Civil War in a traditional (if not always socialist) realist manner, such as Mikhail Sholokhov's *And Quiet Flows the Don* (*Тихий Дон*) or Alexander Serafimovich's *The Iron Flood* (*Железный поток*).

The central problem of *Red Cavalry* is alienation. We can relate this theme to the author's own position, both as a Jew — the traditional outsider in Russian as well as Western societies — and as an intellectual in a militantly anti-intellectual climate. More fundamentally, Babel' was one of those writers in the 1920s labelled 'fellow travellers' by Trotskii;

that is, one who did not profess political adherence to the Bolsheviks, but whose work was tolerated. Indeed, for Babel' literary style was more important than a work's social or political content. Babel' was himself ultimately unable to conform to the new society of Stalin's social engineering, or to the literature of socialist realism.

As both a writer and an individual, Babel' embodied the conflict of art and politics in twentieth-century Russia. Not surprisingly, this conflict is the central one in *Red Cavalry*, where the central character, Liutov, tries to be accepted by the Cossacks with whom he is serving but finds himself at odds with a closely-knit and aggressively prejudiced collective. The book, then, is about acceptance by one's fellow men, the move from adolescence and entry into the adult world (it is no accident that Liutov's experiences are accompanied by maternal images, symbolizing warmth and comfort amid the carnage of war). Liutov, like Babel', is Jewish, and serves as a political commissar in the Red Cossack cavalry commanded by Budennyi. Liutov obviously shares many of his creator's experiences, but Babel' is also careful to distance himself from his hero, for instance by use of *skaz* (of which more below). Furthermore, not all the stories in the cycle feature Liutov.

The Cossacks are violent, and think nothing of killing civilians, prisoners, even their own wounded (to prevent them from falling into the hands of the enemy). In 'The Death of Dolgushov (Смерть Долгушова)' Afon'ka Bida shoots the badly wounded Dolgushov because Liutov cannot bring himself to do so. In 'The Life and Adventures of Matthew Pavlichenko (Жизнеописание Павличенки, Матвея Родионича)', Pavlichenko repays his former lord for a lifetime of abuse, including the rape of his wife, by trampling him to death for over an hour ('and in that time I got to know life through and through (и за это время я жизнь сполна узнал)', he confesses).[5] Attention should be paid to the formulation of the story's Russian title, as it is reminiscent of the style in which the lives of the medieval saints were recounted. Indeed, Pavlichenko was a shepherd, but the idyll of his life was destroyed by his master. In 'Prishchepa's Vengeance (Прищепа)', Prishchepa returns to his village a year after he had left, and proceeds to massacre all those who stole the belongings and property of his parents after they were killed by the Whites. His path from house to house is recognizable by the trail of blood, as he is watched impassively by the rest of the village. Then he drinks heavily for two days, sets his house on fire, and leaves, never to return. Kudria cuts the throat of an old Jew in such a way as to avoid splashing himself with blood (rather like slaughtering an animal). The Cossacks also attack their own infantry, smacking them with the flat of their swords 'for fun' (p. 115) ('для смеху', p. 81).

Liutov's inability to kill his fellow man is regarded with contempt by
the Cossacks, and is one of the reasons why they cannot accept him (the
others are his Jewishness and his incompetence on horseback). In 'After
the Battle (После боя)' there is a passage that combines both Liutov's
own helplessness when faced with this challenge and an appropriately
grotesque yet vivid description of the nearby village:

> The village was swimming and swelling, and blood-red clay was oozing
> from its dismal wounds. The first star glimmered above me, and fell into the
> clouds. Rain lashed the willows and spent itself. Evening flew up to the sky
> like a flock of birds, and darkness crowned me with its watery wreath. I felt
> my strength all ebbing away. Bent beneath the funereal garland, I continued
> on my way, imploring fate to grant me the simplest of proficiencies – the
> ability to kill my fellow-men. (p. 163)

> (Деревня плыла и распухала, багровая глина текла из ее скучных
> ран. Первая звезда блеснула надо мной и упала в тучи. Дождь
> стегнул ветлы и обессилел. Вечер взлетел к небу, как стая птиц, и
> тьма надела на меня мокрый свой венец. Я изнемог и, согбенный
> под могильной, пошел вперед, вымалывая у судьбы простейшее из
> умений – уменье убить человека.) (p. 124)

The Cossacks are proud, arrogant and utterly ruthless, and these
qualities offer a contrast to the humility and acceptance of suffering that
characterizes the Jews. But the Cossacks are also capable of heroism
and personal sacrifice. Squadron commander Trunov shoots a Polish
prisoner in cold blood, and thrusts his sword through the throat of
another. Then he and the young Cossack Vos'miletov engage in unequal
combat with an American plane, condemning themselves to certain
death, in order to allow their comrades to escape. The Cossacks do have
a spurious code of honour: in 'Salt (Соль)' the desecration of the
concept of motherhood is punished when Balmashev shoots a woman
who had saved herself from rape by pretending to be cradling her babe-
in-arms. The Cossacks had respected her as a mother, but Balmashev
shoots her when he finds out that her bundle was in fact salt, which she
was hoping to sell on the black market.[6]

The main symbol of Cossack virility – his freedom, bravery and
independence – is the horse, without which the Cossack feels that he is
not a man. The Cossacks certainly need their horses more than they
need a woman. Women are treated as a disposable commodity: in
'Zamoste (Замостье)' Liutov is billeted with Volkov, who is writing a
letter to his fiancée. She may have forgotten him, and Liutov confesses
that his wife left him. At that moment the Poles attack, and their losing
the battle is equated with losing the battle of the sexes. The horse,

though, is more reliable and trustworthy. In 'The Remount Officer (Начальник Конзапаса)' the relationship between man and horse is exemplified as D'iakov, a former circus athlete, coaxes an exhausted horse to its feet. The horse looks at him with loving eyes, and we are in no doubt about the mutual understanding and trust between man and mount. The loss of a horse is tantamount to castration: in 'The Story of a Horse (История одной лошади)' Savitskii takes away Khlebnikov's horse, and Khlebnikov goes mad and is eventually invalided out of the army. Afon'ka Bida spends a week going round villages in search of a new horse after his own mount Stepan is killed, burning and killing and himself losing an eye in the process. Amid rumours that he has been killed, he returns to his unit on a chestnut-coloured stallion.

The horse Argamak, in the story of the same name, proves instrumental in getting Liutov finally accepted by the Cossacks. The horse had belonged to Tikhomolov, but was taken away from him as a punishment for killing two Polish officers he had been escorting as prisoners. Argamak is a Cossack horse, and is used to speed and sudden bursts of flight. Liutov cannot handle him, and soon the horse's back is covered in sores and weals from the saddle. Other Cossacks disapprove, and Tikhomolov eventually takes back his horse. Still, in this time Argamak had taught Liutov how to ride, and the Cossacks no longer watch him with contempt as he rides past on his new horse.[7]

Another major theme is religion, both Jewish and Catholic. Liutov comes into contact with several Jews in the course of the work, and witnesses atrocities committed against Jews both by the Poles and the Cossacks; this contact makes him acutely aware of his own ties with them. He identifies with them, and is thus unable fully to commit himself to the cause for which the Cossacks are fighting. On the other hand, he rejects the Jewish traditions that are rooted in the past and offer nothing for the future, as exemplified in the Rebbe Motale and Gedali's old shop. At the end of 'Discourse on the *Tachanka* (Учение о Тачанке)', essentially a treatise on the type of cart of the title, and its driver Grishchuk, there is a doleful account of the suffering of the Jews:

Hidden away behind scattered huts, a synagogue squatted upon the barren soil – sightless, dented, round as a Hasidic hat. Narrow-chested Jews hung mournfully about the crossways. The image of the stout and jovial Jews of the South, bubbling like cheap wine, took shape in my memory, in sharp contrast to the bitter scorn inherent in these long bony backs, these tragic yellow beards. In these passionate, anguish-chiselled features there was no fat, no warm pulsing of blood. The Jews of Volhynia and Galicia moved jerkily, in an uncontrolled and uncouth way, but their capacity for suffering was full of a sombre greatness, and their unvoiced contempt for the Polish gentry unbounded. Watching them, I understood the poignant history of this region: the stories of Talmudists renting taverns, of Rabbis carrying on usury, of young girls raped by Polish troopers and over whom Polish magnates fought pistol duels. (p. 75)

(Прикрытая раскидистыми хибарками, присела к нищей земле синагога, безглазая, щербатая, круглая, как хасидская шляпа. Узкоплечие евреи грустно торчат на перекрестках. И в памяти зажигается образ южных евреев, жовиальных, пузатых, пузырящихся, как дешевое вино. Несравнима с ними горькая надменность этих длинных и костлявых спин, этих желтых и трагических бород. В страстных чертах, вырезанных мучительно, нет жира и теплого биения крови. Движения галицийского и волынского еврея несдержанны, порывисты, оскорбительны для вкуса, но сила их скорби полна сумрачного величия, и тайное презрение к пану безгранично. Глядя на них, я понял жгучую историю этой окраины, повествование о талмудистах, державших на откупу кабаки, о раввинах, занимавшихся ростовщичеством, о девушках, которых насиловали польские жолнеры и из-за которых стрелялись польские магнаты.) (p. 43)

Nevertheless, as in 'The Rebbe (Рабби)', Jewish rituals and Motale are described with reverence bordering on awe. When Liutov returns to the 'agit-train' on which he is serving and the realities of the Red Army, he becomes aware of the disparity of the two worlds of which he is part. The Rebbe's son Il'ia does not share the beliefs of his father and wholeheartedly embraces the new order, unlike Liutov. In 'The Rebbe's Son (Сын рабби)' Liutov finds Il'ia dying in an environment typifying the dilemma Liutov himself faces:

His things were strewn about pell-mell – mandates of the propagandist and notebooks of the Jewish poet, the portraits of Lenin and Maimonides lay side by side, the knotted iron of Lenin's skull beside the dull silk of the portraits of Maimonides. A lock of woman's hair lay in a book, the Resolutions of the Party's Sixth Congress, and the margins of Communist leaflets were crowded with crooked lines of ancient Hebrew verse. They fell upon me in a mean and depressing rain – pages of the Song of Songs and revolver cartridges. (pp. 167–8)

(Здесь все было свалено вместе – мандаты агитатора и памятки еврейского поэта. Портреты Ленина и Маймонида лежали рядом. Узловатое железо ленинского черепа и тусклый шелк портретов Маймонида. Прядь женских волос была заложена в книжку постановлений шестого съезда партии, и на полях коммунистических листовок теснились кривые строки древнееврейских стихов. Печальным и скупым дождем падали они на меня – страницы «Песни песней» и револьверные патроны.) (p. 129)

Il'ia lies dying amid remnants of Jewish culture and Bolshevik agitation, filling the void between the Jewish past and the new world, and in death becomes Liutov's 'brother'; that is, Liutov carries on his line.[8]

The Jew and the Revolution is an issue highlighted again in the figure of the old Jewish tradesman Gedali. Gedali is surrounded by death and images of decay, part of the old world from which Liutov — and Il'ia — would like to escape. Gedali is blind, but can see things his fellow men are unable to grasp. He laments the violence of the new world, thinking that the revolution would be 'sweet', created by 'good men'. His reasoning is disarmingly simple, as he explains his doubts to Liutov:

> You shoot because you are the Revolution. But surely the Revolution means joy. And joy does not like orphans in the house. Good men do good deeds. The Revolution is the good deed of good men. But good men do not kill. So it is bad people that are making the Revolution. But the Poles are bad people too. Then how is Gedali to tell which is Revolution and which is Counter-Revolution? (p. 62)

> (Вы стреляете потому, что вы – революция. А революция – это же удовольствие. И удовольствие не любит в доме сирот. Хорошие дела делает хороший человек. Революция – это хорошее дело хороших людей. Но хорошие люди не убивают, революцию делают злые люди. Но поляки тоже злые люди. Кто же скажет Гедали, где революция и где контрреволюция?) (p. 30)

For Gedali and thousands of other suffering innocents, far from offering light and freedom, the Revolution brings death and destruction.

Jewishness is the main cause of Liutov's isolation from the Cossacks and from history, the anti-Semitism and the persecution of Jews represent the prejudice of the past, the old world. But the Jew is also the saviour of the world, as in 'In St Valentine's Church (У святого Валента)'. When Liutov sees a picture of a young Jew as Christ, it is 'the most extraordinary image of God I had ever seen in my life' (p. 124) ('самое необыкновенное изображение Бога из всех виденных мною в жизни', p. 88).

Catholicism is also treated ambivalently. A Catholic church is defiled by the Cossacks, churches are sacked, a nurse is nearly raped in a church, dead bodies lie all around, the drunken Afon'ka Bida bashes out some cacophony on the organ. The other-worldly strangeness of Catholicism is conveyed in 'The Church at Novograd (Костел в Новограде)', when Liutov's descent into the bowels of the church is described as a descent into hell. Father Romual'd is executed as a spy, the church's biscuits smell of 'the crucifixion'. Yet there is an ambivalence on Liutov's part: the sacking of the church is akin to the 'beggar hordes' invading civilized Poland and raping the Madonna. The Catholic Church is seen as the repository of hundreds of years of European culture. In his 1920 diary Babel' explicitly expresses his indignation at the Red Army's sacking of Catholic churches. He constantly berates the barbarism of Russia and longs for the civilization of the West. Elsewhere, in 'Pan Apolek (Пан Аполек)', for instance, the Catholic church stands accused of hypocrisy and of oppressing the poor by its harsh piety and condemnation of sin.

Babel' further pokes fun at Christian values and myths when he introduces the character Sashka the Christ. Sashka, a shepherd, has been given the nickname 'Christ' because of his meekness. He is therefore a pastoral figure, and so becomes a saint for his village. At the age of fourteen, however, he was infected with syphilis, along with his stepfather Tarakanych (derived from the word for 'cockroach'), when they both slept with a crippled beggar woman. Here the ideal and pure image of Christ is besmirched and thus debunked, as is the myth of sainthood. Babel' once more shows the intrusion of the ugly reality of the human world into the idyll of nature. Sashka was accepted by the Cossacks because they loved his songs, and so they protected him as their bard. This theme can be transferred to the broader, symbolic plane: the Revolution was meant to do away with backwardness and ignorance, but war destroys the distinction between good and evil. Babel' undoubtedly sympathizes with Gedali's words.

It is through the portraits on the walls of the Catholic churches that the theme of art, and the role of the artist, is approached. Art is here subversive, challenging the established order, and the artist is a man of the people giving free expression to the lives of the people. Pan Apolek is a painter who for thirty years has used local people as models for his religious portraits that adorn the local Catholic church, using a local prostitute for the portrait of Mary Magdalene and a cripple for St. Paul. Locals pay to have their portraits on the frescoes, and by so doing achieve a sense of immortality. The Church officials accuse Apolek of heresy and blasphemy. Yet, as the cemetery watchman Vitol'd remarks to the vicar, echoing no doubt the author's own view: 'And isn't there more truth in the pictures of Pan Apolek, who satisfies our pride, than in your words so full of blame and aristocratic wrath?' (p. 53) ('И не больше ли истины в картинах пана Аполека, угодившего нашей гордости, чем в ваших словах, полных хула и барского гнева?', p. 23).[9]

The Church's hypocrisy is further revealed in Apolek's story of the apocryphal seduction of Deborah by Jesus, and the subsequent birth of their child. The child is hidden by priests who are afraid to admit any tarnishing of the ideal. In the story 'In St. Valentine's Church' the narrator marvels at the 'heretical and ecstatic' Apolek's 'blasphemous' picture of John the Baptist as one of unbridled sensuality: 'The Baptist's beauty in that picture belonged to the reticent and equivocal type for the sake of which the concubines of kings are ready to lose their already half-lost honour and abandon their sumptuous mode of life' (p. 123) ('На изображении этом Креститель был красив той двусмысленной, недоговоренной красотой, ради которой наложницы королей теряют свою наполовину потерянную честь и расцветающую жизнь', p. 88). Apolek's challenge to the Church and established wisdom lies in his appeal to the masses, rather like that of Jesus Christ in his time (it is thus no accident that Apolek's picture of the Jewish Christ so impresses Liutov). Apolek has no time for established hierarchies or dogma, and paints for the common man; he therefore brings 'high' art to the people, and also gives their humdrum lives meaning and immortality.[10]

In *Red Cavalry* we are faced with a series of paradoxical concepts that are juxtaposed in such a way as to convey a grotesque, upside-down world. History is on the move, the Revolution marches on, but the past is trampled on and drowned in blood. In 'Berestechko (Берестечко)', for instance, the old Polish line of the Ratsiborskii family is dying out. But there is also an awareness of the parallels of history, for in this same story the Cossacks kill an old Jew in much the same way as Bogdan Khmel'nitskii's Cossacks had committed atrocities against the Jews in the seventeenth century.

The contrast of the politically conscious and the emotionally spontaneous is also apparent, expressed through the relationship of the 'straight line' and the 'curve'. As Galin says: 'The Cavalry Army is the social focus effected by the Central Committee of our Party. The revolutionary curve has thrown into the first rank the free Cossacks still soaked in many prejudices, but the Central Committee's manoeuvring will rub them down with a brush of iron' (p. 113) ('Конармия есть социальный фокус, производимый ЦК нашей партии. Кривая революции бросила в первый ряд казачью вольницу, пропитанную многими предрассудками, но ЦК, маневрируя, продерет их железною щеткой', p. 79). Such a statement could serve as the epigraph for the whole novel. The 'revolutionary curve' represents the Cossacks and their unthinking violence and prejudices (for example anti-Semitism); the 'straight line' is the path to the future, the new world being created by the Cossacks who use the methods of the old world to achieve this goal. The new world is created by unthinking, elemental beings. There is thus irony at work in this incongruously beautiful and violent moment in history. In 'My First Goose (Мой первый гусь)' Liutov is finally allowed to read to the Cossacks Lenin's speech as reported in *Pravda*, described as 'the secret curve of Lenin's straight line' (p. 67) ('таинственная кривая ленинской прямой', p. 34), because the road to the future is far from straight and direct.

Style and Imagery

Red Cavalry is about life on the edge, where death is ever present and everyday life is experienced in its extreme manifestations of violence and sex. The work looks at the makers of history and the victims of history, although often there is no clear-cut distinction between the two. The stories are not presented in chronological order: rather, they are arranged in order to highlight the development of the work's themes, especially that of the horror and disillusionment of war. Thus the first story, 'Crossing into Poland (Переход через Збруч)', recounts the Cossacks crossing the river Zbruch and entering a war-torn village in heroic terms of reference and martial imagery. The Cossacks are proud and bear themselves as victors. As the stories continue, the Cossacks as well as the narrator become increasingly war-weary, and lose much of their heroic stature as they suffer terrible and debilitating wounds and injuries. By the time we reach the last story, 'The Kiss (Поцелуй)', the tone is downbeat, the narrator is disillusioned and war promises not glory and a new world but destruction and dashed hopes.

Whereas most of the stories are related from the point of view of Liutov, the author's *alter ego*, some are not. It is interesting to note that Liutov is the pseudonym Babel' gave himself when working as a journalist during and after the Civil War. There is more than a hint of irony here, for 'лютый' means 'fierce', an adjective that can not be applied to the hero of *Red Cavalry*, with his doubts, inner conflicts and aversion to violence. But the irony does not stop there, for in giving his narrator a Russian name (his first names were Kirill Vasil'evich), Babel' is asking for himself to be accepted as a Russian and, as a Red Army commissar, to be part of the new world of the Revolution.

Liutov is not present in some stories, so we cannot rely on his point of view as the focal base of the novel. In 'A Letter (Письмо)', for instance, the narrator reproduces a letter written by Vasilii Kurdiukov to his mother, complete with colloquialisms and grammatical mistakes. The verbatim account serves to intensify the horror of the story how Vasilii's father Timofei hacked his own son Fedor to death – they were in opposing armies. The rest of the letter relates how Vasilii and his other brother Semen hunted down their father and killed him in return.

The story is related dispassionately, without any comment or attempt at a moral judgment by Liutov. But this story is also a metaphorical indicator of the nature of the Revolution and Civil War: the sons rebel against the patriarchal oppression typified by their father, who was a policeman under the old regime.

Other stories in the form of letters, where Liutov again is not involved in the narrative, are 'The Story of a Horse, Continued (Продолжение истории одной лошади)' (here Liutov makes a fleeting appearance introducing the correspondence between Savitskii and Khlebnikov) and 'Treason (Измена)'. 'The Life and Adventures of Matthew Pavlichenko' is recounted in the first person by Pavlichenko himself, complete with reverential forms of reference for the former landowners on whom he is at the time avenging himself.[11] Similarly, only at the very end of 'Konkin's Prisoner (Конкин)' do we learn that the story of how the political commissar Konkin killed a Polish general is actually related by Konkin himself; 'Treason' is in the form of an indignant letter to the prosecutor Burdenko from Cossacks who comically fail to see that hostilities cease when in a military hospital; and 'Salt (Соль)' is told not by Liutov but by Balmashev, the Cossack who shoots the female speculator. The disparity of narrative voices not only allows the reader to see the Cossacks as they see themselves and to learn about them through their own words, thus balancing the picture we get of them from Liutov, but also subverts the work's narrative integrity, giving it a disjointed, fragmentary structure.[12]

The above stories are all examples of *skaz*, which is characterized as 'a special type of narrative structured as emanating from a person distanced from the author (whether concretely named or presumed), and one who possesses a distinct manner of discourse)'.[13] In *Red Cavalry* the 'distinct manner of discourse' is in the form of colloquialisms, comical political bombast and sub-standard grammatical forms, which all serve to bring the narrative close to the genre of oral story-telling, in contrast to the standard literary Russian of Liutov himself.

This disparity is further in evidence when Liutov himself does the telling. He gives us nature description, bloody accounts of death and wounds, a treatise on Jewishness, mock romantic apostrophe ('O Regulations of the Russian Communist Party! (О устав РКП!)', as in 'Evening (Вечер)'), objective, documentary-like accounts of battles and troop movements (as in 'Afonka Bida (Афонька Бида)'). Add to this the fact that it is through Liutov that the major themes are filtered — art, Jewishness, the Catholic church, the Revolution, women and the Cossacks — and we can see that the scope of the narrative discourse is extremely broad.

The very first story in the cycle, 'Crossing into Poland (Переход через Збруч)', contains most of these elements, and serves to synthesize and give direction to the disparate themes in the other stories. The story is only just over one and one-half pages long, and begins with the description of the Red Army crossing the river Zbruch. It is a highly evocative description, with both vivid and grotesque imagery:

> Fields flowered around us, crimson with poppies; a noontide breeze played in the yellowing rye; on the horizon virginal buckwheat rose like the wall of a distant monastery. The Volyn's peaceful stream moved away from us in sinuous curves and was lost in the pearly haze of the birch-groves; crawling between flowery slopes, it wound weary arms through a wilderness of hops. The orange sun rolled down the sky like a lopped-off head, and mild light glowed from the cloud-gorges. The standards of the sunset flew above our heads. Into the cool of the evening dripped the smell of yesterday's blood, of slaughtered horses. The blackened Zbruch roared, twisting itself into foamy knots at the falls. The bridges were down, and we waded across the river. On the waves rested a majestic moon. The horses were in to the cruppers, and the noisy torrent gurgled among hundreds of horses' legs. Somebody sank, loudly defaming the Mother of God. The river was dotted with the square black patches of the wagons, and was full of confused sounds, of whistling and singing that rose above the gleaming hollows, the serpentine trails of the moon. (p. 37)

> (Поля пурпурного мака цветут вокруг нас, полуденный ветер играет в желтеющей ржи, девственная гречиха встает на горизонте, как стена дальнего монастыря. Тихая Волынь изгибается, Волынь уходит от нас в жемчужный туман березовых рощ, она вползает в цветистые пригорки и ослабевшими руками путается в зарослях хмеля. Оранжевое солнце катится по небу, как отрубленная голова, нежный свет загорается в ущельях туч, штандарты заката веют над нашими головами. Запах вчерашней крови и убитых лошадей каплет в вечернюю прохладу. Почерневший Збруч шумит и закручивает пенистые узлы своих порогов. Мосты разрушены, и мы переезжаем реку вброд. Величавая луна лежит на волнах. Лошади по спину уходят в воду, звучные потоки сочатся между сотнями лошадиных ног. Кто-то тонет и звонко порочит богородицу. Река усеяна черными кватратами телег, она полна гула, свиста и песен, гремящих поверх лунных змей и сияющих ям.) (p. 6)

The motifs of colour and sound give the scene a filmic quality; the alliteration and onomatopoeia of the last sentence (at least in the original) in particular reinforce the vividness of the scene.[14] Striking similes and metaphors add a majestic dimension to the terse, compact description, as well as offering a contrast in styles. The description is both beautiful, even romantic, and grotesque.

The treatment of nature in this passage is also of note. Both nature and man have the same qualities of aggression and tumultuousness, part of the same cataclysm. Man's revolution is part of nature's revolution. Elsewhere in the work we find that war is often described as 'a desert', the Cossacks are likened to animals, especially the wolf, and even bullets become animated. Life and death coexist, and sex is reduced to rape, or at best an animal lust. In 'Evening (Вечер)', for instance, the Cossack Galin tries to woo the laundress Irina with tales of how the former Tsars were killed. He then stands by as she is seduced by the cook Vasilii. In 'The Widow (Вдова)' Shevelev lies dying as his 'wife' Sashka is seduced nearby by the Cossack Levka.[15]

The story 'Crossing into Poland' contains other themes, such as senseless killing and the concept of Jewishness. Liutov is billeted with a Jewish family in a squalid and dirty house, and lies next to what he initially believes to be a sleeping Jew. The Jew, however, is dead, killed by the Poles in front of his own pregnant daughter. War is heroic, but killing is shocking and sordid. The Jew had begged the Poles to kill him outside, so that his daughter would not witness the murder, but they killed him in front of her all the same. As she says to Liutov: 'I should wish to know where in the whole world you could find another father like my father?' (p. 39) ('Я хочу знать, где еще на всей земле вы найдете такого отца, как мой отец . . .', p. 7). Amid the squalor of the house we get a picture of dignity, and in the pregnant Jewess there is a metaphor of hope for the future.

Further instances of Babel''s startlingly original descriptive powers abound. For instance, in the story 'Italian Sunshine (Солнце Италии)' Liutov regards the moon as 'Romeo' about to come on to the stage, whose light can be switched off at any moment by the downcast electrician standing behind the scenes. He further muses that 'blue roads flowed past me like streams of milk spurting from many breasts' (p. 57) ('голубые дороги текли мимо меня, как струи молока, брызнувшие из многих грудей', p. 26), and as he dozes, dreams dance around him like kittens. The story 'The Road to Brody (Путь в Броды)' contains an ornate description of the sunset, again as witnessed by Liutov: 'And we were moving towards the sunset, whose foaming rivers flowed along the embroidered napkins of peasant fields. The stillness grew roseate. Like a cat's back the earth lay overgrown with the gleaming fur of crops' (p.72) ('И мы двигались навстречу закату. Его кипящие реки стекали по расшитым полотенцам крестьянских полей. Тишина розовела. Земля лежала, как кошачья спина, поросшая мерцающим мехом хлебов', p. 40). Conversely, in the story 'Zamost'e' the dawn flows down on Liutov and his comrades 'like waves of chloroform' (p. 148) ('как волны хлороформа', p. 111). In the story 'Afon'ka Bida' we are told that 'the rainbow web of heat shimmered in the air' (p. 114) ('в воздухе сияла радужная паутина зноя', p. 80). In all of these instances, beautiful, sensuous imagery is used in contrast to the horror of war.

Babel''s treatment of people is similarly highly idiosyncratic: as she walks a Cossack woman's breasts move 'like an animal in a bag' (p. 97) ('как животное в мешке', p. 63); the Cossack leader Maslak has a belly 'like a big tomcat' (p. 115) ('как большой кот', p. 81). Liutov dreams of buxom women and admits that he looks on the world 'as a meadow in May – a meadow traversed by women and horses' (p. 99) ('как на луг в мае, как на луг, по которому ходят женщины и кони', p. 65). Indeed, lust and sex are on the level of the animal world, and sex is simply a physical act. In 'The Widow' sex is described in the same way as horses eat their food, and in 'Chesniki (Чесники)' two horses mate as do humans. Here too men and women belong to the same elemental world as do animals.

But there is sexual ambiguity, too. Note the homoerotic description of Savitskii at the beginning of 'My First Goose':

> Savitsky, Commander of the VI Division, rose when he saw me, and I wondered at the beauty of his giant's body. He rose, the purpose of his riding-breeches and the crimson of his little tilted cap and the decorations stuck on his chest cleaving the hut as a standard cleaves the sky. A smell of scent and the sickly sweet freshness of soap emanated from him. His long legs were like girls sheathed to the neck in shining riding-boots. (p. 64)

> (Савицкий, начдив шесть, завидев меня, и я удивился красоте гигантского его тела. Он встал и пурпуром своих рейтуз, малиновой шапочкой, сбитой набок, орденами, вколоченными в грудь, разрезал избу пополам, как штандарт разрезает небо. От него пахло духами и приторной прохладой мыла. Длинные ноги его были похожи на девушек, закованных до плеч в блестящие ботфорты.) (p. 32)

Such a description bears witness to Liutov's (and Babel''s) fascination with the authoritative demeanour of the Cossack commander, seen here as a powerful, phallic figure. Savitskii is elsewhere described as being 'captivating' (p. 81).

Liutov is both repelled by the unthinking brutality of the Cossacks and attracted by their elemental sensuality. In the story 'My First Goose' the Cossacks insult and humiliate Liutov, making it clear that he will only be accepted if he rapes a woman ('and a good lady, too', p. 65 ('самую чистенькую даму', p. 33)). Instead, Liutov kills a goose, blood spurting out and its white feathers ground into the mud as he crushes its head under his boot. The killing of the goose obviously signifies Liutov's degradation of an image of purity, and the Cossacks subsequently have no qualms about letting him partake of their soup. He then reads the newspaper reports of Lenin's speech to them, and they all fall sleep together, legs intertwined in an image of male bonding (complete with homosexual overtones).

Further paradoxes occur in the vivid nature description, set alongside scenes of immense carnage; Liutov's attitude to his own Jewishness and to other Jews he comes across; the mixture of grotesque and realism, picturesque and horrific; the nature of the Revolution, which should bring about peace and harmony but instead causes death and suffering. Above all, the Cossacks are presented as brave and violent, elemental creatures in a world turned upside down. They are not politically conscious or articulate, but neither do they bear malice. They simply do what they have to do in the context of war. Death is meted out quickly, without sadism or torture (unlike the actual atrocities witnessed in the diaries). But they too are wounded and maimed at the end of the work, and we are left with a deromanticized picture in stark contrast to the picture of them which we get in 'Crossing into Poland'.

Conclusion

It remains to be said that Liutov is the only rounded character, and that the various Jews, Cossacks and Poles we meet are mere projections of certain qualities. There is much symbolism in how these various groupings are described: the Cossacks are often associated with black clothing, suggesting that they are angels of death, although they are also seen by Liutov as heroes. Similarly, the physical weakness of Apolek, Gedali and Sashka Khristos is actually their main virtue. So the work features two types of men: the physically strong and cruel, who bring about destruction, and the weak, who are creative and possess spiritual insight.

The last story, 'The Kiss', suitably brings the cycle to a close. Liutov kisses Tomilina, the woman with whom he is billeted, in a sexual embrace. Significantly, this is the reader's first emotional contact after so much blood. Just as significantly, the Cossacks are leaving Poland; the first story, 'Crossing into Poland', sees them entering the country. Liutov tells her and her family about Lenin and the Revolution, allaying their fears about the Bolsheviks and so establishing the book's ideological credentials. But to himself Liutov ponders the paradox of the present:

> The future seemed ours for the asking, the war like an impetuous prologue to happiness, and happiness the hallmark of our character. All that remained to be defined were the details, and we used to discuss them for nights on

end, nights when the candle-end was reflected in the opaque glass of the vodka-bottle. (p. 322)

(Будущее казалось никем не оспариваемой нашей собственностью, война – бурной подготовкой к счастью, и самое счастье – свойством нашего характера. Нерешенными были только его подробности, и в обсуждении их проходили ночи, могучие ночи, когда огарок свечи отражался в мутной бутыли самогона.) (pp. 137–8)

Liutov sees the ruined walls trace 'a long curve swollen with crimson blood' (p. 322) ('кривая, набухшая рубиновой кровью линия', p. 138) against the sky, a symbol of his own doubts about 'the future'.

But Tomilina places her faith in Liutov to take her and her family to Moscow, and away from the war. Liutov lets her down as he leaves without her. The future, then, is one of disappointment, disillusion and betrayal. The work is perhaps best summed up by Milton Ehre:

For a world torn by the rival claims of culture and power, compassion and violence, he [Babel'] finds no comfortable solution. He stands with the rabbi's son (sic), in stoic determination to live with ambiguity. The resolution of *Red Cavalry* does not lie in the triumph of any single allegiance, but in an assertion of the will to live in a discordant world.[16]

Babel' in the 1920s already had an insight into what the future held, and felt that the 'straight line' towards the future would remain 'a curve', and would lead away from happiness and justice to further terror and death.

In conclusion, we can say that *Red Cavalry* is based on the constant interplay of paradox and contrast, incongruous yet beautiful imagery, characters as symbols of opposing world-views, nowhere better exemplified than in the wanton, wild and violent Cossacks and the old, resigned and passive Jews. Violence is juxtaposed with the serenity of Church symbols, although these are often defiled in the chaos of war. There is no political uplift; the Cossacks at the end seem demoralized, as war ultimately serves up horror and tragedy, and the new world is one of pain and blood.

Notes

1. Milton Ehre, *Isaac Babel*, Boston, 1986, p. 19.
2. Isaak Babel', '«Ненавижу войну». Из дневника 1920 года

Исаака Бабеля', ('"I hate war". From Isaak Babel"s 1920 Diary'), *Druzhba narodov*, no. 4, 1989, pp. 238–52; no. 5, 1989, pp. 247–60. In particular, the entry for 21 July reads as follows: 'We are the vanguard – but of what? The population waits for people to deliver them, the Jews wait for freedom – but the men from Kuban' come instead...' ('Мы авангард, но чего? Население ждет избавителей, евреи свободы – приезжают кубанцы...') (no. 4, p. 243). On the diary, see Carol J. Avins, 'Kinship and Concealment in *Red Cavalry* and Babel's 1920 Diary', *Slavic Review*, vol. 53, no. 3, 1994, pp. 694–710.

3. The stories 'Argamak' and 'The Kiss' were added in 1932 and 1937 respectively. The 1966 Khudozhestvennaia literatura edition, the first in Russia since Babel"s rehabilitation, ended the cycle with 'Argamak'; the 1990 two-volume edition, however, ends the cycle with 'The Kiss' (for bibliographical details see note 5).

4. Shentalinskii also affirms that twenty-four files from Babel"s archive were confiscated at the time of his arrest, none of which have subsequently, even in post-Soviet times, been recovered. There is also no document testifying to their destruction. See Vitalii Shentalinskii, '«Прошу меня выслушать...». Последние дни Исаака Бабеля' ('"I Ask to be Heard Out...".: Isaak Babel"s Last Days'), *Znamia*, no. 7, 1994, pp. 135–64 (p. 163).

5. Isaac Babel, *Collected Stories*, trans. Walter Morison, Harmondsworth, 1983, p. 92; Isaak Babel', *Сочинения в двух томах (Works in Two Volumes)*, Moscow, 1990, vol. II, p. 54. All further references to the work will be taken from these editions, with relevant page numbers incorporated directly into the text.

6. Milton Ehre notes of the Cossacks:

As in Tolstoy's *War and Peace*, history is made by men who have no idea what they are making. The Cossacks, not without codes of honour and principles of justice, are yet creatures of impulse. Revolution appeals to them by the opportunity it gives for free exercise of their powers, which they manifest in indiscriminate violence and mindless vengeance. The consciousness of the heroes of *Red Cavalry*, like the prose that conveys their progress, is riveted to the immediate present, the act of the moment, the event as pure event. Consequently, they are children of nature and their march, which is the march of history, is a kind of natural occurrence (Ehre, *Isaac Babel*, p. 70).

7. From his 1920 diary:

I understood what a horse was for the Cossack and cavalryman.
Dismounted horsemen on the burning, dusty roads, Their saddles in their

hands, sleep like dead men in the carts of others, everywhere there are rotting horses, the talk is only of horses, the ritual of changing, the excitement, horses are martyrs, horses are sufferers, they are epic, I myself became infused with this feeling – at every crossing I feel the horses' pain

(Я понял – что такое лошадь для казака и кавалериста.
 Спешенные всадники на пыльных горячих дорогах, седла в руках, спят как убитые на чужих подводах, везде гниют лошади, разговоры только о лошадях, обычай мены, азарт, лошади мученики, лошади страдальцы, об них – эпопея, сам проникся этим чувством – каждый переход больно за лошадь) (Babel', 'I hate war', p. 258).

8. Patricia Carden notes that 'in Ilia we find the author's construction of the perfect man, a man combining the intellectual gifts of the best Jewish tradition with the valor of the Cossacks. Thus does Babel bring together the two chief strands in *Red Cavalry*' (Patricia Carden, *The Art of Isaac Babel*, Ithaca, NY, 1972, p. 105). The contrast between the Jews and the Cossacks is not only in the times they respectively represent but also in the space they occupy. Efraim Sicher notes that 'Jewish areas visited by the narrator of the Red Cavalry stories are almost always located in enclosed, confined space and contrast with the open, unbounded areas that lie outside' (Efraim Sicher, *Style and Structure in the Prose of Isaak Babel'*, Columbus, OH, 1985, p. 85). Furthermore, the 'open areas of physicality and nature' (ibid., p. 87) are inhabited by the Cossacks.

9. Efraim Sicher actually sees art as the work's most important theme:

The theme of the intellectual torn between irreconcilable commitments to the Revolution and to the past was one that preoccupied Fedin, Aleksei Tolstoi, Olesha, Pil'niak, Zamiatin and other Russian writers after 1917, but Babel' presents the collisions, dichotomies and dilemmas in his Red Cavalry stories as an aesthetic confrontation. Babel' does this partly by juxtaposing the physical beauty with the repulsiveness of human nature and by distancing the narrator in order to shock the reader into realizing the horrors of war fought in the name of a revolutionary ideal (Sicher, *Style and Structure in the Prose of Isaac Babel'*, p. 113).

10. Milton Ehre equates the vision of Apolek with that of Gedali: 'Apolek's artistic vision is but a variant of the Hasid Gedali's prophetic dream of the coming Revolution of Joy and the International of Good People. Polish village artist and Jewish shopkeeper represent the aesthetic and ethical imaginations, respectively. Engulfed by violence, both cling to dreams of universal compassion' (Ehre, *Isaac Babel*, p. 79). We should not

forget that Babel' himself provides vivid pictures and images, showing the inner truth of reality and so replicating Apolek's art in words.

11. Milton Ehre remarks that 'the story is a fable on the making of a revolutionary warrior, detailing Matvey's progress from submissiveness to violent aggression . . . Though the action is terribly brutal, the tone is closer to "black comedy" than melodrama' (Ehre, *Isaac Babel*, p. 65).

12. Patricia Carden points out that 'the most brutal happenings are usually narrated by the men who take part in them. In fact, it is striking that all stories in *Red Cavalry* that are told by a secondary narrator are concerned with acts of violence' (Carden, *The Art of Isaac Babel*, p. 119). She notes as examples 'A Letter', 'Italian Sunshine', 'The Life and Adventures of Matthew Pavlichenko', 'Salt', 'Konkin's Prisoner' and 'Treason'.

13. Victor Terras (ed.), *Handbook of Russian Literature*, New Haven, 1985, p. 420.

14. On the further use of colour in *Red Cavalry*, see Sicher, *Style and Structure in the Prose of Isaak Babel'*, pp. 47–9.

15. Of the concurrence of the animal and human worlds, Sicher says: 'The world comes alive, and this recreates the illusion of the immediacy of the visual and psychological impressions of the narrator who apprehends these metaphoric metamorphoses as real. Metaphor transplants human attributes to the animal kingdom, it animates the inanimate. The impression is multi-sensory, kaleidoscopic' (Sicher, *Style and Structure in the Prose of Isaak Babel'*, pp. 43–4).

16. Ehre, *Isaac Babel*, p. 86.

—3—

Iurii Olesha (1899–1960), *Envy* (*Зависть*)

Introduction and Background

Iurii Karlovich Olesha is best known for his short novel *Envy*, published in 1927, although he also wrote many poems and short stories, some plays and another novella *The Three Fat Men* (*Три толстяка*, 1928). In his autobiographical last work, *No Day Without a Line* (*Ни дня без строчки*), on which he was still working at the time of his death, he showed that he was aware of the importance of this work: 'I have the conviction that I have written a book, "Envy", which will live for centuries' ('У меня есть убеждение, что я написал книгу «Зависть», которая будет жить века').[1] The reception of *Envy* has been, at least in the Soviet Union, ambivalent, for some critics have seen it as a satirical attack on those who refuse to accept the new world, while others have been justifiably worried by the various levels of ambiguity regarding the so-called 'positive' characters in the novel. Western critics have tried to see it as a defence of individualism. However, both Soviet and Western critics, including those of the 1920s, even those opposed to its ideological standpoint, generally agreed on the quality and originality of its language, structure and style.[2]

After 1932 Olesha published almost nothing original, and remained virtually silent until after Stalin's death. He earned a living doing translations, working on stage adaptations of the Russian classics and writing film scenarios (his adaptation of Dostoevskii's *The Idiot* was finally produced at the Vakhtangov Theatre in 1958). His last work, *Ни дня без строчки*, containing his reflections on his own work and career and that of others, appeared after his death in 1965.

Olesha lived for most of his childhood in Odessa, where he also went to school. He then attended university in Novorossiisk.[3] It was here that he met the future writers Il'ia Il'f, Valentin Kataev and Eduard Bagritskii. In 1919 he volunteered for the Red Army, and worked as a journalist; in 1922 he settled in Moscow, where he began working on the railway newspaper *Gudok* (*The Siren*) under the pseudonym 'Zubilo' (Chisel). At this time other writers, such as Babel', Bulgakov, Il'f and Petrov, were also working on this newspaper, and Olesha became acquainted with all of them; indeed, he shared an apartment with Il'f. He was to remain in Moscow until his death, apart from spending the war years in evacuation in Ashkhabad. Although never actually imprisoned, Olesha was effectively expunged from Soviet literary history between 1941 and 1956.[4]

Plot, Theme and Characterization

In order to understand fully *Envy*, Olesha's own statement from the 1934 Soviet Writers' Congress should be borne in mind. He opened his address as follows:

> In every person there is good and there is bad . . . Every person can feel within himself the sudden appearance of a double. In an artist this is manifest particularly clearly, and this is one of the artist's amazing qualities: to experience the passions of others.
>
> Inside each person lie hidden the shoots of the most varied passions — both dark and light. The artist is able to draw out these shoots and turn them into trees.

> (В каждом человеке есть дурное и есть хорошее . . . Каждый человек может почувствовать в себе внезапное появление какого-угодно двойника. В художнике это проявляется особенно ярко, и в этом — одно из удивительных свойств художника: испытать чужие страсти.
>
> В каждом заложены ростки самых разнообразных страстей – и светлых и черных. Художник умеет вытягивать эти ростки и превращать их в деревья.)[5]

This statement of the 'duality' of man explains much about the method of characterization in *Envy*. Another statement from the same speech helps us to understand Olesha's own attitude toward his far from positive hero, Kavalerov, and the subsequent hostility towards him of orthodox socialist realist critics:

> Yes, Kavalerov looked at the world with my eyes. Kavalerov's colours, hues, images, comparisons, metaphors and conclusions belong to me. And they were the freshest and most vivid colours that I saw . . . As an artist, I revealed in Kavalerov the purest strength, the strength of the primary entity, the strength of retelling one's first impressions.

> (Да, Кавалеров смотрел на мир моими глазами. Краски, цвета, образы, сравнения, метафоры и умозаключения Кавалерова принадлежат мне. И это были наиболее свежие, наиболее яркие краски, которые я видел . . Как художник проявил я в Кавалерове наиболее чистую силу, силу первой вещи, силу пересказа первых впечатлений.)[6]

Envy, like Babel''s *Red Army*, Zamiatin's *We* and most other major works of the 1920s, is about alienation and isolation, ultimately the individual's relationship to the collective. The novel is divided into two parts, a first-person narrative as seen through the eyes of Nikolai Kavalerov, the main character, and a conventional third-person narrative related by the author himself. The plot is little more than an account of Kavalerov's 'envy' of Andrei Babichev and others who belong to the new, post–1917 world, and his and others' inability, or unwillingness, to accept this new world.

Nikolai Kavalerov is a young poet, homeless and destitute, temporarily living in the home of Andrei Babichev, a 'new Soviet man', a former Civil War commissar and now famous as a manufacturer of sausages. Kavalerov's observation of Andrei washing at the very beginning of the novel reflects his fascination with the older man's sheer physicality. Andrei is 'a model, masculine specimen'[7] ('образцовая мужская особь', p. 13); his groin is 'magnificent', it is 'the groin of a producer', and Kavalerov muses that Andrei would set any girl's heart a-flutter by merely looking at her. The first thing Kavalerov describes, and the first thing we read in the book, is Andrei's morning routine in the toilet, followed by his exercises. Andrei gargles so loudly that people in the street below stop and look up at the source of the sound. We are then treated to a description of Andrei's snoring and eating habits. It is not therefore surprising that Andrei's business is food, and Kavalerov furnishes us also with details of the new sausage for which Andrei is responsible.

Kavalerov is fascinated both with Andrei's sexuality and his efficiency as an industrialist. Kavalerov's picture is initially positive, and is imbued with admiration and respect. However, a less respectful attitude creeps in after a few pages. Kavalerov remarks that Andrei is 'greedy and jealous' (p. 6) ('он жаден и ревнив', p. 15), as Kavalerov thinks that Andrei, through his encouragement of communal eating halls, is destroying the centre of family life, the kitchen. This is the first indication we get of Kavalerov's envy, as Andrei is undoubtedly quite an important figure. He even has his own seat in the Vesenkha (the Supreme Economic Council). Furthermore, Kavalerov is prepared to admit his own inadequacy before Andrei. However, Andrei also resembles the 'double' Olesha mentions above: his sexuality is ambiguous, for while Kavalerov's picture of him emphasizes his virility and strength, Olesha the author describes him as having breasts like a woman's and wearing liberal amounts of eau-de-cologne. Furthermore, his very name, Babichev, is derived from the word *baba* (wench).[8]

Andrei represents the state and, indeed, embodies the state, for he acts as surrogate father and mother to Kavalerov, although he himself denies the importance of the family in the new world. But his invention of the giant sausage is described as his 'child', and Kavalerov asserts that Andrei would like to 'give birth' to food. Andrei's delight on seeing his new sausage is likened to the delight felt by the groom when he gazes on his bride on his wedding night.

Andrei had literally picked Kavalerov up from the street, where he was lying drunk and despondent. Kavalerov's emotions towards Andrei are mixed: he feels envy (the 'envy' of the title), as Andrei actively contributes to and is assimilated into the new post-revolutionary society, but he also feels intimidation, contempt and arrogance. Kavalerov's problems with the modern world are subsumed into his inability to cope even with the simplest aspects of everyday reality:

> Things don't like me. Furniture tries to trip me. Once some sort of lacquered corner literally bit me. With my blanket I always have complex interrelations. Soup which is served me never cools. If some kind of trinket – a coin or a cuff link – falls off the table, it usually rolls under some piece of almost immovable furniture. I crawl along the floor and, raising my head, I see how the sideboard is laughing. (p. 4)

> (Меня не любят вещи. Мебель норовит подставить мне ножку. Какой-то лакированный угол однажды буквально укусил меня. С одеялом у меня всегда сложные взаимоотношения. Суп, поданный мне, никогда не остывает. Если какая-нибудь дрянь – монета или запонка – падает со стола, то обычно закатывается она под трудно отодвигаемую мебель. Я ползаю по полу и, поднимая голову, вижу, как буфет смеется.) (p. 14)

This is a classic persecution complex. Kavalerov thinks that things do not like him because he is alienated from his immediate environment. Elizabeth Beaujour comments: 'Kavalerov's assertion "Things don't like me" is a way of avoiding responsibility for his inability to deal with things and for his fear of them.'[9] Kavalerov wants to be the centre of things, he needs to feel that he can control his surroundings. His name is derived from the word *kavaler* ('knight'), suggesting a romantic, chivalrous idealist belonging to another age. He wants to be famous and admired, but feels that the new Soviet world is inimical to him, that he can never find his niche in it:

> In our country the roads to glory are obstructed by barriers . . . A talented man must either abate or dare to raise the barrier with a big scandal. I, for example, would like to argue. I like to show the strength of my personality. I want my own glory. We're afraid to give a man attention. I want more attention. I would like to have been born in a small French town, to have grown up in daydreams, to have set myself some sort of high goal, and one

fine day to have walked out of that small town and come to the capital on foot, and there, working fanatically, to have reached my goal. But I wasn't born in the West. Now they've told me: it's not that it's yours – even the most remarkable personality is nothing. (pp. 17–18)

(В нашей стране дороги славы заграждены шлагбаумами ... Одаренный человек либо должен потускнеть, либо решиться на то, чтобы с большим скандалом поднять шлагбаум. Мне, например, хочется спорить. Мне хочется показать силу своей личности. Я хочу моей собственной славы. У нас боятся уделить внимание человеку. Я хочу большего внимания. Я хотел бы родиться в маленьком французском городке, расти в метаниях, поставить себе какую-нибудь высокую цель и в прекрасный день уйти из городка и пешком прийти в столицу и там, фанатически работая, добиться цели. Но я не родился на Западе. Теперь мне сказали: не то что твоя – самая значительная личность – ничто.) (p. 23)

On the other hand, Kavalerov's words have a ring of truth about them, for indeed the new world favours not individual skills or talents but collective effort, expediency and purpose. This becomes clear in the football match in Part Two of the novel (see below). Kavalerov's attitude towards Andrei is most ungracious, as Andrei had given him shelter out of the goodness of his heart and with no ulterior motive, and even provided him with some part-time clerical work. When he is unceremoniously bundled out of Andrei's flat, having insulted him, Kavalerov decides to kill his former protector.

The world as we see it in Part One is poetic and unusual, for we see it through Kavalerov's eyes. Thus at the aerodrome Kavalerov describes planes that no longer resemble birds, but fish sprawled helplessly along the ground. Kavalerov is refused access to Andrei's circle of acquaintances, as the guard sees immediately that he does not belong in such company. 'You're not from there' (p. 31) ('вы не оттуда', p. 34), he asserts, correctly. Elsewhere his descriptions are almost always accompanied by a simile, no matter how outlandish (for instance, 'yawning shook me like a dog' (p. 35) ('зевота трясла меня, как пса', p. 37)). Kavalerov's letter to Andrei is a masterpiece of quixotic intent, chivalry and romanticism, but with no root in reality; instead, he talks of his dreams and fantasies, in starkly original language and imagery. Kavalerov berates himself for speaking in images, and for not being able to speak simply.

Kavalerov meets Ivan Babichev, who is a clear contrast to his brother, Andrei. Ivan is a pathetic Chaplinesque figure, who opposes what he sees as the dehumanizing morality of the day with his own 'conspiracy of feelings' ('заговор чувств').[10] Ivan is a hopeless dreamer who creates legends and illusions about himself. Ivan's reality is really fantasy. Why, for instance, is he arrested and detained for ten days? Is it, as he claims, because Andrei had him arrested as a political undesirable, or was he simply drunk and disorderly? The neutral observer may incline towards the latter conclusion. Significantly, both Ivan and Kavalerov are thrown out of bars after causing a row.

Volodia Makarov is a young footballer who also lives with Andrei, and whose fierce collectivism is at odds with Kavalerov's hopeless individualism. There are also two women in the story: Valia is Ivan's daughter, and the object of affection of both Kavalerov and Makarov; Anechka Prokopovich is a fat and sexually aggressive middle-aged widow, first seen tearing pieces of meat 'as a princess tears through a cobweb' (p. 20) ('как принцесса [раздирает] паутину', p. 25). Kavalerov rents a corner of her room, most of which is taken up by her huge bed. In the end, Kavalerov and Ivan take it in turns to share her sexual favours. Their world is reduced to one of sordid sex, alcoholism and indifference.

The plot, then, is based on the clash of contrasting characters and their opposing world views. Andrei and Ivan, Makarov and Kavalerov, Valia and Anechka are all contrasting pairs, one representing the new world, the other the old. Characters are associated with certain symbols: Andrei's vision is of the Chetvertak, a huge dining room that will cater for all families, where a two-course meal will cost a quarter of a rouble: a *chetvertak*. Thus the household drudgery of everyday cooking would be removed. Ivan's dream is to build a corresponding machine called Ophelia, which will do battle with and destroy the Chetvertak. There are further correspondences in the minor characters Shapiro, who tests Andrei's sausages and is integrated into the new world, and Getske, the German footballer, an individualist who plays only for personal glory and not for the victory of the team. Furthermore, Shapiro's dignity and conviviality are emphasized, while Getske feels only contempt for everyone else around him. If Andrei is further associated with the giant sausage (which has obvious phallic overtones), Ivan carries with him a pillow, a symbol of the human warmth he feels is disappearing in the modern world. The pillow can also be seen as a metaphor for Ivan's eventual defeat, as he is to resign himself to a lifetime in Anechka's bed. When we first see Andrei and Ivan together, their stature is contrasted: Andrei is large and imposing, his shadow falls across the town 'like a Buddha' as he confronts his brother from the balcony of his flat, whereas Ivan is small and fat, looking up to his brother above him (both literally and metaphorically). Ivan appeals to his daughter Valia, clutching his pillow, to come back to him, but she prefers the tutelage of her progressive-minded uncle.

However, things are not so clear cut as they may initially appear. The novel is divided into two parts, the first largely narrated through Kavalerov's eyes and told in the first person and the second told by a third-person narrator, who nevertheless shares many of Kavalerov's thoughts and feelings.[11] Thus, descriptions and perceptions are similarly original and unusual. Andrei may be a builder of the new world, but his major contribution is to produce a new jumbo sausage – hardly an achievement of grandiose significance. Volodia Makarov chides Andrei for his hospitality towards Kavalerov as giving in to sheer human compassion, thereby revealing his own jealousy. (Makarov saved Andrei's life during the Civil War, and since then they have been together like father and son.) Andrei is certainly not the unfeeling brute Kavalerov would have us believe, but is rather a sensitive and compassionate man driven by humanistic rather than ideological concerns.

We are also taken into Andrei's mind when he is suddenly assailed by self-doubt over his way of life and the values he lives by. Andrei, it turns out, has just those human weaknesses and emotions that Ivan thinks are disappearing. Nevertheless, we are told more about Ivan's childhood than we are about Andrei's. All we learn of Andrei's past is that he was in exile in the Tsarist period and lived abroad before the Revolution. Ivan, however, was a talented child, with imagination; we get the distinct impression that the author is more sympathetic towards Ivan than he is to Andrei.

Another example of Olesha's ambivalence is in his two female characters. Valia is young, bright-eyed and innocent, a symbol of the new generation with its bright hopes and aspirations, but Kavalerov sees her in decidedly erotic terms, with her legs parted in a posture of sexual availability or her dress billowing up over her body. Kavalerov further claims that Andrei also entertains not entirely chaste intentions towards her. Anechka Prokopovich may represent humbling sexuality of the worst kind – she is portrayed as wielding a huge knife, as if to castrate the men she sleeps with – but Kavalerov would like to see in her a mother-figure. She feels pity for both Ivan and Kavalerov, and in the end is the only haven of warmth and affection they can find.[12]

Makarov may seem to be the perfect example of the new Soviet man, but he sees himself as a 'machine', exactly the type Ivan fears, as he writes in a letter to Andrei:

I am a man-machine. You won't recognize me. I've turned into a machine. If I haven't already turned, then I want to turn. The machines here are beasts. Thoroughbreds! Remarkably indifferent, proud machines. Not what's in your sausage works. You're using primitive means. You only have to cut up calves. I want to be a machine. I want to consult with you. I want to become proud from work, proud because I work. In order to be indifferent, you understand, to everything that's not work! Envy toward the machine has taken hold – that's what it is! How am I worse than it? We invented it, created it, but it turned out much more ferocious than we. Give it a start – it's away! It'll work so that there's not a squiggle extra. And I too want to be like that. You understand, Andrei Petrovich – so there's not a squiggle extra. How I'd like to talk with you. (p. 46)

(Я – человек-машина. Не узнаешь ты меня. Я превратился в машину. Если еще не превратился, то хочу превратиться. Машины здесь – зверьё! Породистые! Замечательно равнодушные, гордые машины. Не то что в твоих колбасных. Кустарничаете. Вам только телят резать. Я хочу быть машиной. С тобою хочу посоветоваться. Хочу стать гордым от работы, гордым, – потому что работаю. Чтоб быть равнодушным, понимаешь ли, ко всему, что не работа! Зависть взяла к машине – вот оно что! Чем я хуже ее? Мы же ее выдумали, создали, а она оказалась куда свирепее нас. Дашь ей ход – пошла! Проработает так, что ни цифирки лишней. Хочу я быть таким. Понимаешь ли, Андрей Петрович, – чтоб ни цифирки лишней. Как хочется с тобой поговорить!) (p. 45)

The style of this letter is in sharp contrast to Kavalerov's flowery letter to Andrei, as it is full of colloquial, over-familiar language and brutish phrases.

Makarov is the collectivist of whom the new Soviet regime could be proud and, when his team plays against a visiting German team, he is the consummate team-player. The Germans play as individuals, exemplified by the skill of Getske. Makarov's almost super-human efforts are applauded by his team-mates, and he is lifted up by them when he concedes a goal and generally supported throughout the game. We do not know the final score; the last we hear is that the Germans are leading 1–0 at half-time. However, Soviet collectivism is obviously superior to the Germans' individualist skills, a symbolic representation of the ultimate victory of Russian socialism over Western capitalism. Kavalerov watches the game and returns home drunk, now convinced of his own defeat, Makarov's superiority and the latter's legitimate right to Valia.

In the end, Valia chooses to be with Makarov and with Andrei her adopted father. Indeed, she hardly gets to know her other erstwhile suitor, Kavalerov, who merely looks on her from a distance and fantasizes about her. Kavalerov dreams not only of her, but of other girls getting into bed with him. Makarov the man-machine triumphs over the poet, just as Andrei the pragmatic sausage-maker triumphs over his brother, the energetic but hapless dreamy inventor. Makarov is an unattractive character, unfeeling and somewhat coarse towards his benefactor Andrei, but he is a good footballer and his efforts are directed towards the good of the collective.

Olesha, however, is much more interested in Kavalerov and Ivan. Ivan defines himself as 'the last dreamer on earth' ('последний мечтатель земли'), 'the leader of an army of many millions' ('вождь многомиллионной армии'), that is, of all those who belong to the past, 'the children of the dying century' ('дети гибнущего века'), those who care for feeling and emotion and who cannot fit into the present. He sees himself as a Christ-like figure being led to Golgotha, a Don Quixote doing battle with windmills. Lonely and lost, he speaks of desolation, deserts, trenches and abandoned objects in them. Significantly, his conversations on these topics with Kavalerov are usually held in a bar. He tries to rouse his troops, in the bar, in the name of his 'conspiracy':

'We – that is humanity – having reached the last limit,' he said, banging a mug against the marble like a hoof. 'Powerful personalities, people who've decided to live their own way, egoists, stubborn people, I turn to you as the more intelligent – my vanguard! Listen, you who are standing in the lead! An epoch is ending. The wave is breaking against the rocks, the wave bubbles, the foam sparkles. Just what do you want? What? To disappear, to come to nought like droplets, like petty water bubbling? No, my friends, you don't have to die like that! No! Come to me, I will teach you.' (p. 64)

(– Мы – это человечество, дошедшее до последнего предела, – говорил он, стуча кружкой но мрамору, как копытом. – Сильные личности, люди, решившие жить по-своему, – эгоисты, упрямцы, к вам обращаюсь я, как к более умным, – авангард мой! Слушайте, стоящие впереди! Кончается эпоха. Вал разбивается о камни, вал закипает, сверкает пена. Чего же хотите вы? Чего? Исчезнуть, сойти на нет капельками, мелким водяным кипением? Нет, друзья мои, не так должны вы погибнуть! Нет! Придите ко мне, я научу вас.) (p. 56)

In a rare moment of lucidity Ivan admits his own envy, thus calling into question the legitimacy of his 'conspiracy': 'We envy the approaching epoch. If you wish, here is the envy of old age. Here is the envy of the first human generation to have grown old', p. 76 ('Мы завидуем грядущей эпохе. Если хотите, тут зависть старости. Тут зависть впервые состарившегося человеческого поколения', p. 65).

Not for nothing does he give his imaginary vengeful machine the name of Ophelia, for Ophelia in *Hamlet* is a beacon of love and devotion in a cruel and treacherous world. However, her name also suggests madness and suicide. Ivan asserts that his Ophelia has human characteristics, has emotions and picks flowers. Only in his dreams and fantasies can Ivan, the 'little man', defeat Andrei, the 'giant'. In reality, he can do nothing but feel envy.

Style and Imagery

The most arresting feature of *Envy*, however, is not the plot or characterization but the imagery and style. To be sure, the work's myriad and diverse images are not mere embellishments, but provide added texture and meaning to the subject matter. Kavalerov views Andrei taking his toilet in Part One and likens him to all sorts of animals: he is like a flamingo, his 'magnificent' groin is like that of a male antelope. Elsewhere similes are similarly outlandish: Kavalerov sees Andrei as a 'wild boar', a truck crawls along like 'a beetle'. Plants, trees, animals and birds are all used in comparisons and metaphors. Especially in the first part, narrated by Kavalerov himself, we get a poetic and stylized picture of reality, or rather, reality as Kavalerov would like to see it.

Perhaps the most important stylistic feature of the work is the preoccupation with modes of seeing and perceiving. Indeed, the Russian title, *Зависть*, comes from the verb завидовать, 'to envy', which has at its root the verb видеть: 'to see'. Light and colour are recurring motifs, so that the narrative has a vivid and immediate effect. Kavalerov and Andrei look at the world through telescopes and binoculars, Andrei in order to see the finer details of things, Kavalerov in order to see things in a distorted way. By making things seem small and miniature, he can thus assert his superiority over them. Whereas Kavalerov is always seeing the world in reflection (mirrors, pieces of metal, buttons, water, dishes), Andrei has no need of illusory reflections.[13] Consequently, there are many references to things as they *seem* or *appear* to be.[14]

Mirrors are especially important. Anechka's bed has a huge mirror attached to it, a mirror that has not only a realistic function – for heightened sensuality – but also a metaphorical one: in this bed, their final refuge, Ivan and Kavalerov can introvert their gaze, their attention is turned in on themselves and not on the outside world. When Ivan and Kavalerov first meet, it is near a street mirror, and this mirror serves as the bridge between the end of Part One and the beginning of Part Two, a bridge which marks the end of a fantasy world and the beginning of the actual world.

Eyes are also important motifs. Feeling threatened by him, Kavalerov does not see Andrei's eyes but merely 'two stupidly, mercurially shining plates of the pince-nez' (p. 32) ('две тупо, ртутно сверкающие бляшки пенсне', p. 35); in other words, Kavalerov dehumanizes Andrei by seeing him as a machine and by so doing, reduces him as a figure of authority and status (at least in his own eyes). Ivan also sees only the glass of Andrei's pince-nez when addressing his brother. Both insist on seeing not the person, but external characteristics. Kavalerov and Olesha further associate Andrei with inanimate or mechanical objects, by portraying him standing or sitting next to electric lights, at an aerodrome or on a moving crane on a building site.

Conversely, when Ivan Babichev finally realises that emotions such as love and tenderness still thrive, and that his 'conspiracy' is futile and his 'machine' merely a figment of his imagination, he can look on reality no more:

> 'Valya, pluck out my eyes. I want to be blind,' he said breathlessly, 'I don't want to see anything: neither lawns, nor boughs, nor flowers, nor knights, nor coward – I have to become blind, Valya. I was mistaken, Valya . . . I thought that all feelings had perished – love and devotion and tenderness . . . But everything's remained, Valya . . . Only not for us, and for us remained only envy and envy . . . Pluck out my eyes, Valya, I want to become blind.' (p. 100)

> (– Валя, выколи мне глаза. Я хочу быть слепым, – говорил он, задыхаясь, – я ничего не хочу видеть: ни лужаек, ни ветвей, ни цветков, ни рыцарей, ни трусов, – мне надо ослепнуть, Валя . . . Я думал, что все чувства погибли – любовь, и преданность, и нежность . . . Но все осталось, Валя . . . Только не для нас, а нам осталось только зависть и зависть . . . Выколи мне глаза. Валя, я хочу ослепнуть . . .) (p. 82)

Kavalerov also looks out on the real world through windows, whether at clouds racing across the sky or at Andrei driving to work. Perspective and angles of vision make things seem different, depending on whether they are viewed from afar, from above, from below or from the side; only thus is Kavalerov able to cope with things. He looks down at a tugboat on the river which at first strikes him to be like an almond; as he watches an aeroplane take off and recede into the distance, the object changes shape and resembles different things as it gets further away. It is thus no surprise that for Kavalerov things that are threatening seem disproportionately huge (like Andrei himself, or Anechka's bed). Sounds, too, are different when heard from various distances, such as twenty bells heard from a distance, or noises in a restaurant that seem to Kavalerov to become like a little tune. The bell-ringer he likens to Quasimodo, and the tune sounds to him like 'Tom-vir-lir-li'. He then conjures up an image of an imaginary Tom Virlirli (or Dick Whittington), who then turns into the concrete Volodia Makarov, whom he sees for the first time standing before him in the real, tangible world. The fantasy world is invariably broken up by the real world.

Kavalerov undoubtedly speaks for Olesha himself on the validity of seeing the world differently. Towards the end of Part One the 'I' of the narrative comments that looking at a landscape through the wrong end of binoculars makes colours and contours more precise and makes familiar objects small and unusual, like a dream. Furthermore:

> The distance opens before you. Everyone's sure: that's a house, a wall, but to you has been given the advantage: that's not a house! You've discovered a mystery: here's not a wall, here's a mysterious world where everything you've just seen repeats and at the same time repeats with that stereoscopy and vividness which is subject only to the distancing lenses of binoculars. (p. 51)

> (Перед вами открывается даль. Вы уверены: это дом, стена, но вам дано преимущество: это не дом! Вы обнаружили тайну: здесь не стена, здесь таинственный мир, где повторяется все только что виденное вами, – и притом повторяется с той стереоскопичностью и яркостью, которые подвластны лишь удаляющим стеклам бинокля.) (pp. 48–9)

Kavalerov can only dominate his environment if he makes it small. Later, at the football match, Kavalerov feels superior to Makarov because he is looking down at him from the stand. The author later explicitly identifies himself with Kavalerov, asserting the legitimacy of individual perception, however distorted, for this vision gives access to that 'mysterious world' that exists side by side with the everyday.[15]

As an example of this similarity of vision of both Kavalerov and the author, let us consider two passages. The first is from Part One, narrated by Kavalerov:

> I amuse myself with observations. Have you ever noticed how salt falls off the end of a knife without leaving a trace – the knife shines as if it were never touched; that a pince-nez runs over the bridge of a nose like a bicycle; that a person is surrounded by little inscriptions, a sprawling anthill of small inscriptions: on forks, spoons, plates the rim of a pince-nez, buttons, pencils? No-one notices them. They struggle for existence. (p. 6)

> (Я развлекаюсь наблюдениями. Обращали ли вы внимание на то, что соль спадает с кончика ножа, не оставляя никаких следов, – нож блещет, как нетронутый: что пенсне переезжает переносицу, как велосипед: что человека окружают маленькие надписи, разбредшийся муравейник маленьких надписей: на вилках, ложках, тарелках, оправе пенсне, пуговицах, карандашах? Никто не замечает их. Они ведут борьбу за существование.) (p. 15)

Andrew Barratt has noted that in this passage 'Kavalerov is unconsciously projecting his own neuroses upon the world of objects'. Furthermore, because he indicates the kind of minutiae nobody else would notice, 'he is, in effect, drawing attention to his own pitiful position in Andrei's household, where he is not even taken for granted'.[16]

The second passage is from Part Two, narrated in the third person. Note in particular the emphasis on colour imagery in the first sentence, and the treatment of inanimate objects:

> Black was the evening, white and spherical the lanterns, the bunting showed unusually red, the gaps beneath the wooden slips were deathly black. The lanterns swung clanging their wires. As if the shadow was fluttering its eyebrows. Around the lanterns gnats flew and perished. From far off, forcing the windows along the way to blink, the contours of the surrounding houses, torn away by the lanterns, were carried and dashed against the structure – and then (until the lantern swung by the wind came to rest) the woods violently enlived, everything came into motion – and, like a many-tiered sailing-ship, the structure floated onto the crowd. (p. 90)

> (Был черен вечер, белы и шаровидны фонари, необычайно алели полотнища, провалы под деревянными сходнями были смертельно черны. Раскачивались, звеня проволоками, фонари. Тень как бы размахивала бровями. Вокруг фонарей летала и гибла мошкара. Издалека, заставляя мигать попутные окна, неслись сорванные фонарями контуры окрестных домов и кидались на постройку, и тогда (до тех пор пока не успокаивался раскачанный ветром фонарь) бурно оживали леса, все приходило в движение – – и, как многоярусный парусник, плыла на толпу постройка.) (p. 75)

Nils Åke Nilsson has commented on the 'invisible' world in Olesha:

> What we learn from Oleša's stories is that there exist two worlds – the world we ordinarily live and act in, and an 'invisible world'. This 'invisible world' is part of our common, everyday reality, only we do not usually notice it. One has to know the trick. Window-panes, street-mirrors, binoculars, rain, wind, unusual angles, optical illusions – all these things are keys with the magic power of opening the closed door to this fantastic world, a world which to Oleša is as real and important as the 'visible' one.[17]

Distortion for Kavalerov, as for Olesha, is the key to poetic vision for, paradoxically as it may seem, it actually makes reality clearer and easier to cope with. But because it is distorted, it is also artificial, a pretence, an illusion.

Light and darkness are also important motifs in this respect. Verbs denoting shining, sparkling, flashing (сиять, сверкать, блестеть) and their compounds recur throughout the book. Furthermore, light glistens on surfaces, people and things 'shine', light plays tricks with the eyes and illusions occur – but only with Ivan and Kavalerov. To them, things seems different in different shades of light. Even in his dream, Ivan sees Ophelia loom overhead as he confronts Andrei, but Andrei sees only a passing shadow. For Ivan, light represents the old world and so is accompanied by verbs such as тускнеть and потухать ('to grow dim', 'to become extinguished'), and the new world brings about only darkness: thus his preferred blindness would bring darkness to him. Yet Kavalerov sees Ivan's world, and Anechka's bedroom, as one of unrelieved gloom (мрак and сумрак). When Ivan and Kavalerov walk through Moscow, they walk through alternate patches of shadow and light:

> Sunday morning – one of the best aspects of a Moscow summer. The illumination, not shattered by traffic, remained whole, as if the sun had just risen. Thus they walked along the geometrical maps of light and shadow more likely: through stereoscopic bodies, because the light and shadow crossed not only the flat surfaces but in the air as well. Not yet reaching the Mossoviet, they found themselves in full shadow. But into the space between two buildings fell a large massif of light. It was thick, almost dense; here it was already impossible to doubt that light is material: dust carried in it could have been taken for the vibration of the ether. (p. 96)

> (Воскресенье утром – один из лучших видов московского лета. Освещение, не разрываемое движением, оставалось целым, как будто солнце только что взошло. Таким образом, они шли по геометрическим планам света и тени, вернее – сквозь стереоскопические тела, потому что свет и тень пересекались не только по плоскости, но и в воздухе. Не доходя до Моссовета, они очутились в полной тени. Но в пролет между двумя корпусами выпал большой массив света. Он был густ, почти плотен, здесь уже нельзя было сомневаться в том, что свет материален: пыль, носившаяся в нем, могла сойти за колебание эфира.) (p. 79)

Ivan is mistrustful of electricity, for it brings about artificial light, artificial energy and the artificial life of the new world. He talks of the new world as a light bulb that will sooner or later burn itself out, to be followed by darkness. Significantly, at home Andrei always sits or stands near the lampshade, and indeed we see him at such an angle that his head seems to be replaced by it. After the success of his sausage, he too 'shines'.

Another feature of Olesha's vision is the qualities with which he invests inanimate objects. Just as humans are likened to animals and plants, so shadows and clouds become animate, causing storms in bushes and a shadow across the city 'like Buddha', as already mentioned, or a cloud to hover 'with the outline of South America' (p. 47) ('с очертаниями Южной Америки', p. 46). Just as people become like machines (and Kavalerov sees a machine-like Andrei coming towards him at the aerodrome), so machines such as Ophelia become like people.

Space is an important motif. Ivan addresses Andrei and Valia from the street, looking up to them on the balcony as if pondering a higher reality. Andrei is always described as large; Ivan is always small. Kavalerov looks down on Makarov at the football match, feeling superior (but not for long). Andrei fills up the spaces he occupies; he dominates his surroundings, and Kavalerov always feels suffocated by him. At both the aerodrome and the building site, Kavalerov views Andrei from afar, over a distance, and still feels humbled by him; at the building site Andrei flies past and above Kavalerov on a swinging crane, with Kavalerov looking up at him, helpless and bewildered.

Both Kavalerov and Ivan have dreams. Ivan dreams of victory over his brother, where Andrei begs to be allowed to die on Ivan's pillow: Kavalerov has a dream which represents the eventual resolution of the plot, as Valia floats into Makarov's arms on a breath of wind, borne along by the sounds of an orchestra. In this same cataclysmic dream Kavalerov also sees Ivan killed by Ophelia, his own machine, transfixed to a wall by a needle in an image of mock crucifixion, and turning on his own axis so that he becomes like a machine himself.[18] This is a grotesque dream, but one that highlights the sad futility of Ivan's reality and Kavalerov's rebellion.

Conclusion

Зависть, then, is about the clash of the old and the new worlds, and therefore all aspects of reality are two-sided. Although there are diametrically opposed pairs of characters, none of them is portrayed by the author in simple unequivocal terms. Distortion, of images, of perceptions, of light, of romance, is a central structural feature, and the text is beset with contradictions and ambiguities. The concentration on optical effects and modes and angles of perception, as well as the narrative viewpoint itself, blur the distinction between what *is* and what *seems to be*. The use of reflected images, reflected reality, comes to assume a greater importance within the work's overall scheme.

But, more fundamentally, the novel is also about literature, creativity and the role of the artist in the new world. The role of literature is changing, reduced to stage repertoires such as monologues and rhymes about NEP types of the day, the kind that Kavalerov is currently writing.

Such a statement is surely not without irony: Olesha, like Kavalerov, is afraid that the great Russian literary tradition, like everything else of the nineteenth century, has no place in the modern world. Ivan comes to advocate indifference, but we do not in the end know whether Kavalerov accepts his offer to share Anechka.

In this respect *Envy* embodies the same concerns as Bulgakov's *Мастер и Маргарита*. Mention has been made of the references to *Don Quixote* and *Hamlet*; Andrew Barratt has also noted parallels with Dostoevskii's *Notes from Underground* (the conflict of the rational and the irrational, the romantic and the utilitarian, the individual and the collective), and further notes that the scene in Kavalerov's nightmare where Ophelia impales Ivan on a spike is reminiscent of a passage in H. G. Wells' *War of the Worlds*, with which Olesha was certainly acquainted. The theme of man against the machine is also in Karel Capek's *R.U.R.*, again a work which Olesha knew well.[19] D. G. B. Piper has also remarked on the work's indebtedness to Wells' *The Time Machine*. The literary references and transparent influences suggest that the novel is not just about the fate of the artist in the post–1917 society, but also of literature itself. The section 'The Tale of the Meeting of the Two Brothers' (*Сказка о встрече двух братьев*) is a narrative within a narrative, told seemingly by a different narrator with its own distinctive style and point of view. The very structure of the novel – divided into contrasting halves, told in differing narrative styles – clearly demonstrates the novel's own self-conscious status. The letters of Kavalerov and Makarov to Andrei offer two differing modes of thought and writing. The novel is indeed about a writer, a poet, and his vision of the world; it is also about the notion of writing itself. The fact that Olesha himself explicitly identified with this writer figure, showing how a writer's vision can transform 'objective' reality, gives further justification for regarding the novel as a narrative essentially concerned with the future destiny of the writer and of literature in general.

Notes

1. Iu. K. Olesha, *Избранное* (Selected Works), Moscow, 1974, p. 451. All further references to Olesha's works, unless otherwise indicated, are taken from this edition, with page numbers incorporated into the text.

2. A useful survey of the critical responses to *Envy* can be found in Andrew Barratt, *Yurii Olesha's 'Envy'*, Birmingham Slavonic Monographs, 1981, pp. 1–6.

3. Olesha has also benefited from the post-Gorbachev literary thaw in the sense that not only have his works been reprinted, often for the first time in seventy years (for instance his poems from 1917–18), but also memoirs of him by other writers that have shed light on his life. Thus, Nikolai Starshinov, 'В Голыцино, в былые годы' ('In Golytsino, in Past Years'), *Iunost'*, no. 12, 1988, p. 89, recalls Olesha telling him that he began writing poems while still at school.

4. Boris Iampol'skii recalls Olesha at this time as thoroughly demoralized and sad, shunned by all the people in the writing fraternity he used to know, living in poverty, dependent on advances from theatres, circuses and film studios. Furthermore, he had substantial psychological problems: 'And he, an old, grey, hungry child, recalled to the point of hallucination "the twilight in the canteen, the canteen on Grecheskaia Street, which looked out on to Orlov's wall and window". Iurii Karlovich, nice, dear Iurii Karlovich!' ('И он, старый, седой, голодный ребенок, вспоминал до галлюцинаций «сумерки в столовой, той столовой на Греческой, выходящей в стену, в окно Орлова»'. Юрий Карлович, милый, дорогой Юрий Карлович!'): Boris Iampol'skii, 'Да здравствует мир без меня (Long Live the World Without Me)', *Druzhba narodov*, no. 2, 1989. Iampol'skii goes on to assert that Olesha was destroyed in the 1930s. Margarita Aliger recalls how Olesha in 1936 denounced Shostakovich's opera *Леди Макбет Мцхенского уезда* (*Lady Macbeth of Mtskhensk District*) in the wake of the vicious *Pravda* attack on the composer's music. She paints a picture of a man trying to convince himself of the correctness of *Pravda*'s reasoning and coming to terms with his own artistic capitulation. She adds: 'I realised that from that tragic evening Olesha wrote and bequeathed to people nothing significant, nothing essential. Art does not forgive betrayal' ('Я поняла, что с того трагического вечера Олеша ничего значительного, ничего существенного не написал и не оставил людям. Искусство не прощает измен'). Margarita Aliger, 'Печальная притча' ('A Sad Parable'), *Znamia*, 1987, no. 10, pp. 102–9 (p. 108). Arkadii Belinkov's long and often rambling monograph discusses Olesha as a writer, but more fundamentally as a symbol of the Soviet intelligentsia who compromised and sold his soul: see *Сдача и гибель советского интеллигента. Юрий Олеша* (*The Submission and Demise of a Soviet Intellectual. Iurii Olesha*), Madrid, 1976.

5. *Первый Всесоюзный Съезд писателей СССР. Стенографический Отчет* ('The First USSR Writers' Congress. A Stenographic Record'), Moscow, Khudozhestvennaia literatura, 1934; reprint edition, Moscow, Sovetskii pisatel', 1990, p. 234.

6. *Первый Всесоюзный Съезд*, p. 235.

7. Yury Olesha, *Envy*, trans. T. S. Berczynski, Ann Arbor, 1975, p. 3. All translations from the novel are taken from this edition, with page numbers incorporated into the text.

8. William Harkins sees Andrei as a eunuch or hermaphrodite:

> This confused array of traits, some masculine, others which suggest an effeminate man or eunuch, puzzle us until we grasp the essential principle which Andrei represents: he is a hermaphrodite figure. As hermaphrodite he combines masculinity with femininity, but a masculinity and femininity which tend to neutralize one another: for masculine sexuality Andrei substitutes an intense career drive, while his feminine sexual tendency satisfies itself as latent homosexuality through the adoption of young men. He combines in himself the roles of provider (father) and nourisher (mother), and this is the inner reason why he is characterized as hermaphroditic'. (William E. Harkins, 'The Theme of Sterility in Olesha's *Envy*', in Edward J. Brown (ed.), *Major Soviet Writers: Essays in Criticism*, Oxford, 1973, p. 282).

9. Elizabeth Klosty Beaujour, *The Invisible Land: A Study of the Artistic Imagination of Iurii Olesha*, New York, 1970, p. 40.

10. Recent archival publications show Ivan originally as the most important character in the novel. Indeed, early versions did not make mention of Andrei or even Kavalerov. Even in the early versions Ivan is depicted carrying his pillow. I. Ozernaia notes the evolution of Ivan's significance: 'But if in the final version of the novel Ivan's inventions are merely the fruits of his unrestrained fantasy, in the beginning, at the novel's genesis, Ivan Babichev's "little things" are very serious and fill up the whole of Moscow as soon as he appears . . . And all of these actions culminate in insane consequences and phantasmagoric events' ('Но если в окончательном варианте повести изобретения Ивана являются лишь плодами безудержной его фантазии, то вначале, при зарождении книги, «штучки» Ивана Бабичева на полном серьезе и всецело заполняют Москву, как только он появляется в ней . . . И все эти его действия обязательно завершаются безумными последствиями и фантасмагорическими событиями'). I. Ozernaia, '«Штучки» Ивана Бабичева в первых вариантах повести Юрия Олеши «Зависть»' ('Ivan Babichev's "Little Things" in early versions of

the novel "Envy"'), *Literaturnaia ucheba*, no. 2, 1989, pp. 158–69.
11. Neil Cornwell, among others, has noted the inconsistencies in Olesha's narrative method: in Part One, Kavalerov appears to know (or imagines he knows) what Andrei is doing in his absence; in Part Two, the narrator is not omniscient and Kavalerov, Ivan and the third-person narrator all perceive Andrei in the same negative terms. See Neil Cornwell, 'Olesha's "Envy"', in J. Andrew (ed.), *The Structural Analysis of Russian Narrative Fiction*, Essays in Poetics Publication no. 1, Keele, no date, p. 119.
12. Harkins notes: 'And the widow's enormous and terrible bed is likewise sexual in its symbolic implications: it is at once the goal of Kavalerov's yearnings and the symbol of his fear of and disgust at sexuality, his fear of his own impotence. The bed itself is a vaginal symbol in its implicit connection with its owner and its function in the sexual act' (Harkins, 'The Theme of Sterility in Olesha's *Envy*', p. 289).
13. Elizabeth Beaujour notes: 'The ultimate tool for those Olesha heroes who desire to control and appropriate the world and turn it into their personal possession through tricks of vision is the mirror. The mirror first reassures them of their own existence. The mirror also gives one the power to project one's image – *my* reflection . . . Men of action do not need mirrors . . . Andrei Babichev is reflected back to himself by the activity of his co-workers' (Beaujour, *The Invisible Land*, pp. 53–4).
14. Neil Cornwell has commented on the high incidence in the narrative of the verb 'казаться' ('to seem'). See Cornwell, 'Olesha's "Envy"', p. 124.
15. Don Piper explicitly links Olesha with Kavalerov and Ivan: 'If Olesha is both Kavalerov, who narrates the events of the first half of the book, and also Ivan, whose biography and fantasies comprise most of the second half, then we see more than three-quarters of the action through the eyes of Olesha, who, in Mirsky's words, is also unreal. In short, *Zavist'* becomes an extremely subjective poetic fantasy' (D. G. B. Piper, 'Yuriy Olesha's *Zavist'*: an Interpretation', *Slavonic and East European Review*, vol. 48, no. 1, 1970, p. 28).
16. Barratt, *Yurii Olesha's 'Envy'*, p. 15.
17. Nils Åke Nilsson, 'Through the Wrong End of Binoculars: An Introduction to Jurij Oleša', in Brown (ed.), *Major Soviet Writers*, p. 263.
18. Harkins sees the needle as a phallus, and Ophelia's rebellion against her master as a kind of castration to illustrate Ivan's impotence. See Harkins, 'The Theme of Sterility in Olesha's *Envy*', p. 292.
19. Barratt, *Yurii Olesha's 'Envy'*, pp. 10–11.

4

Nikolai Ostrovskii (1904–36), *How the Steel was Tempered* (*Как закалялась сталь*)

Introduction and Background

How the Steel Was Tempered (1930–4) is the socialist realist novel *par excellence*. Its schematic plot, easily identifiable heroes and villains and heroic, self-sacrificing central character make it a classic work of what became in 1934 the 'basic method of Soviet artistic literature and literary criticism'. Indeed, partially because the biography, and in particular the trials and physical ordeals undergone, of Pavel Korchagin, the 'positive hero' of the narrative, are based on those of the author himself, the book has been phenomenally popular in the USSR and was required reading for Soviet schoolchildren up to the late 1980s. Korchagin himself became a symbol of revolutionary energy: the standard school textbook on Soviet literature makes the point that 'the writer links the biography of Pavel Korchagin with the fate of the whole generation that brought about the proletarian revolution' ('биографию Павла Корчагина писатель связывает с судьбой целого поколения, свершившего пролетарскую революцию').[1] Furthermore: 'N. Ostrovskii opened up man's inexhaustible spiritual possibilities, proving that devotion to social ideals and communism engenders a sublime, genuine morality, and spiritually enriches a person' ('Н. Островский открыл неисчерпаемые духовные возможности человека, доказав, что преданность общественным идеалам, делу коммунизма рождает высокую, подлинную нравственность, духовно обогащает человека').[2] Korchagin's immense energy, his strength of will and commitment to the cause of Bolshevism, and his qualities of leadership and self-abnegation have been seen as ideal material for emulation by the young and a source of inspiration for future generations.

Nikolai Ostrovskii was the son of a labourer. He joined the Komsomol, the Communist Youth Union, at the age of fifteen in 1919, and the Communist Party in 1924. He was seriously wounded during the Civil War, and in the late 1920s went blind and became paralysed and bedridden. Only then did he began writing. The experience of Pavel Korchagin therefore can be seen to be squarely based on that of his creator. Before further discussion of the novel, however, a few words on the prevailing cultural and political environment are necessary.

By the early 1930s the experiments and considerable variety in the literary and cultural fields of the 1920s had come to an end. RAPP (the Russian Association of Proletarian Writers), established in 1928, campaigned against all 'fellow travellers' in literature as well as other literary groups, and called for the promotion of proletarian writers and values. Its pronouncements initially had the stamp of official Party approval, but by 1932 this and all other groups had been abolished and a single Union of Soviet Writers was set up. In 1934 the Union held its first Congress, at which socialist realism was adopted as the fundamental theory underpinning and determining the future development of Soviet literature.

The formula which encapsulates the main tenets of socialist realism is contained in the Writers' Union Constitution, pronounced at the Congress by Andrei Zhdanov, Stalin's cultural spokesman and subsequent hatchet-man, and runs as follows:

> Socialist Realism, the basic method employed by Soviet artistic literature and literary criticism, demands from the writer an authentic, historically specific depiction of reality in its revolutionary development. This authenticity and historical specificity in the depiction of reality should be combined with the task of ideologically reshaping and educating the toilers in the spirit of socialism.
>
> Socialist Realism guarantees the creative artist exceptional opportunities for the manifestation of his creative initiative, for the choice of various forms, styles and genres.[3]

The consequent practice of this rather vague and ill-defined theory showed that works which came to be regarded as socialist realist exemplars revolved around a central 'positive hero', who in the course of his life graduates from a state of ideological ignorance (i.e., innocence) to political commitment and devotion to the Bolshevik cause (i.e., consciousness). Moreover, the positive hero was usually physically strong, symbolizing also a strength of spirit which would be unbroken despite the hardships visited upon the body.

In her seminal analysis of the structures and myths of socialist realism, Katerina Clark pays particular attention to the 'master plot' of the Soviet novel as 'a sort of parable for the working out of Marxism-Leninism in history'. She continues:

> The novel takes as its focus a relatively modest figure, usually a Soviet worker, administrator or soldier. This subject is known as 'the positive hero'. However modest he may be, the phases of his life symbolically recapitulate the stages of historical progress as described in Marxist-Leninist theory. The novel's climax ritually re-enacts the climax of history in communism.[4]

Under these conditions, Soviet writers in the 1930s no longer had the privilege of observing and commenting on society from the outside; they now had to engage themselves consciously in the construction of a socialist society, thereby actively participating in the historical process. After 1934 a work of Soviet socialist realism had to contain impeccable ideological commitment (*ideinost'*), be infused with 'Party spirit' (*partiinost'*) reflecting the Party's thinking, and be true to the interests of 'the people' (*narodnost'*). Crucially, socialist realism need not show the actual victory of Bolshevik reason and commitment over the forces of reaction, but had to imply or indicate the ultimate (or at least symbolic) vanquishing of enemies. Furthermore, no one must doubt that the foundations had been laid for conflicts to be resolved in the future. In other words, the artistic depiction of reality should indicate not what actually was, but what should be according to a particular ideological formula (and thus, by implication, what will be in the 'radiant future').

Plot, Theme and Characterization

How the Steel Was Tempered was first written in 1928, but was lost in the post as Ostrovskii sent it to a publisher. He rewrote it, and the completed version was at first rejected by the journal *Molodaia gvardiia* as being 'unreal' and 'defective' (забракована). It was accepted only after a second review.[5] Its original journal publication went unnoticed, as did its first appearance in book form six months later. In 1934 Part Two was published, and again was largely ignored by reviewers. The beginning of the 'storm' was marked by an article in 1935 in the Party newspaper *Pravda* by M. Kol'tsov, which was followed by essays and reviews by other newspapers and journals. Six months later Ostrovskii was a household name: 'In the course of half a year he changed from being an unknown novice writer to becoming a living classic' ('В течение полугода из безвестного начинающего литератора он превращается в живого классика').[6]

Ostrovskii's novel, perhaps better than any other written in Stalin's time, serves as the ideal socialist realist model. We are first introduced to Pavel Korchagin as a twelve-year-old boy when he is expelled from the parish school. He lives in the Ukrainian town of Shepetovka, a major railway junction not far from the Polish border. The geographical position of the town is important for subsequent plot development, as it is occupied successively by Germans, Red Guards, White forces, Ukrainian nationalists, Polish soldiers and, finally and victoriously, the Red Army. Shepetovka thus acts as a microcosm of the greater struggle going on in the Ukraine and its occupation by various forces, and the whole course of war during the years 1914–21.

The novel has a clear, chronologically based structure with little stylistic variation or imagery, and is often crudely didactic. In literary terms, according to western aesthetic criteria the novel is thus simplistic, two-dimensional and lacking in all manner of complexity. However, the aesthetics of socialist realism are different and should be viewed from a different perspective. The emphasis here is on the development of the hero; as events in the narrative unfold, then Pavel's psychology progresses correspondingly. As this psychological development is at the crux of *How the Steel is Tempered*, it is best to look at the novel in its chronological progression.

We are introduced to the injustices of the pre-October years from the outset. Pavel is expelled from the parish school as a result of putting tobacco in the food of the hated Father Vasilii (and is also beaten). When he finds work in the railway station buffet, he is angered at the injustices suffered by the kitchen workers at the hands of the waiters who can 'buy' and 'sell' the girls. Such arbitrary cruelty can also be seen as a representation of the exploitation within the country as a whole, but the first explicit indication of political repression occurs when a newspaper seller is arrested for selling illegal literature. Pavel then goes to work as a stoker's apprentice, thereby joining the industrial proletariat, and it is now that the single most formative event of his youth occurs: the Revolution.

In 1917 Pavel is about seventeen years old, and so his coming of age coincides with the onset of a new age and the dawning of political consciousness. The shifting political realities of Shepetovka throughout the turmoil of 1917 are seen through the politically uncomprehending eyes of Pavel, although as a true proletarian he does spot the essential feature of the 'bourgeois' February revolution: even after the Tsar's abdication things remain very much as they were in class terms, with the same owners of shops, the same laws and the same rich officers. When he first catches sight of some Red Guards, they are smiling and friendly, confident of their role as the custodians of the new order, and altogether less distant and more accessible than their White counterparts.

Pavel is not only representative of the working class, in Marxist-Leninist ideology the most 'progressive' class, but is also one of the people. Ostrovskii gives him some musical talent, such as the ability to play the accordion, thus demonstrating both Pavel's intuitive grasp of folk musical tradition and his link with the people. Ostrovskii also attempts to give Pavel human characteristics by describing his first stirrings of sexual attraction for his neighbour Galina. Pavel, however, controls his elemental urges and chastity becomes another proletarian virtue.

He then meets and is attracted to Tonia, a middle-class girl, and their relationship becomes symbolic of the growing alliance, in Marxist-Leninist terms, of the working class and the middle class in the fight against the landowners and exploiters of labour. Their burgeoning relationship is analogous to that of Gavrik, the working-class boy, and Petya, the son of a civil servant, in Valentin Kataev's *A White Sail Gleams* (*Белеет парус одинокий*), another novel of high Stalinist culture (1936). The relationship between Pavel and Tonia does not last long, and Ostrovskii is above all at pains to demonstrate the differences between the two, from at first Tonia's point of view and then from Pavel's:

> Having said farewell to Pavel, Tonia headed for home. She was thinking about the meeting she had just had with this black-eyed youth, and without knowing why, was glad of it.
>
> 'How much fire and strength he has! And he's not at all the ruffian I used to think. In any case, he's not at all like those drivelling grammar-school boys . . .'
>
> He was of another breed, from another environment, with which Tonia had hitherto not had any close contact.

> (Расставшись с Павлом, Тоня направилсаь домой. Она думала о только что прошедшей встрече с этим черноглазым юношей и, сама того не сознавая, была рада ей.
>
> Сколько в нем огня и упорства! И он совсем не такой грубиян, как мне казалось. Во всяком случае, он совсем не похож на всех этих слюнявых гимназистов . . .»
>
> Он был из другой породы, из той среды, с которой до сих пор Тоня близко не сталкивалась.)[7]

This is how Pavel regards the worthiness of his origins:

> Having grown up in poverty and hunger, Pavel felt animosity towards those he understood as rich. Pavel treated his feeling with caution and anxiety, he did not regard Tonia, like Galina the stonemason's daughter, one of his own, one who could be understood, and so looked on her with mistrust, ready to

give a sharp rebuff to any mockery or scorn that this pretty and educated girl may give him.

(Выросший в нищете и голоде, Павел враждебно относился к тем, кто был в его понимании богатым. К своему чувству подходил Павел с осторожностью и опаской, он не считал Тоню, как дочь каменотеса Галину, своей, простой, понятной, и недоверчиво относился к Тоне, готовый дать резкий отпор всякой насмешке и пренебрежению к нему, со стороны этой красивой и образованной девушки.) (p. 51)

Pavel begins to educate Tonia in the ways of the world, in particular the working-class realities of his own life. He also reveals to her that his favourite reading is about Giuseppe Garibaldi, the revolutionary, freedom-fighter and working-class hero.

It is at this time that Pavel comes under the influence of Zhukhrai, a Bolshevik left behind by the retreating Red Guards to work with the local population as the Germans advance. Zhukhrai's agitation amongst the workers has its effects in the form of discontent when the landowners return, partisan attacks on German soldiers, and strikes in protest at repression and arrests. Pavel meets Zhukhrai through Artem, his elder brother, but it is Zhukhrai who teaches Pavel how to look after himself; he teaches him to box so that he can defend himself from the grammar-school bully Sukhar'ko, and also assumes the responsibility of Pavel's political education. Zhukhrai, indeed, becomes Pavel's ideological mentor. Of the role of the mentor in socialist realism, Katerina Clark observes:

> A character who has already attained 'consciousness' presides and helps the hero shed the last vestiges of his individualistic consciousness and cross over to 'there' . . . The character who assumes the role of elder should be of proletarian origins or at least have been in the Party for some time and hold a fairly high rank in the local administration.[8]

Zhukhrai was a sailor with the Baltic Fleet and a Party member since 1915. Under Zhukhrai's influence Pavel commits his first politically conscious act: stealing a German officer's revolver. Zhukhrai, when he is on the run from Ukrainian nationalists, hides with Pavel for eight days and during that time reveals to him the 'truth' of the political situation. This is Pavel's real conversion, and when he frees Zhukhrai from captivity he crosses the threshold and becomes an active fighter for the Bolshevik cause. He further demonstrates that he is not afraid of self-sacrifice and physical pain by being subsequently imprisoned and tortured.

As the tumult of the Civil War mounts, the Ukraine becomes

engulfed in 'an acute, merciless class struggle' ('острая, беспощадная борьба классов', p. 56). The image used to describe social unrest, the метель (snowstorm), is a traditional one in Russian literature and comes down to us from Pushkin (in *The Captain's Daughter*). The occupation of Shepetovka by anti-Semitic Ukrainian nationalists under the leadership of Semen Petliura offers an opportunity for Ostrovskii to stress the true internationalist spirit of the novel, with condemnation of the pogroms and anti-Jewish hatred of the aggressors. Pavel Korchagin is imprisoned, released, and then escapes to join Budennyi's cavalry corps, and while he is absent from the narrative his friend Serezha Bruzzhak replaces him as its focal point. Serezha has many Jewish friends, and Mendel', the leader of a group of Jewish workers, serves as a father figure to him. Jews, like Russians and Ukrainians, are poor and repressed, victims of an unjust society; also like their Russian or Ukrainian brethren, they have their own exploiters in their midst in the form of Bliumshtein, the owner of the printing-shop where they work. Serezha is later wounded defending an old Jew during a pogrom which is inspired by an officer merely to improve the morale of his men. Bolshevik internationalism is further emphasized when the Reds take the town; the first Bolshevik Serezha sees is not a Russian, but of Chinese nationality. Serezha also joins the Reds, and is later killed in battle. Another character who extends Pavel's proletarian credentials, and who emerges later in the narrative, is Ivan Zharkii.

Following his escape from the Petliura prison, Pavel joins the Red Cavalry. Word gets back to Shepetovka that he has been killed, but he is in fact only wounded. He also contracts typhus, and this is the first of his several encounters with physical debilitation. Nevertheless, his unit is friendly and assured and the soldiers all respect one another as equals, including the commander and the commissar. Pavel transfers to Budennyi's cavalry unit. It is now 1920. At the front he meets his brother Artem, who is now the driver of an armoured train, and is then blown up by an artillery blast. Once more Pavel faces death.

There is now an abrupt shift of narrative point of view. Ostrovskii tends to shift perspective throughout the novel so that the reader sees events and characters through the eyes of individuals; thus we see both Tonia's view of Pavel and vice versa. Another such example is when Pavel frees Zhukhrai: we see his action both through his own eyes and then through the eyes of Liza Sukhar'ko, who watches from a distance and then tells Viktor Leshchinskii, who in turn informs the authorities. Elsewhere Ostrovskii assumes an Olympian viewpoint so that an all-seeing author informs the reader of troop movements, offensives and withdrawals, and thus demonstrates from a Marxist-Leninist perspective the overall working out of history. When Pavel is again wounded, we see his suffering and recovery through the eyes and notes of the doctor treating him. The doctor is amazed that Pavel has survived, and he recovers without complaining despite his serious head wound. His survival is due to an almost superhuman effort of will. He is also treated by the nurse Frosia, with whom he used to work in the Shepetovka railway buffet in the immediate pre-revolutionary years.

On his release from hospital, Pavel breaks with Tonia. Their conversation is worth recording as an indication of the extent to which Pavel has now travelled on his way to total commitment to the Party:

Tonia looked at the golden rays and said, with deep sadness:
'Will our friendship really die out, as the sun is dying out now?'
His gaze did not flinch from her; his brow tightly knit, he replied in a quiet voice:
'Tonia, we've already talked about this. Of course, you know that I have loved you and even now my love may return, but for that you must be with us. I'm not that little Pavlusha of before. And I would be a bad husband if you consider that I should belong first to you and then the Party. I will belong to the Party first, and then to you and the rest of my family.

(Тоня смотрела на золотые лучи и проговорила с глубокой грустью:
«Неужели наша дружба угаснет, как угасает сейчас солнце?»
Он смотрел на нее не отрываясь; крепко сдвинув брови, тихо ответил:
«Тоня, мы уже говорили об этом. Ты, конечно, знаешь, что я тебя любил и сейчас еще любовь моя может возвратиться, но для этого ты должна быть с нами. Я теперь не тот Павлуша, что был раньше. И я плохим буду мужем, если ты считаешь, что я должен принадлежать прежде тебе, а потом партии. А я буду принадлежать прежде партии, а потом тебе и остальным близким.») (pp. 157–8)

Pavel then joins Zhukhrai in the Cheka, fighting Vrangel' and the only White forces not yet defeated by the Reds. It is here that Serezha Bruzzhak is killed, fighting alongside Pavel. Pavel is then transferred to a production line to work as a Komsomol secretary, and is able to return home for a couple of weeks; while he is at home he makes the acquaintance of Ivan Zharkii, another 'mirror image', a machine gunner decorated for his actions who has survived the Civil War unscathed. With the end of the Civil War, Part One of the novel comes to an end, and Part Two follows the remainder of Pavel's life through Lenin's New Economic Policy of the early 1920s, a policy that was designed to enable the country to recover economically after the devastation of war by permitting the partial re-establishment of capitalism. The novel is at pains to show, in line with Stalinist thought, that this policy, far from being a betrayal of Marxist-Leninist ideals, was purely a pragmatic move to provide short-term relief from deprivation and acute hardship.

Part Two begins with another character's view of Pavel: that of Rita Ustinovich, whose diary contains a fulsome evaluation of Pavel's character. The return to small-scale private trading and the free market that marked the NEP is regarded in a negative light by the author. For example, the description of an NEP market contains no reference to the availability and wide variety of goods, as in later Soviet fiction dealing with the NEP period, but rather depicts the market as a festering pit of speculation, greed and evil:

(Life in the town wound its usual way. Throngs of people swarmed around five markets in tumult. Here two ambitions dominated: one was to fleece as much as possible, the other to give away as little as possible. Here rogues of all different calibres showed off the whole range of their powers and abilities. Like fleas, nifty types in their hundreds scurried about, in whose eyes you could see everything except conscience. Here, as in a dung-heap, gathered all the unclean elements of the town in a united effort to swindle the greenhorn novice. The occasional trains disgorged from their bellies crowds of people loaded down with bags. All of these people headed for the markets.)

(Жизнь в городе плелась обыденным ходом. На пяти базарах копошились в гомоне людские скопища. Властвовали здесь два стремления: одно – содрать побольше, другое – дать поменьше. Тут орудовало во всю ширь своих сил и способностей разнокалиберное жулье. Как блохи, сновали сотни юрких людишек с глазами, в которых можно было прочесть все, кроме совести. Здесь, как в навозной куче, собиралась вся городская нечисть в едином стремлении облапошить серенького новичка. Редкие поезда выбрасывали из своей кучи навьюченных мешками людей. Весь этот люд направлялся к базарам.) (р. 176)

This crude, venomous depiction of free trade and enterprise clearly mirrors the official disapproval of NEP in the 1930s, and offers justification for the subsequent introduction of a planned and centralized economy. The novel thus vindicates government policy of the time.

Although it is peacetime, the political struggle carries on. The new Soviet state is but a few years old, and is beset by enemies both external and internal. Official Soviet propaganda always maintained that the enemy never sleeps, and that constant vigilance is required; to illustrate this, Shepetovka, due to its geographical position, becomes the centre of a counter-revolutionary plot hatched by White officers, the remains of Petliura's band and bandits, aided by Poland. Father Vasilii, Pavel's old foe, is also among the conspirators, but the plotters are routed by

Pavel and Zharkii. Subsequently the main enemies are provided by the elements: cold and hunger.

Pavel volunteers to help lay a railway line from the town to the forest that will enable fuel to get to the town before the winter sets in. The enemy to be conquered is now nature, although a group of bandits led by a certain Orlik also present occasional problems. Pavel and the volunteers labour amid incredible hardship in the rain, mud and cold, with an irregular food supply. They are meant to work in two-week shifts, but their replacements do not arrive and so they have to work on. Zhukhrai comments on their tremendous reserves of fortitude: 'That's where the steel is tempered!' ('Вот где сталь закаляется!', p. 201). Here, Pavel once again drops out of the narrative focus for a while, and he becomes just one of the workers making tremendous efforts to lay the track. He is not one of those who decide things, but who do them. Ostrovskii instead concentrates on the efforts of the leadership: Zhukhrai, Tokarev, Pankratov, Dubava and Patoshkin.

Pavel is a man of resolute action, and his strength and powers of self-abnegation are qualities to be admired by all. No matter what the physical privations, his strength of will enables him to carry on. He has no boots, only galoshes, and one of his feet swells up. He has no coat, only a jacket that belongs to someone else; this despite the severe cold. He is briefly reunited with Tonia, who emerges from a train that has stopped nearby. Ostrovskii emphasises her bourgeois tastes, her luxurious clothes, fur boots, thick coat and warm hat. She is now married, and is shocked by Pavel's unkempt, poorly dressed and filthy appearance. She thinks only of externals, and is surprised that Pavel is still only a worker, when he could have advanced up the career ladder. She is struck, though, by his eyes, with their 'undimmed fire' ('незатухающий огонь,' p. 208). The reader, Tonia and Pavel now all realise the gulf between them, and that they no longer have anything in common. The railway is completed on 1 January 1922: symbolically, the new year is full of hope and optimism for a better world.

Pavel, though, is struck down with typhus. Everyone fears that he will die, but he recovers by the spring. Spring is also a symbolic time, as it suggests that the deadness of winter has been conquered and life returns to the world. In the socialist realist context, just as life conquers death, so the natural elements that offer resistance to the Bolsheviks' plans for industrialization are overcome through the sheer force of will and commitment of the volunteers, with Pavel Korchagin as their exemplar.

Pavel now devotes his whole being to the cause, which is greater than his own family: he does not even attend his brother Artem's wedding. Pavel later visits Artem, and is struck by the petit-bourgeois affluence of his home: Artem has abandoned his proletarian origins and now lives the life of a well-off peasant. Pavel further sees the difference between the superstitious and backward peasantry and the forward-looking, dynamic life of the city. He thus looks forward to the collectivization of agriculture, Stalin's solution (catastrophic as it was to prove) for bridging the gap between town and village.

Further contrasts occur when he accidentally meets Nelli Leshchinskaia, sister of his arch-enemy Viktor, on a Polish diplomatic train. Nelli is a perfect illustration of the decadence and moral corruption of the West: arrogant and haughty, she wears exotic clothes and perfumes and is addicted to cocaine. Pavel is by now a pure embodiment of will, with relatively few identifiable human characteristics left. His idea of a good night out is not at a party with other young people, but attending a plenum of the city *soviet*. He still plays the accordion, however, to emphasize his link with the masses. He develops a relationship with Anna Borkhadt and kills an attacker one night as he walks her home. Pavel thinks nothing of killing an enemy, but he cannot bring himself to love a woman. He is steadily losing all the vestiges of humanity that he thinks weaken him, such as smoking, and vows also to refrain from swearing. He later relates to Rita Ustinovich his idea of a revolutionary, based on his reading of L. Voynich's classic socialist realist novel *The Gadfly*:

> But I support the basic principle in *The Gadfly* – his courage and boundless endurance, the type of person who can bear suffering without showing it to each and everyone. I support the image of a revolutionary for whom the private is nothing in comparison to the general.

> (Но я за основное в Оводе – за его мужество и безграничную выносливость, за этот тип человека, умеющего переносить страдания, не показывая их всем и каждому. Я за этот образ революционера, для которого личное ничто в сравнении с общим.)
> (p. 302)

Pavel helps solve a number of peacetime conflicts, and in so doing points to the future. He helps two villages settle their differences over the boundaries between their lands, and remarks that collective farms will help solve such problems in the future. He also helps root out class enemies in the countryside, such as *kulaks*, and thus affirms the legitimacy of the campaign of the late 1920s against the *kulaks*. He also persuades, with the help of his accordion playing, many of the young people of the villages to join the Komsomol, awakening in them political awareness. During military exercises Pavel again undergoes physical deprivation and goes without sleep, but his battalion performs brilliantly.

There is a curious digression from the plot that takes place on the Soviet-Polish border. There are two border guards, one Soviet, one Polish. The Polish guard is poorly dressed, the Soviet guard is impressive and huge, like a богатырь, a hero from an epic poem. Seen entirely through the eyes of the Polish guard, the whole episode is designed to show that across the Soviet border life is more humane and the people are in control of their own destiny, whereas in the capitalist West they are downtrodden by a repressive system. The Polish guard accepts a match from his Soviet counterpart, but cannot keep the box as it would cost him two years in prison if found out, and he watches with envy the fraternal greeting of the Soviet major come to inspect the border post.

The years 1923–4 in the narrative revolve around the political background of the rout of Trotskii and his followers, of whom Dubava, now married to Anna Borkhadt, is one. Pavel is hounded from the stage of a Party conference by Trotskyists, an incident which serves to increase his heroism and ideological correctness in the reader's eyes. Dubava and Anna have political differences and these, rather than any suggestion of personal incompatibility, lead to their marriage breaking down. Pavel's political instinct is here shown to be unerring, as he had always suspected Dubava's reliability. The Trotskyists are portrayed as having been given a fair chance to be heard by the Stalinist majority, but they nevertheless seek to subvert and disrupt the political process for their own ends. Lenin's death in January 1924 is a pivotal moment in the life of the working class, for Artem resolves to join the Party and live nearer the railway station, so reasserting his closeness to the industrial proletariat. Old Zakhar Bruzzhak also joins the Party, no longer bowed by the death of his son and daughter. Indeed, it is a solemn, momentous occasion, like a lowly individual joining a great family in marriage.

Style and Imagery

The treatment of 'us' and 'them', the workers and the exploiters, is predictably hidebound. Petliura's men are a drunken and ill-disciplined rabble, and a military parade held in honour of the arrival of Petliura himself turns out to be a disaster. They are rarely individualized, and when we are introduced to them as individuals, such as the brute Salomyga, we see that they are little better than beasts. The nationalists lose the battle with the Reds for the town, and the entry of the Red forces is marked by the sound of their cheerful laughter, which is contrasted to the evil and mocking guffaws of the Petliura bands. The Reds in turn have to abandon the town, and Polish troops occupy it. The perfidy of the upper classes is shown in the figure of Viktor Leshchinskii, Pavel's sworn enemy and the son of a rich lawyer; it is he who is Tonia's suitor, it is he who constantly informs on Pavel and it is he who is responsible for Pavel's eventual arrest. Furthermore, Leshchinskii is not bound by any patriotic feeling for his Ukrainian homeland: of Polish descent, he eagerly awaits the arrival of the Polish troops.

Mention should also be made of the female characters, as they too conform to type. The brutal treatment of women, such as the female workers in the buffet in which Pavel works before the Revolution, demonstrates the inherent iniquity of that society. During the turmoil of the Civil War, it is women's suffering that reveals the true depths to which enemies of the proletariat will sink. When Pavel is in prison, the peasant girl Khristina offers her virginity to him rather than have it forcibly taken by the prison commander, but Pavel is still dominated by his love for Tonia and cannot bring himself to besmirch her memory. The Jewish girl Riva is also raped during the pogrom. Valia Bruzzhak, sister of Serezha, is raped, beaten, tortured and then hanged by the Poles, but as a committed Bolshevik offers resistance to the last. On the other hand, the morality of the Reds is beyond question: three Latvians attempting to rape the wife of a Polish officer are shot by their own officer. Women of the future, fighting for the Bolshevik cause, are portrayed as resilient and committed, prepared to die for what they believe in. Such women are Valia Bruzzhak and Rita Ustinovich, throwing off the vestiges of their downtrodden past to adopt active political roles and become fully integrated with the emerging new order.

Although there is little imagery in the novel, one striking example occurs towards the end of the narrative. Pavel meets Rita again after three years, at the Sixth Russian Komsomol Congress, held in the Bolshoi Theatre. The opening of the Congress is depicted in constructivist or futurist style, with the full stock of politically charged bombast and metaphors:

Pavel and Rita rose. It was time to take up their places nearer to the stage. They headed for the seats of the Ukrainian delegation. The orchestra struck up. Huge red canvases shone forth, and the luminous letters cried: 'The future belongs to us'. Thousands of people occupied the stalls, boxes and upper circle. These thousands merged together here in a united and mighty transformer of never-ending energy. The gigantic theatre admitted into its walls the flower of the young guard of the great industrial tribe. Thousands of eyes, and in each pair flashes the reflection of the message burning over the heavy curtain: 'The future belongs to us'.

(Павел и Рита встали. Пора было занимать места поближе к сцене. Они направились к креслам, где усаживалась украинская делегация. Заиграл оркестр. Горели алым огромные полотнища, и светящиеся буквы кричали: «Будущее принадлежит нам». Тысячи наполняли партер, ложи, ярусы. Эти тысячи сливались здесь в единый мощный трансформатор никогда не затухающей энергии. Гигант-театр принял в свои стены цвет молодой гвардии великого индустриального племени. Тысячи глаз, и в каждой паре их отсвечивает искорками то, что горит над тяжелым занавесом: «Будущее принадлежит нам».) (р. 302)

The emphasis here is on the impersonal, the merging of the personal with the social, and the deliberate (and contrived) use of metaphors from industry. To Pavel (and Ostrovskii) this is the culmination of his struggle, 'the victorious triumph of the young guard of Bolshevism' ('это победное торжество молодой гвардии большевизма,' p. 303), the justification of his many years of hardship and suffering.

Conclusion

The last few pages of the novel see the further deterioration of Pavel's health. As a result of over-work he suffers a nervous disorder, and has his right knee crushed in a motor accident. At the age of twenty-four Pavel is walking with the aid of a stick and is given an invalid's pension. Having failed to establish a relationship with Rita or Anna, Pavel eventually gets married to Taia Kiutsam, a Latvian he meets while recuperating on the south coast. Taia adores Pavel, and under his guidance she undertakes political work and joins the Party, so becoming in the terms of this novel a real woman: a devoted wife and political activist. Pavel becomes totally blind, his left arm and both legs paralysed, only kept in touch with the real world through the radio which informs him of the momentous changes taking place, such as the completion of the huge Magnitostroi metallurgical complex and the decision to collectivize agriculture.

Pavel's return to active participation in the social process, despite his physical frailties, is brought about, as with Ostrovskii himself, by writing. He writes a short novel and sends it to a Leningrad publisher, and even when one copy of the first three chapters is lost, he carries on and rewrites them. The fortunes of Korchagin are thus also those of his creator. Korchagin's new weapon is the pen, as he dictates his words to his amanuensis Galina, his former neighbour.

The field of propaganda and the task of educating the masses through his own example are the culmination of Pavel's life. Although his body is broken as a consequence of the battering it has taken from both political foes and the elements, his spirit remains strong and his commitment and faith are like a beacon to future generations. In conclusion, it is worth quoting Hans Günther's remarks on Korchagin's development:

> His growth consists of an arduous learning process under the guidance of Party mentors and the attainment of awareness and understand of existing necessities . . . The development of the young hero involves a number of exemplary conflicts. Every conflict he withstands leads to an ideal virtue that is often mentioned explicitly.[9]

Lev Anninskii is in no doubt about Korchagin's significance as a symbol of his generation:

> Pavel Korchagin became one of the most vivid symbols of that generation . . . Korchagin was created for the epoch which seized him. It is even difficult to say who created whom – did the epoch create Korchagin, or Korchagin the epoch; Nikolai Ostrovskii's book is inseparable from the historical moment that gave birth to it.

> (Павел Корчагин стал одним из ярчайших символов этого поколения . . . Корчагин создан для той эпохи, которая подхватила его. Трудно даже сказать, кто кого создал – эпоха Корчагина или Корчагин эпоху: книжка Николая Островского неотрывна от породившего ее исторического момента.)[10]

Furthermore, Korchagin is the prototype for the positive hero in Soviet literature. He was the first character to embody the traits outlined above, and the standard Soviet literary history for pedagogical colleges is characteristically forthright about Korchagin's influence on subsequent generations:

> The influence of N. Ostrovskii's novel on the development of Soviet literature is great – primarily in giving form to the heroic image of Soviet man.
> The traditions of N. Ostrovskii are particularly strongly felt in literature of the Great Patriotic War . . . The writer who depicts the heroic feat, who wishes to understand the nature of this feat and grasp the character of the new man, cannot bypass the literary legacy of Nikolai Ostrovskii.

> (Велико влияние романа Н. Островского на развитие советской литературы – главным образом на дальнейшее воплощение героического образа советского человека.
> С особенной силой сказались традиции Н. Островского в литературе Великой Отечественной Войны . . . Писатель, рисующий героический подвиг, желающий понять природу этого подвига,

постичь характер нового человека, не может пройти мимо литературного наследия Николая Островского.)[11]

The novel has many drawbacks in terms of its composition – black-and-white characters whose personalities are shaped by their political allegiances, schematic plot development that serves merely to canonize its hero, and the crude, bombastic authorial overview that often intrudes into the text itself – but it is the perfect example of socialist realism whereby the aesthetic merits of creative literature are reduced to questions of ideological correctness and a 'progressive' world-view. This was made abundantly clear in the many Soviet studies of the novel, and just how well the novel met the demands of socialist realism can be judged by the evaluation of the Stalinist critic Vengrov (complete with obligatory fulsome praise of the Great Leader):

N. Ostrovskii completed his novel at the time when Comrade Stalin for the first time defined the method of Soviet literature as the method of socialist realism. Bolshevik party-mindedness in the evaluation of reality; the abundance in the novel of progressive ideas which determine its genuine popular spirit; a truthful, realistic depiction of socialist reality in its revolutionary development; the revelation in images of the contradictory processes in the life and consciousness of people; the illumination of the present through the light of the future and the loving depiction of the growth of the new, to which this future belongs; the huge educative role of N. Ostrovskii's work – all this is characteristic of the novel 'How The Steel Was Tempered' as a work of socialist realism.

(Н. Островский заканчивал книгу в то время, когда товарищ Сталин впервые определил метод советской литературы как метод социалистического реализма. Большевистская партийность в оценке изображаемых явлений действительности: насыщенность романа передовыми идеями, определяющими его подлинную народность: правдивое, реалистическое отображение социалистической действительности в ее революционном развитии: раскрытие в образах противоречивых процессов в жизни и сознании людей; озарение событий настоящего светом будущего и любовное изображение ростков нового, которому принадлежит это будущее; огромная воспитывающая роль произведения Н. Островского – все это характерные черты романа «Как закалялась сталь» как произведения социалистического реализма.)[12]

How the Steel Was Tempered can be seen as the culmination of that rationalist, utilitarian tradition in nineteenth-century Russian literature exemplified by the socially conscious poetry of Nikolai Nekrasov, Chernyshevskii's *What is to be Done?* and the literary criticism of Belinskii and Dobroliubov, where the importance of content over form was asserted and civic consciousness became the dominant criterion of merit.[13] The novel thus exemplifies an artistic method that places ideological content above what we in the West would ordinarily claim as 'aesthetic' criteria; but the socialist realist novel has its own aesthetic code, of which the following five points are perhaps the most significant. Firstly, as Katerina Clark has shown, character development must show how the positive hero proceeds from a psychological state of innocent spontaneity to one of political consciousness and outright commitment to the Party's cause. Secondly, he must struggle with nature, impose his will over it and control it, at the same time as vanquishing his ideological foes. Thirdly, the Party becomes his real and extended family; Pavel explains this to Tonia, and later even his brother Artem joins the Party. Fourthly, as we see in the Komsomol meeting at the Bolshoi theatre, the new world is dominated by massive, impersonal imagery, where individuals are belittled and finally engulfed by the machine of society. Finally, the drama that takes place in Pavel's soul, his battles and his eventual victory, are but a microcosm of the greater struggle going on in society, and here the use of Shepetovka, as a railway junction and therefore the home of a powerful industrial proletariat, which is occupied by Poles, Germans, Whites, Ukrainian nationalists and finally Reds, can be seen as a microcosm of the whole Civil War. It should not of course be forgotten that Ostrovskii's novel and its immense popularity demonstrate the extent to which the utilitarian ethic came to eclipse all other literary considerations for a quarter of a century in Russia, that of the Stalin and immediate post-Stalin years.

Notes

1. V. A. Kovalev (ed.), *Русская советская литература: 10* (*Soviet Russian Literature: 10*), 2nd edn, Moscow, 1977, p. 222. All translations from the Russian in this chapter are my own.
2. *Русская советская литература*, p. 227.
3. *Первый всесоюзный съезд Союза писателей СССР. Стенографический отчет* (*The First All-Union USSR Writers' Congress: Stenographic Record*), Moscow, 1934, p. 716.
4. Katerina Clark, *The Soviet Novel: History as Ritual*, 2nd edn, Chicago, 1985, pp. 9–10.

5. Lev Anninskii, *«Как закалялась сталь» Николая Островского* (*Nikolai Ostrovskii's "How the Steel Was Tempered"*), 3rd corrected edn, Moscow, 1988, pp. 7–9.
6. Anninskii, *«Как закалялась сталь»*, p. 18.
7. Nikolai Ostrovskii, *Как закалялась сталь (How the Steel Was Tempered)*, Leningrad, 1980, p. 50. All further references to the novel are taken from this edition, with relevant page numbers incorporated into the text.
8. Clark, *The Soviet Novel*, p. 168.
9. Hans Günther, 'Education and Conversion: The Road to the New Man in the Totalitarian *Bildungsroman*', in Hans Günther (ed.), *The Culture of the Stalin Period*, Basingstoke, 1990, pp. 196, 200.
10. Anninskii, *«Как закалялась сталь»*, p. 93. This was written relatively recently, and it is interesting to compare this judgment with one written during the Stalin years (if only to demonstrate the fact that Soviet assessment of this novel, despite the changing political climate, remained essentially unchanged):

The sense of history does not desert the young author in the course of the whole narrative. The truthful historicism of the novel finds its reflection in Ostrovskii's constant desire to show reality moving on, to portray his hero and his comrades in the process of their spiritual evolution. The lives of the characters and all the decisive events are linked with stages of the revolutionary struggle and the growth and consolidation of Soviet power. In the changes the characters undergo and in the consciousness of the young generation the artist managed to reflect the essential and distinctive features of the age. The novel gives an authentic picture of life because it presents a historically accurate picture of the changing tactics of the people's war, and has a clear . . . eye for the changes in the way the young people regard life, work and socialist property, because it reveals a profound understanding of inter-party and Komsomol life, the struggle with the Trotskiite traitors and, finally, because it conveys the pathos of the socialist offensive, as related in the last few pages of the novel.

(Чувство истории не покидало молодого автора на протяжении всего его повествования. Правдивый историзм романа находит выражение в постоянном стремлении Островского показать действительность в ее движении, изобразить своего героя, его товарищей в процессе их духовного роста. Жизнь ее героев, все решающие события в ней связаны с этапами революционной борьбы, с ростом и укреплением советской власти. В изменении характеров и сознании молодого поколения художник сумел отразить существенные и отличительные черты эпохи. Жизненная убедительность его романа обусловлена исторически правдивым показом меняющейся тактики народной войны, зорко увиденными . . . изменениями в отношении молодежи к насущным вопросам жизни, труду, социалистической собственности, глубоко понятыми событиями внутрипартийной и комсомольской жизни, борьбы с предателями-троцкистами и, наконец, передачей в романе пафоса социалистического наступления, о котором рассказывают последние страницы романа.) See N. Vengrov, Николай Островский (*Nikolai Ostrovskii*), Moscow, 1952, p. 69.

11. A. I. Metchenko and S. M. Petrov (eds), *История русской советской литературы (1917–1940)* (*The History of Soviet Russian Literature (1917–1940)*), 2nd edn, Moscow, 1983, p. 461.
12. Vengrov, *Николай Островский*, p. 99. I have deliberately tried to maintain the particular Soviet tone of the original in the translation.
13. The nineteenth century's contribution to the development of socialist realism is well documented and analysed in Rufus Mathewson, *The Positive Hero in Russian Literature*, 2nd edn, Stanford, 1975, especially pp. 25–83.

5

Mikhail Bulgakov (1891–1940), *The Master and Margarita* (*Мастер и Маргарита*)

Introduction and Background

Mikhail Bulgakov is one of the most important Russian writers of the twentieth century, a writer who is equally at home in theological argument and in biting satire, and who can turn his hand to anything from the fantastic to knockabout comedy. His great novel *The Master and Margarita* (1929–40), which remained unfinished on his death and which in the course of its composition went through several redactions, reveals all these aspects of his talent.[1] Bulgakov began work on the novel in 1929, and it is estimated that there may have been as many as six different redactions. Certainly it is known that Bulgakov himself destroyed some versions, and the loss of others has not been as yet satisfactorily explained (and may never be).[2] Although completed in 1940, the novel was published in the Soviet Union only in 1966, at first in an incomplete form (the 1969 Posev edition published in Germany was also incomplete) and then in 1973, in what is now seen as the definitive version.[3]

It must be borne in mind that by the mid–1960s Khrushchev had been deposed as General Secretary of the Communist Party, and his replacement Leonid Brezhnev was bringing to an end the policy of de-Stalinization. The conservatives now had the upper hand, and monthly journals such as *Novyi mir*, edited by Alexander Tvardovskii and for over ten years the mouthpiece of liberal thought in the USSR, were fighting very much a rearguard action to retain some vestige of independence. The reception of *The Master and Margarita* in the Soviet Union in the 1960s must thus be seen against the background of the struggle between 'liberals', especially those publishing in *Novyi mir* such as Igor' Vinogradov and Vladimir Lakshin, and 'conservatives' such as Mikhail Gus' and Liudmila Skorino, determined to implement the post-Khrushchev freeze in the arts. Whereas the 'liberals' emphasized the novel's moral issues within the context of de-Stalinization, the neo-Stalinists poured scorn on what they saw as the novel's ideological heresy and its obvious divergence from the tenets of socialist realism. Andrew Barratt speculates that its publication was allowed in the first place as a kind of 'safety-valve', a sop to liberal sentiment with 'the purpose of relieving some of the pressure which had built up against party and state'.[4] Discussion of the work's considerable aesthetic qualities had to wait until the relatively calmer times of the 1980s, with the publication in Moscow of books by Lidiia Ianovskaia and Marietta Chudakova (both listed in the bibliography at the end of this book).

Mikhail Afanas'evich Bulgakov was born in Kiev, the son of a professor of comparative religion at Kiev University. He was by training a doctor (like Chekhov before him), and began writing during the years of the Russian Civil War. He moved to Moscow in 1921, where he continued his literary career writing journalistic articles, prose and, in the late 1920s, plays. Much of his prose and drama was banned in the Stalin years, and Bulgakov was subjected to merciless criticism in the periodical press throughout the 1930s. Even so, it is said that *The Days of the Turbins* (*Дни Турбиных*, 1926), based on his novel *The White Guard* (*Белая гвардия*, 1924, 1924) was highly regarded by Stalin. He managed to find work from 1930 to 1936 in the Moscow Art Theatre alongside the highly respected director Konstantin Stanislavskii, with whom he nevertheless had many quarrels; in 1936 he moved to the Bolshoi Theatre. After the death of Stalin many of his works were republished, or even published or performed for the first time, but it was only as a result of Gorbachev's policy of *glasnost'* in the arts from 1986 that his entire *oeuvre* has been returned to the Russian literary canon. Previously banned or neglected works appeared in Soviet periodicals in 1986–9, and the Moscow publishing house Khudozhestvennaia literatura published a five-volume edition of Bulgakov's collected works in 1989–90.

Plot, Theme and Characterization

The novel eschews realism – both critical and socialist – from its very first pages. The novel opens with the arrival of the Devil, whom we later learn goes by the name of Woland, in Moscow some time in the late 1920s. Two literary figures, the bureaucrat Berlioz and the erstwhile poet Bezdomnyi, are strolling in a Moscow park when they are confronted by a strange, foreign-looking professor who speaks to them of Christ's meeting with Pontius Pilate and then foretells the death of Berlioz, down to its finest details. Berlioz is indeed killed when he slips on some oil at the tram stop, falls under the approaching tramcar, and is beheaded – all exactly as predicted by Woland, the mysterious stranger. Bezdomnyi witnesses this, and, horror-stricken, chases the stranger around Moscow, believing him to be a dangerous spy. Here he encounters strange things: a huge black cat boarding a tram and tendering its fare; a radio playing the opera *Evgenii Onegin*; he himself loses his clothes as he swims in the Moscow river. Carrying an icon, a candle and a piece of paper, Bezdomnyi is himself apprehended and, believed to be in deep shock at Berlioz's death, temporarily hospitalized. It is in the asylum that he makes the acquaintance of the Master. The Master (whose real name we never get to know) is a historian; he knows five languages and, until he won 100,000 roubles in a lottery, worked in a museum. He has no family or relations in Moscow. Since this windfall, he has devoted himself entirely to writing a novel about Christ's meeting with Pontius Pilate, a novel he then burned in despair at its negative reception by the critics.

This brief synopsis of the opening chapters of the novel serves to bring together the two main strands of the plot, the Biblical and the contemporary. However, the second part of the novel is largely devoted to Margarita, lover of the Master, who is invited by Woland to be the hostess of his ball, and in return is provided with her wish to be re-united with her beloved.

The Holy Land and Moscow are brought closer in other ways, for the full moon shines in Moscow in the 1920s as it does almost two thousand years earlier in Ierashalaim (Jerusalem), and there are images (the heat and the smell of roses) that occur in both episodes. Furthermore, the action of both stories takes place over the same four days in the year. In the asylum, Bezdomnyi compares Professor Stravinskii to Pilate because of the solemnity with which he is regarded by those who work for him. However, the narrative styles of these sections are very different: the Moscow chapters are generally light-hearted, ironic and racy, while the Ierashalaim chapters are more sombre and formally poetic. Moreover, the Ierashalaim chapters are related from three different sources: Woland, Margarita reading from the Master's manuscript and Bezdomnyi's dream in the asylum.

In the course of Bulgakov's narrative whole chapters from the Master's novel-within-a-novel are quoted verbatim, so that we are introduced to Pilate, Christ (here called Ieshua Ha-Notsri, after the Aramaic), his follower Matthew the Levite, the secret police official Afranius, Judas and the Judean high priest Caiaphus as actual literary characters.[5] In the central scene Pilate sentences Ha-Notsri to death by crucifixion, and refuses to intercede on his behalf when the possibility arises that one of the three condemned men can be released.

Pilate is struck by Ha-Notsri's meekness and his insistence that all men are 'good'; he is also struck by the fact that Ha-Notsri knows of his (Pilate's) headaches and even dares to give him advice as to how to cure them. Pilate becomes aware in the course of his interrogation that Ieshua has indeed done nothing wrong, and is quite fascinated by him. After representations from Caiaphus, however, Pilate acquiesces in the death sentence. Pilate's sin is that of moral cowardice: he refuses to risk his own position within Judea and with the Emperor Tiberius in Rome in order to vouch for Ha-Notsri. Caiaphus has made it clear that the Church regards Ha-Notsri's teachings as subversive and threatening, and he is resolutely against setting him free. Instead, the robber Var-a-van (Barrabas) is set free.

The motif of moral cowardice also brings the Biblical aspect of the novel closer to that set in contemporary Moscow, for here, too, the morality of the populace is under scrutiny. Here it is the Devil, Woland, who is doing the scrutinizing. Woland's retinue includes Behemoth, a huge talking black cat, the regent Fagot Korov'ev, the sinister Azazello who has fangs instead of teeth, and Hella, an alluring and lascivious vampire seen throughout the narrative in various stages of undress. Korov'ev and Behemoth in particular cause havoc in Moscow, but their adventures are not haphazard or simply fun. Korov'ev tricks Bosoi, the chairman of the housing cooperative where Berlioz used to live, into signing away the flat to him. Korov'ev then rings the police and Bosoi is found with a sum of money in hard currency and arrested. Bosoi later has a dream which resembles a Stalinist show trial in which he is accused of possessing hard currency (a criminal offence in the USSR). The Variety Theatre's accountant Lastochkin is also arrested when he is found with hard currency. Prokhor Ivanovich, the head of the finance office, disappears into thin air after a visit by Behemoth: he exclaims 'Let the devils take me!' ('Черти б меня взяли!'), and so they do, although his empty suit remains, writing, shouting orders, snoring and even holding telephone conversations. Workers in another office, after a visit by Korov'ev, cannot stop singing.

The targets of this diabolical fun and mischief are all bureaucrats and officials, who also give themselves away as opportunists and self-seekers. (It is difficult, however, to see what punishment Lastochkin and Doctor Kuzmin have deserved, as they are not explicitly accused of anything.) Another such character is Berlioz's uncle Poplavskii, who arrives in Moscow from Kiev in order to secure his deceased nephew's flat (he had received a telegram from the deceased inviting him to the funeral!); after being subjected to humiliation and ridicule in the flat, he is dissuaded from further claims to a Moscow residence by the sight of a huge black cat reading his passport and a vicious-looking Azazello, with a knife, showing him the door. Sokov, the buffet manager of the Variety Theatre, pays a visit to Woland's flat to reclaim money he has earned and which, he thinks, the magician caused to disappear; he, too, is sent packing, with wine spilled on his trousers and his bald head lacerated by Behemoth's claws. We also learn that Sokov himself has over two hundred thousand roubles in various accounts, gold hidden beneath his floorboards, and will die of cancer in nine months.

The most memorable illustration of this devilish mischief is when Woland and his retinue conduct an evening of black magic in the Moscow Variety Theatre, creating fake money and making the clothes people wear suddenly disappear. The cat Behemoth tears off the head of the intrusive and annoying compère Bengal'skii, having been encouraged to do so by the audience, but then replaces it when the audience is upset by Bengal'skii's screams and the gushing blood. Woland actually does nothing, merely comments on the moral make-up of modern society and passes instructions to Behemoth and Korov'ev, but the whole performance is intended to reveal the moral make-up of modern Moscow. What we witness is the vanity and greed of people as individuals and as a mass (including the adultery and venality of the dignitary Sempleiarov, who comes to regret that he self-importantly addressed the stage from his place in one of the boxes). In short, concludes Woland, people are the same as ever. In other words, black magic actually reveals the truth about people.[6] Still, people are also still capable of compassion − as when a woman sheds tears over the decapitated Bengal'skii. The whole performance in the theatre is told with great wit, irony and gusto, and the subsequent adventures of Woland's entourage in Moscow are equally uproarious.

The theatre administrator Varenukha, a bully and a boor, is abducted by Behemoth and Azazello, beaten up and taken to a flat, where he is kissed by the naked but ice-cold Hella. He turns into a vampire and, accompanied by Hella, that night pays a visit to the theatre's financial director Rimskii. This is indeed quite a frightening scene, in the best tradition of Gothic horror, and although Rimskii beats off his attackers as the cock crows to announce the dawn, the experience turns his hair completely grey. Rimskii races to the Leningrad Station in a taxi, only to be swallowed up in the darkness. Likhodeev, the director of the Variety Theatre, having been told by Korov'ev that he is a pig, drunkard and womanizer, and furthermore is incompetent, is spirited away to Yalta. Likhodeev used to share a flat with Berlioz, a flat with a history of tenants who disappear, and it is no surprise to anyone when Likhodeev himself vanishes. It should be remembered that in Stalin's Russia there was nothing fantastic about people suddenly disappearing, and others were not encouraged to ask questions.

There are further scenes of mayhem in Griboedov House, the Writers' Union headquarters (based on the actual Herzen House), which is set on fire as Behemoth and Korov'ev have a gunfight with police, and in a hard currency shop, which is also razed to the ground. Both of these episodes can be seen in terms of the author exacting his own revenge on a hierarchical and intolerant system of official privilege and exclusivity reserved for sycophants and hacks. Behemoth and Korov'ev also accuse a foreigner of theft from the shop, and incite the passing public against him in a parody of official 1930s state xenophobia. The foreigner, it turns out, speaks perfect Russian; similarly, when Berlioz and Bezdomnyi first meet Woland, they are struck by how well he speaks Russian although he seems to be a foreigner. As everywhere else in the novel, all is not as it seems.

As in the Variety Theatre performance, there is a complex relationship between black magic and what passes for truth. The fact that Woland's retinue can make people disappear is not at all fantastic in the Soviet Union of the 1920s. Nor does Bulgakov need to resort to the fantastic to satirize life in the USSR; he attacks the very paucity of material existence, whether this be in the form of the bullying petty officials, Sokov's sandwiches 'of secondary freshness' ('бутерброды второй свежести'), the fact that certain restaurants are reserved only for a certain *nomenclatura*, or the severe housing shortage. The result is the brutalization and sheer opportunism of the majority of the populace.

Woland, though, is clearly a figure of considerable supernatural power. He has power over human time; his ball begins and ends at midnight, although for Margarita it lasts for hours, and we know that he was present at the meeting of Ieshua and Pilate nearly two thousand years previously. He can also control physical space, as he extends the boundaries of the flat he appropriates so that it resembles a huge, dark cavern, and his guests appear out of the fire. Above all, Woland is primarily interested in literary affairs and spiritual questions, and he lets his retinue have fun with lesser mortals.

Bulgakov's satirical ire is particularly directed at the literary establishment. Not only does he figuratively burn down its headquarters through the supernatural agency of Behemoth and Korov'ev, but he also pulls no punches in his ridicule of the nonentities who inhabit it. The classical literary tradition is held up as a counterpoint (note the deliberately ironic use of Griboedov's name to designate a building and institution whose intrigues and mediocrities are not worthy of the great Russian classical tradition.[7] In Griboedov House itself, the following extended dialogue between Behemoth and Korov'ev suggests the author's own squaring of accounts with the writing community of his time:

'Look, there's the writer's club. You know, Behemoth, that house has a great reputation. Look at it, my friend. How lovely to think of so much talent ripening under that roof.'

'Like pineapples in a hothouse,' said Behemoth, climbing up on to the concrete plinth of the railings for a better look at the yellow, colonnaded house.

'Quite so,' agreed his inseparable companion Koroviev, 'and what a delicious thrill one gets, doesn't one, to think that at this moment in that house there may be the future author of a *Don Quixote*, or a *Faust* or who knows — *Dead Souls*?'

'Frightening thought,' said Behemoth.

'Yes,' Koroviev went on, 'think what astonishing growths may sprout from the seedbeds of that house and its thousands of devotees of Melpomene, Polyhymnia and Thalia. Just imagine the furore if one of them were to present the reading public with a *Government Inspector* or at least a *Eugene Onegin*!'

'It could easily happen,' said Behemoth.

'Yes,' Koroviev went on, wagging a warning finger, 'but — but, I say, and I repeat — *but*! . . . provided that those hothouse growths are not attacked by some micro-organism, provided they're not nipped in the bud, provided they don't rot! And it can happen with pineapples, you know! Ah, yes, it can happen!'

(Ба! Да ведь это писательский дом. Знаешь, Бегемот, я очень много хорошего и лестного слышал про этот дом. Обрати внимание, мой друг, на этот дом! Приятно думать о том, что под этой крышей скрывается и вызревает целая бездна талантов.

– Как ананасы в оранжереях, – сказал Бегемот и, чтобы получше полюбоваться на кремовый дом с колоннами, влез на бетонное основание чугунной решетки.

– Совершенно верно, – согласился со своим неразлучным спутником Коровьев, – и сладкая жуть подкатывает к сердцу, когда думаешь о том, что в этом доме сейчас поспевает будущий автор «Дон Кихота», или «Фауста», или, черт меня побери, «Мертвых душ»! А?

– Страшно подумать, – подтвердил Бегемот.

– Да, – продолжал Коровьев, – удивительных вещей можно ожидать в парниках этого дома, объединившего под своей кровлей несколько тысяч подвижников, решивших отдать беззаветно свою жизнь на служение Мельпомене, Полигимнии и Талии. Ты представляешь себе, какой поднимется шум, когда кто-нибудь из них для начала преподнесет читающей публике «Ревизора» или, на самый худой конец, «Евгения Онегина»!

– И очень просто, – опять-таки подтвердил Бегемот.

– Да, – продолжал Коровьев и озабоченно поднял палец, – но! Но, говорю я и повторяю это – но! Если на эти тепличные растения не нападет какой-нибудь микроорганизм, не подточит их в корне, если они не загниют! А это бывает с ананасами! Ой-ой-ой, как бывает!)[8]

If there were any authors of such classics, which in their own ways challenged the established contemporary order and its conventions, they would certainly not be allowed to ripen and flourish today. The metaphor of ripening fruit is loaded with irony but the gastronomic flavour is appropriate, as we have already seen how the writers in the restaurant greeted the news of Berlioz's death: with shock and sadness, but not for too long, lest the food grow cold. Thus, we may assume, they are in permanent thrall to the Waist!

When Behemoth and Korov'ev attempt to gain access to the restaurant, they are stopped at the door by a woman who asks for proof of their status. Korov'ev replies:

> But look here – if you wanted to make sure that Dostoyevsky was a writer, would you really ask him for his membership card? Why, you only have to take any five pages of one of his novels and you won't need a membership card to convince you that the man's a writer. I don't suppose he ever had a membership card, anyway! (p. 398)

> (Так вот, чтобы убедиться в том, что Достоевский – писатель, неужели же нужно спрашивать у него удостоверение? Да возьмите вы любых пять страниц из любого его романа, и без всякого удостоверения вы убедитесь, что имеете дело с писателем. Да я полагаю, что у него и удостоверения-то никакого не было!) (p. 769).

You, the woman points out, are not Dostoevskii. How do you know, retorts Korov'ev. Dostoevskii is dead, she affirms. Korov'ev protests: Dostoevskii is, after all, immortal! The dialogue offers not only an extremely witty vignette on the absurdities of Soviet bureaucratic status. The point is not whether someone is a writer, but whether he or she belongs to the right organization and is therefore entitled to enjoy the material benefits offered to those who have sold their souls, and which are denied to the vast majority of the population. It is also a scathing attack on the nonentities who call themselves writers merely because they possess the right sort of удостоверение (i.e., a membership card is more valuable than actual talent).

We should not forget either the references to Goethe's *Faust*, as the novel's epigraph is taken from that work:

> 'Say at last – who art thou?'
> 'That Power I serve
> Which wills forever evil
> Yet does forever good.'

> (. . . так, кто ж ты, наконец?
> – Я – часть той силы, что вечно хочет зла и вечно совершает благо.)

In Goethe's work, Mephistopheles is once referred to as 'Voland', and this is undoubtedly the source of the name for Bulgakov's Devil. Mephistopheles in the former work makes his first appearance to Faust in the guise of a black poodle, whereas Bulgakov's Woland possesses a cane whose black grip is fashioned in the shape of a poodle's head. The heroine of Bulgakov's work is called Margarita, while Goethe's heroine, who loves just as strongly and innocently, is called Margareta. Interestingly, at Satan's Ball Bulgakov's Margarita asks for Frida, who had murdered her child, to be released from her eternal torment; in Goethe's work Margareta murders her own child.

The Faustian theme extends not only to the witches and devils that stalk modern Moscow; rather, these demons are the external manifestations of a deeper evil.[9] Almost all the writers we meet have sold their souls for material benefit. Afranius has a Mephistophelean ability to read Pilate's innermost thoughts, and also has the gift of making them reality. Before Judas is killed by Afranius' men, Pilate has given him explicit instructions to protect Ha-Notsri's betrayer. Afranius, however, interprets Pilate's anxiety for Judas' well-being as, in fact, an unarticulated but nevertheless very real desire to have him killed; this indeed turns out to be the case. It is Afranius who reports to Pilate Ha-Notsri's last words, which bring Pilate to the brink of his moral purgatory: 'he regarded cowardice as one of the worst human sins' (p. 346) ('в числе человеческих пороков одним из самых главных он считает трусость,' p. 721). Moreover, Andrew Barratt argues convincingly that Afranius may be a secret follower of Ieshua, as his report of Ieshua's death does nothing to lessen Pilate's sense of moral unease. Indeed, it is only through Afranius that Pilate learns of Ieshua's words on moral cowardice; perhaps Ieshua said no such thing, and Afranius is simply gloating over Pilate's discomfort.[10]

Woland is a more substantial Mephistophelean figure, capable of reading men's thoughts and knowing their motivations. No one escapes his gaze or his judgment, he is there to observe modern man and to remind him of his responsibilities and weaknesses. Woland actually does very little in the novel, for the tomfoolery and devilish antics are predominantly carried out by Begemot and/or Korov'ev. He does, however, oversee the antics in the Variety Theatre, and passes comment on the morality of modern Muscovites. Indeed, he eventually brings the Master and Margarita together, and he brings back the manuscript of the Master's novel from the flames. Therefore, as a figure of evil Woland hardly fits the bill; he is, rather, an agent of justice and retribution. Lidiia Ianovskaia comments: 'Woland and his entourage appear as a particular kind of miracle, whose sentence is swift, just and carried out without delay' ('Воланд и его свита оказываются в роли своеобразного чуда, приговор которого скор, справедлив и приводится в исполнение незамедлительно').[11] He links past and present, and he also acts as the bridge between the literary and the philosophical themes of the novel.[12]

The literary theme is arguably the most important in the novel, as it links the novel's moral aspect with its central philosophical argument. References to the classical Russian literary tradition have already been mentioned. In the modern (1920s) context, from the outset the reader is introduced to the bureaucratic shenanigans of the literary administration in the form of Mikhail Aleksandrovich Berlioz, journal editor and chairman of MASSOLIT, one of the most important writers' organizations (presumably modelled on RAPP, the militant and vindictive proletarian writers' organization of the late 1920s). Before the appearance of Woland, he and Bezdomnyi (the affected pseudonym of Ivan Nikolaevich Ponyrev) are discussing the latter's poem about Jesus Christ, with Berlioz earnestly asserting that the only way to describe Christ is to describe him as someone who never existed at all! Minutes later, Berlioz is dead. The 'generals' of MASSOLIT have dachas in the village of Perelygino (obviously a reference to the actual writers' village of Peredelkino). Margarita takes revenge on the critic Latunskii by flooding his flat and then wrecking it and the House of Littérateurs and Dramatists. This violent action can be seen as a metaphor for Bulgakov's own imagined revenge on the hostile critics who condemned him to silence in the 1930s, for Latunskii is primarily responsible for the articles damning the Master's novel. Bulgakov further makes fun of the writing fraternity by giving the MASSOLIT secretariat names that have a comical, Gogolian, ring in Russian: Dvubratskii, Poprikhin, Ababkov, Nepremenova, Zheldybin, Beskud-nikov and others. The most extreme example of Bulgakov's settling scores with what he perceived as a cowardly and ultimately murderous writing fraternity is the execution by Azazello of Baron Maigel' at Woland's ball. Maigel' is described as a 'spy' and 'informer', who had asked to be invited to the ball so that he could report on it to the authorities.[13] We should also take note of composers' names that feature in the novel: Berlioz, Stravinskii and Rimskii, all testifying to the importance of the theme of artistic creativity.

This theme also includes the act of creativity itself, and the truth of the written word. Bezdomnyi is incarcerated in an asylum and diagnosed by the famous professor Stravinskii as schizophrenic, but his friend the poet Riukhin, who accompanies him to the asylum, realizes that he is totally sane. Riukhin is upset that in his ravings Bezdomnyi tells the truth about his (Riukhin's) poetry: it is worthless, Riukhin does not believe in it himself and he will never achieve immortality through it. Bezdomnyi vows never to write poetry again. Riukhin returns to Griboedov House, having indulged in a conversation with Pushkin's monument in Moscow city centre, and gets drunk alone, thoroughly depressed. Riukhin, although less so than Bezdomnyi, also gains an insight into true literary worth, although only a negative one; he realises that his own verses are bad, but he does gain an insight into what constitutes good writing. The Master, Bezdomnyi and Riukhin stand as mirror images to each other as writer figures, gaining a degree of self-knowledge and awareness of the spiritual prerequisites of creativity. Bezdomnyi, however, at the end of the novel is wiser, a professor of philosophy who knows the power and importance of the non-material world and always goes out to watch the full moon.

Throughout the novel the Master remains a figure of great moral authority. He possesses great intuition as, without any physical description, he immediately realizes from Bezdomnyi's ravings that he has met Woland. Woland too accords him considerable respect. As a character, however, he is weak and somewhat insipid, burning his novel in a moment of despair and retiring voluntarily to the asylum. He does nothing to help or save himself; rather, his liberation and the restoration of his faith are effected by the selfless love and efforts of Margarita.

The Master has burnt his novel in desperation, but Woland returns it with the now famous phrase that 'manuscripts don't burn' (p. 326) ('Рукописи не горят!', p. 703). (It is a significant fact that Bulgakov also burnt a draft of this novel in 1930. Indeed, it is one of the ironies of Soviet literary history that Bulgakov's own novel seemed lost but was then returned from oblivion.)

There is also in the novel considerable self-conscious parodying of literary convention. Bulgakov engages in a dialogue with the reader, urging the reader on ('Follow me, reader' (pp. 245, 249) ('За мной, читатель!', pp. 631, 632)), but at every step of the way subverts established expectations. He even uses his own favourite medium of the stage, both in the black magic show and in Bosoi's dream, to suggest the morbid theatricality of the Stalin show trials.

But more importantly, Bulgakov at several points disputes the authenticity of the written word as recorded in the Gospels, just as Ha-Notsri disputes the accuracy of Matthew's note-taking. The figure of Jesus is not the one to which we are accustomed from the Bible; Bulgakov's Ha-Notsri fears violence and shrinks from the beating of the giant centurion Mark Krysoboi, and the reader is not spared the gruesome and unseemly details of his slow and agonizing death. The effect is to remove any saintly aura from this hero: Ha-Notsri is simply a man, with all his frailties. Similarly, Judas is not a misguided follower, but a mercenary who is interested only in the money he earns for the betrayal, and who does not commit suicide, as described in the Bible, but is ambushed and murdered. Matthew is not so much a devoted servant of Jesus as a vain young man who wants to share in some of his master's glory. The author is thus asking fundamental questions about truth and reality, not only historical truth but also the basis of faith in the Christian world, and thus the nature of the world we live in.

Did Christ exist? Berlioz thinks not, and Matthew's writings are unreliable. Bulgakov's version of the confrontation of Christ and Pilate is markedly different from that in the Bible, as is his characterization of Christ, Matthew and Judas, and the events with which their names are now historically linked. Does the Devil exist? Again, Berlioz thinks not. Bulgakov is asserting the primacy of literature and the creative imagination to arbitrate in matters of truth/fiction/reality/illusion. Literature gives access to the higher reality, the 'fifth dimension'.

An important but overlooked theme in the novel is that of living space and accommodation, for here too there is an important moral and ethical issue.[14] Throughout the novel Woland and his entourage comment on how Muscovites have become corrupted through their desire for more living space, a remark directed not so much at the individuals as at a regime that keeps its subjects in such obeisance. Korov'ev goes so far as to suggest that an individual's ability to increase the size of his or her accommodation and exchange it for something still bigger is akin to knowledge of the fifth dimension. Moreover, the state's reward for loyalty is more living space. A dacha in Perelygino, we learn, is a particularly prized possession. Similarly, when Berlioz has met his unhappy end, Bosoi receives in two hours thirty-two requests for the three rooms he used to inhabit. We have seen how Poplavskii arrives from Kiev to claim his nephew's flat; and we also learn that the Master was denounced by his friend Aloizii Mogarych so that the latter could claim his flat. The issue of living space, as in the work of Iurii Trifonov in the 1960s and 1970s, reveals the moral essence of people, for if an individual is prepared to do anything to get a larger flat or a dacha, then he or she is lost as a human being.[15] It is exactly the issue of living space that determines the nature of the Soviet present in Bulgakov's novel.

Egotism and selfishness, also as with Trifonov, seem to be the main attributes of the Muscovites we meet in the novel. The exception is Margarita, who is prepared to die for the Master and will do anything to alleviate his distress. She attends Woland's ball, and is granted a wish as a result. Instead of asking for something for herself, she asks that the murderess Frida, who had killed her own child and whom she had seen at the ball, be set free from her torment. Woland is impressed by her compassion, as he had been by the compassion of the women in the

Variety Theatre, and grants her another wish; this time she asks to be with her beloved. Woland even gives her a present (a golden horseshoe).

The treatment of the character of Bezdomnyi is of interest as the only example of character development in the novel. When we first meet him in Patriarchs' Ponds he is a conformist and pliant member of the literary community. With Berlioz's death he quickly changes, as he is the only person who grasps who or what exactly Woland is. He renounces hack verse, dreams of episodes from the Master's novel and becomes the Master's pupil. At the end of the novel he has a different profession and seems happily married, although his sleep is troubled and every month he is drawn to the full moon. He is one of the few characters who remain profoundly affected by the events in the novel.

Style and Imagery

The narrator self-consciously utters words and phrases previously used by his characters: 'Oh gods – poison, I need poison!' (p. 75) ('О боги, боги, яду мне, яду!', p. 477), he says as he surveys the food on offer in the Griboedov House restaurant (also at several other points in the novel), thus repeating Pilate's words as he complains of his headache. The Master also utters the words 'Oh, ye gods' when Woland returns his manuscript to him, and Bezdomnyi uses the same words at the end of the novel as he stares out at the full moon. The author may offer to be our guide, but things in the novel never turn out as we think they should. For instance, the Master is introduced as the hero of the novel, but his self-characterization is ridiculously pompous ('I am a master' (p. 159) ('я – мастер', p. 552)). Self-pitying and weak, he hardly cuts a heroic figure. Similarly, Woland may be the Devil, but he is hardly an evil character; on the contrary, he brings about justice and reconciliation. Those who suffer, as we have seen, largely deserve their rough treatment. Indeed, the only person actually killed by the servants of the Devil is Maigel', an informer and spy; Berlioz dies in an accident. Bulgakov also flouts the conventions of belletristic writing, for there is no happy ending; while the Master and Margarita may be reunited, they are actually dead, for happiness is possible for them only in the other world. Earthly life is characterized by failure, deceit and danger, and love and self-sacrifice are attainable only in this other world.

The work's rich cultural borrowings also extend to minor characters: the head waiter at the restaurant in Griboedov House, Archibal'd Archibal'dovich, with his dark eyes and dagger-like beard, is likened to a pirate; when Margarita is transformed into a witch, she flies to an island where creatures from both Slavic and Western folklore, satyrs, witches, frogs and water-maidens, are enjoying a feast. The real reason for Woland's arrival in Moscow is not only to look at modern Muscovites, but to hold his annual ball. It is at the ball that he really shows his powers of life and death, and his dominance of the realm of darkness. Villains from world history make their fleeting appearance: Caligula and Messalina, Maliuta Skuratov, unnamed jailers, poisoners, murderers, traitors, madmen, even vampires. Musical instruments are played by a variety of animals (chimpanzees, gorillas, orangutans, mandrills, gibbons, marmosets, polar bears, tigers, salamanders and butterflies). Berlioz's head is transformed into a skull from which Woland and then Margarita drink the spilled blood of Maigel'. Woland conducts a dialogue with Berlioz's severed head, and duly despatches it to the oblivion Berlioz himself had asserted was awaiting everyone after death. Thus the atheist Berlioz receives after death the fate he had obviously craved. Furthermore, the festivities of Woland's ball offer a bitter parody of the dancing and carousing previously described in Griboedov House (both events begin at midnight), for these too are described as 'hell' by the author.[16]

Woland's powers and the behaviour of his entourage are the focus of the magical aspect of the novel. Towards the end of the novel Behemoth has a gunfight with the police, yet no one is hurt as a result. Azazello gives Margarita some cream to apply to her body which makes her ten years younger and allows her to fly like a witch, complete with broom. Naked and free, she walks on moonbeams. Her housekeeper Natasha also becomes a witch, and flies astride the lustful neighbour Nikolai Ivanovich, who has turned into a pig and calls her his 'goddess', his 'Venus'. This episode in particular is surprisingly erotic, but from a feminist viewpoint the tables are turned on the lecherous male, who is dominated and mocked while straddled by a sexually independent woman.

Moreover, Woland exists outside of time and human history. He brings the fifth dimension of the supernatural to Moscow, he brings about what for mortals is impossible, and he shows up the vanities and limitations of people with pretensions. His chessboard consists of living pieces, and he also has a globe that moves and shows up various places and wars in detail: a clear symbol of his omnipotence.

The novel's structure is characterized by contrasting imagery, be it of colour or of contrasts of dark and light, the sun and the moon, or fire and water. Pilate wears a white gown with a blood-red hem, and drinks and spills red wine which lies at his feet like the blood of the innocent Ha-Notsri. In Judea it is blisteringly hot, as it is in Moscow in the opening chapters. Judas runs through alternating moonlight and shadow as he rushes towards the ambush prepared for him by Afranius; when he dies, moonlight falls on his foot. Pilate spends several hours looking at the moon on the night of Judas' death, as does his dog Vanda; here too, as already mentioned, there is a link with Moscow, for Satan's ball takes place at the time of the full moon. Woland's apartment is ominously dark, but at the ball the staircase that leads endlessly upwards is bathed in light. The moon and the night finally transform Woland and his retinue into their true selves as they prepare to leave Moscow at the end of the novel; all pretence at buffoonery disappears, and they reveal their true demonic selves.

A black cloud descends upon Jerusalem when Ha-Notsri has been killed, and a storm seems to tear the sky apart. Pilate dreams that he walks up a moonbeam with Ha-Notsri, the two of them in deep debate. The moonlight gives Pilate no peace, and when Afranius informs him of Judas' death and then leaves, candles are brought in to replace the moonlight. He falls asleep as the dawn is about to break. The guests at Satan's ball come out of the fire (i.e. the flames of hell), and the Master consigns his novel to the flames of hell (whence Woland reconstitutes it). At the end of Woland's stay in Moscow, the flat he had used as a base also goes up in flames, as does the hard-currency shop visited by Korov'ev and Behemoth, and Griboedov House itself. Finally, the house that the Master and Margarita share is itself burned down, as Azazello asserts that everything begins and ends in fire, and with it burns the returned manuscript of the Master's novel. The novel is again lost to the world. Woland leaves Moscow in the midst of a storm, with dark clouds and a gloom that cuts the sun in two. In the darkness that ensues, houses, bridges, everything disappears in a fitting apocalyptic finale. Korov'ev and Behemoth cause more chaos with their whistling that uproots trees, kills birds, causes earth tremors, sends restaurants into the river and drives a passenger boat onto land. The sun is reflected in a thousand windows, representing the shattering of stability and all accepted perceptions of reality. However, as in Behemoth's gunfight with the police, no one is hurt. Just as the material world is transformed, so too are Woland and Ieshua in the spiritual realm: this is, indeed, the real culmination of the novel.

Throughout the novel, contrast is used as a stylistic device, and as a thematic one, as best summed up by Woland in conversation with Matthew, himself now Ha-Notsri's emissary between the light and the shadows:

> You spoke your words as though you denied the very existence of the shadows or of evil. Think, now: where would your good be if there were no evil and what would the world look like without shadow? Shadows are thrown by people and things. There's the shadow of my sword, for instance.

But shadows are also cast by trees and living things. Do you want to strip the whole globe by removing every tree and every creature to satisfy your fantasy of a bare world? You're stupid. (p. 405)

(Ты произносишь свои слова так, как будто ты не признаешь теней, а также и зла. Не будешь ли ты так добр подумать над вопросом: что бы делало твое добро, если бы не существовало зла, и как бы выглядела земля, если бы с нее исчезли тени? Ведь тени получаются от предметов и людей. Вот тень от моей шпаги. Но бывают тени от деревьев и от живых существ. Не хочешь ли ты ободрать весь земной шар, снеся с него прочь все деревья и все живое из-за твоей фантазии наслаждаться голым светом. Ты глуп.) (p. 776)

Characters are also played off against each other or, as in the case of the three writer figures already mentioned, are used as mirror images of each other. Ha-Notsri and Pilate are perhaps obvious examples; they first appear as the condemned man and his judge, but at the end of the novel their roles are reversed. Other characters act as parallels: Judas is to Ieshua as Aloizii Mogarych is to the Master; Matthew is Ha-Notsri's 'pupil' as Bezdomnyi becomes the Master's 'pupil' (perhaps Riukhin will become Bezdomnyi's pupil).[17] Both Ha-Notsri and the Master are men of moral authority and vision, and both suffer at the hands of secular authorities.

Ha-Notsri has sent Matthew to ask that the Master be given peace. Woland grants him this, and permits him to be with Margarita, but, in a phrase that has puzzled critics down the years, insists that he has not earned the right to light.[18] Ha-Notsri and Pilate both share the same immortality, for when people talk about Jesus they also talk about Pilate. Pilate has come to hate his immortality; at the end of the novel he and Ha-Notsri are reconciled, and ascend a moonbeam together towards the moon. The Master has set Pilate free from his torment. This is an act not of historical fact but of artistic truth, of forgiveness for moral weakness. The Master is himself freed by Woland, on Margarita's wish, and both the Master and his Margarita thus achieve their own immortality outside of human life.

Lesley Milne has commented on the link between the Master and Woland:

In 1937, when the title of the novel finally emerged as *The Master and Margarita*, the V in Voland changed to a W, an upturned M. This formal link between the two encodes Woland's second, non-retributive function: the assistance he renders to the Master and Margarita. The Master and Woland are complementary emanations of a literary force which is both other-worldly and combative. As characters they have no 'psychology' but they characterize psychological drives recognizable as those of 'the writer': total inner concentration and outwardly-directed challenge.[19]

There is also a link between Woland and Ha-Notsri, for both challenge secular authority and the systems of rationalist belief they follow.

The spiritual, non-rational dimension – the fifth dimension – is fundamental to the novel. Dream is an important aspect of the non-material world. Bezdomnyi has several dreams: in the first he sees Ha-Notsri's execution, while in the second, Pilate and Ha-Notsri reach agreement, there is no execution and Pilate is freed from his guilt. Pilate himself prophetically dreams of a conversation with Ha-Notsri, both of them ascending a moonbeam, where he himself asserts that cowardice is the most terrible sin; this is also part of Bezdomnyi's second dream. Margarita also has a prophetic dream where she is reunited with her lover. Berlioz thinks he is dreaming when he first glimpses the materialization, from thin air, of Woland and Korov'ev, and Bezdomnyi thinks that Woland's story about Christ and Pilate is nothing but a dream. Bezdomnyi then sees the next chapter of the meeting between Ha-Notsri and Pilate in a dream. Bosoi also has a dream, in which he is accused of hoarding foreign currency. Similarly, Bezdomnyi first sees the Master in the asylum after he has been given a sedative and seems to split in two, into his former self and his new self. From then on Bezdomnyi begins a new life, but more importantly, in his dreams he becomes the Master's 'pupil', just as Matthew the Levite is pupil to Ha-Notsri.

Conclusion

In the Epilogue of the novel, the inanity of the material and rational world is shown up and ridiculed. The police establish that a gang of hypnotizers has been at work in Moscow, therefore black cats and people with similar-sounding surnames have been the main victims. The rational, atheistic world is unable to cope with the supernatural, the 'fifth dimension', on its own terms. Rimskii, Bengal'skii and Likhodeev leave the theatre, Varenukha, as he had promised Korov'ev, is polite to people on the telephone, Aloizii Mogarych now has Likhodeev's job. Bezdomnyi has changed both inwardly and externally, and he shares his fascination for the full moon with Margarita's neighbour Nikolai Ivanovich, who sits waiting for Natasha to return.

The novel achieves a certain symmetry of structure, characterization and style. Characters complement and contrast with each other, and there is a consistent use in both the Moscow and Judea chapters of darkness and light, the sun and the moon, heat and shadows (in particular the use of heat as a metaphor for political oppression). Dream, fantasy and magic reveal the truth about people and the material world. Finally, there are various levels of the novel's preoccupation with literature, from the satirical attacks on the writing community to the calling of the writer and then deeper to the role of literature as a repository of truth.

The novel, then, is more than just an extremely funny and inventive tale of fantasy and the author's squaring of accounts. Lidiia Ianovskaia sees it 'above all as a satirical novel'.[20] It is very much about the act of creativity, the immortality of the written word and the world of the spirit. Although it would be difficult to claim the novel as a defence of Biblical truth (indeed, as Julie Curtis and Andrew Barratt have shown, Bulgakov is claiming the Gospels as a work of fiction),[21] it contains many borrowings from the Bible and Christianity, as well as from the occult. The Master's novel, not the Bible, contains the truth of the Pilate/Christ dialogue, for it is the truth of sin and forgiveness which is at the heart of all human history. Literature is truth because it expresses man's moral essence, and penetrates beyond the superficial concerns of secular tyranny and religious obfuscation. The Master's novel is only complete when Pilate is released from his torment, for it then ends with mercy, reconciliation and love. This is the ultimate truth of human life on this earth, but it is only possible in the supernatural realm.

The relationship of the writer, or any man of ideas, to secular authority is another important motif, for if Pilate holds the power of life or death over Ha-Notsri, the same could be said not only of the Master and Woland, but also of Bulgakov and Stalin. Those who suffer in Moscow are tyrants of the literary and artistic world, and Woland punishes those who have persecuted the Master. There is clearly an identification between Bulgakov and his fictional author, and so too, implicitly, between Woland and Stalin. Undoubtedly, one of Bulgakov's major themes is the paucity of atheistic belief and its sheer inadequacy as an answer to man's spiritual searchings. But the novel is also about the hopelessness of the mundane world, as truth and happiness reside beyond it. Ultimately the novel stands as a testimony to the power of literature to express man's moral searches, and to provide the basis for compassion and love in the here and now.

Notes

1. There are certain inconsistencies in the text which suggest that there was no final revision. For instance, there are differing accounts of how the bodies of the Master and Margarita are disposed of, and Ha-Notsri is described as coming from two different cities. On these and other confusions, see J. A. E. Curtis, *Bulgakov's Last Decade: The Writer as Hero*, Cambridge, 1987, pp. 132, 137. On the other hand, Boris Gasparov regards the novel as 'completed', but Andrew Barratt disagrees. See B. M. Gasparov, 'Из наблюдений над мотивной структурой романа М. А. Булгакова *Мастер и Маргарита*' ('From Observations on the Motif Structure of M. Bulgakov's Novel "The Master and Margarita"'), *Slavica Hierosolymitana*, 3, 1978, pp. 198–251 (p. 248); Andrew Barratt, *Between Two Worlds: A Critical Introduction to 'The Master and Margarita'*, Oxford, 1987, p. 62, and pp. 40–63 for a detailed account of the novel's development.
2. For further discussion, see the introductory essay by the archivist V. Losev, '«Рукописи не горят' ('Manuscripts Don't Burn'), in M. Bulgakov, *Великий канцлер: Черновые редакции романа «Мастер и Маргарита»* (*The Great Chancellor: Early Redactions of the Novel 'The Master and Margarita'*) Moscow, 1992, especially pp. 9–18.
3. Barratt, *Between Two Worlds*, pp. 67–74, lists the major differences between the texts of the various editions.
4. Ibid., p. 36.
5. Julie Curtis notes that Matthew the Levite actually corresponds to two figures from the Bible: the tax-collector Matthew in Matthew (9:9), and Levi in Mark (2:13–14) and Luke (5:27–8); see Julie Curtis, *Bulgakov's Last Decade*, p. 147.
6. Riitta Pittman observes: 'Consequently, it can be deduced that in Bulgakov's novel the sustaining of the mysteries of black magic depends on the maintenance of a lie or lies, while the revelation of these mysteries occurs when the truth comes out. In principle, the magic depends on the individual's or the audience's belief in an illusion and/or a lie!' (Riitta Pittman, *The Writer's Divided Self in Bulgakov's 'The Master and Margarita'*, London, 1991, p. 72).
7. Barratt, *Between Two Worlds*, p. 120, has noted several intertextual references to Griboedov in the novel; in particular, the character Sof'ia Pavlovna, who initially refuses Behemoth and Korov'ev entry to the restaurant, shares her Christian name and patronymic with the heroine of *Woe from Wit* (*Горе от ума*).
8. M. Bulgakov, *The Master and Margarita*, translated by Michael

Glenny, London, 1988, pp. 396–7; *Три романа* (*Three Novels*), Moscow, 1973, pp. 767–8. All further references to the work will be taken from these editions, with corresponding page numbers incorporated directly into the text.

9. For a more detailed examination of Bulgakov's borrowings from Goethe's *Faust*, see Barratt, *Between Two Worlds*, pp. 268–302, and E. Stenbock-Fermor, 'Bulgakov's *The Master and Margarita* and Goethe's *Faust*', *Slavic and East European Journal*, vol. 13, no. 3 1969, pp. 309–25. On the influence of E. T. A. Hoffman, see Pittman, *The Writer's Divided Self*, pp. 94–5, 137–8.

10. Barratt, *Between Two Worlds*, p. 216.

11. Lidiia Ianovskaia, *Творческий путь Михаила Булгакова* (*Mikhail Bulgakov's Creative Path*), Moscow, 1983, pp. 281–2.

12. Julie Curtis' definition of Woland is perhaps the most fitting for this study:

> So Woland figures in the novel as a kind of plenipotentiary ambassador from the supernatural realm; his task is to establish contact with mankind at a moment when it appears to have cut itself off from its spiritual heritage. Soviet man has ceased to see that upon his actions will hang consequences which may not even become apparent until the next life, that he is responsible for determining his own destiny through the choices he makes. In this existentialist vision of the dilemmas of choice confronting the individual, Woland is not empowered to influence the decisions that each person takes. By meting out punishments and allocating rewards, he can only hope to give modern man a salutary reminder of his own responsibilities in the spiritual domain, responsibilities which have not been swept away with the setting-up of a materialist state power (Curtis, *Bulgakov's Last Decade*, p. 173).

See also Ianovskaia, *Творческий путь Михаила Булгакова*, p. 278: 'Воланд не сеет зла, не внушает зла. Он всего лишь вскрывает зло, разоблачая, снижая, уничижая то, что деиствительно ничтожным' ('Woland does not spread evil, does not impose evil. He merely uncovers evil, exposing, belittling and reducing to absurdity that which really is mediocre').

13. Lesley Milne tells us that the American Embassy ball that Bulgakov attended in April 1935 was also attended by the informer Baron von Steiger, who served as the prototype for Maigel'. She also asserts that the opulent description of Woland's ball derives from this event (Lesley Milne, *Mikhail Bulgakov: A Critical Biography*, Cambridge, 1990, p. 250). On other possible prototypes, Riitta Pittman argues that Riukhin may be based on Vladimir Maiakovskii, Bezdomnyi on Sergei Esenin or Ivan Pribludnyi,

Berlioz on Anatolii Lunacharskii (Pittman, *The Writer's Divided Self*, pp. 92–3). Andrew Barratt also makes an attempt to identify the real-life prototypes of the members of the Griboedov club (Barratt, *Between Two Worlds*, pp. 119–23).

14. Referring to the diaries of Bulgakov's third wife Elena, Riitta Pittman points out that Bulgakov himself yearned for a good flat in the 1930s (Pittman, *The Writer's Divided Self*, p. 68).

15. Pittman (*The Writer's Divided Self*, p. 69) concludes: 'The utilitarian aims have failed to bring about material happiness for all. Corruption and bribery are commonplace. Genuine contact between human beings has been sacrificed for the sake of personal, material gain.'

16. Ibid., p. 124: 'Bulgakov's view of the prostitution of the writer's talents is unequivocal: the betrayal of artistic integrity for mercenary ends is a crime against the sanctity of the human spirit. Bulgakov's discovery of the devil's domain, of the fictitious aspect of the tangible reality, renders the literary "merry-go-round" of Moscow transparent and unveils its jesters' monstrous appetite for a life of illusions and "creature comforts".'

17. Riitta Pittman argues that the Master and Bezdomnyi 'represent different regions of creative experience' (Ibid., p. 115). Indeed, both have similar experiences: they are situated in an asylum, they have both written about Jesus Christ, both gain 'peace' and Bezdomnyi dreams of the Master's novel.

18. Julie Curtis comments:

> Beyond Matvey's words we hear Bulgakov invoking all the themes of hesitation, failure and regret which pervade his oeuvre from the earliest days of his literary career. If the phrase is also to be construed as Bulgakov's final judgment on himself, we are invited to sympathize with his weary hopelessness about the possibility of gaining either worldly renown, or any triumphant reward in the next world to compensate for his tribulations; he can envisage no happier prospect than release from persecution, a marvellous final peace (Curtis, *Bulgakov's Last Decade*, p. 182).

On the Master's reward, and the varying critical interpretations, see Barratt, *Between Two Worlds*, pp. 278–81.

19. Milne, *Mikhail Bulgakov: A Critical Biography*, p. 243.

20. Ianovskaia, *Творческий путь Михаила Булгакова*, p. 276.

21. Curtis, *Bulgakov's Last Decade*, pp. 148–50; Barratt, *Between Two Worlds*, pp. 175–83.

6

Boris Pasternak (1890–1960), *Doctor Zhivago* (*Доктор Живаго*)

Introduction and Background

Doctor Zhivago was published in Italy in 1957, and has become perhaps the most celebrated Russian novel of the twentieth century. Because it was published in the West it was, like *We* before it and *Cancer Ward* after it, viewed by the Soviet authorities as providing ideological ammunition to the Western foe, and consequently as an anti-Soviet work. It was therefore regarded as deeply inimical to the regime. The editors of the journal *Novyi mir*, who rejected the manuscript, indicated at the height of the 'Pasternak affair' in 1958 why the novel was unacceptable:

> Printed abroad, Pasternak's book, which presents a libellous picture of the October Revolution, the people who accomplished this Revolution, and the building of socialism in the Soviet Union, has been defended by the bourgeois press and used as a weapon by the forces of international reaction.

> (Будучи издана за границей, эта книга Пастернака, клеветнически изображающая Октябрьскую революцию, народ, совершивший эту революцию, и строительство социализма в Советском Союзе, была поднята на щит буржуазной прессы и принята на вооружение международной реакцией.)[1]

Indeed, the publication resulted in a campaign of vilification of Pasternak in the Soviet Union, the worst since the death of Stalin, with press articles and (carefully channelled) public opinion used to attack the writer and his works.

Pasternak was awarded the Nobel Prize for literature in 1958, but was forced to refuse it when the Soviet authorities suggested that they would not allow him back into Russia and would deprive him of his Soviet citizenship, if he travelled to Sweden to accept the prize. He was also expelled from the Writers' Union, an act which effectively deprived him of earning a living. Pasternak nevertheless continued to write; his novel was translated into all the major languages of the world, and he was admired throughout the world as a symbol of resistance to the tyranny of the Soviet regime. Despite the official opprobrium around his name in the Soviet Union, his funeral was attended by thousands, and his grave in Peredelkino is still a place of pilgrimage for many Russians, young and old. Indeed, for many of today's younger generation of Russians, for whom the country called the Soviet Union is but a vague memory, Pasternak and the poet Anna Akhmatova, who was officially reviled in 1946, but who maintained her dignity and continued to write according to the dictates of her conscience and her heart, remain as literary figures who towered above their times. This was exactly because they did not compromise their artistic integrity or their morality during the dark years of Stalinism. Both suffered persecution and their loved ones were imprisoned (Akhmatova's son Lev Gumilev, Pasternak's lover Ol'ga Ivinskaia), but, despite these deprivations and other substantial material hardships, they kept alive the Russian literary traditions of the nineteenth century and the link with pre–1917 culture.

Pasternak was born in Moscow into a respected and quite wealthy artistic family. His father Leonid was an eminent artist (and remained so after he emigrated to France in the 1920s), and his mother had been a concert pianist. Boris studied at the universities of Moscow and Marburg, and his first poems appeared in 1913. He received acclaim after the publication of his third volume of poems, *My Sister – Life* (*Сестра – моя жизнь*) in 1922. During the years of revolution and civil war he also began writing prose, and several volumes appeared throughout the 1920s and 1930s. In the 1930s and 1940s Pasternak confined himself largely to translation, but even here his genius shines through. His Russian renderings of Shakespeare's tragedies and Goethe's *Faust* are in themselves major Russian poetic works.

The relative easing of cultural policy during the Second World War enabled Pasternak to publish more of his own poetry, and volumes appeared in 1943 and 1945. After the war, however, Pasternak continued with his translating work but also began writing *Doctor Zhivago*.[2] Some of the poems that make up the last chapter of the novel were published in the journal *Znamia* in 1954, but the novel as a whole was rejected by *Novyi mir* in 1956. Pasternak had been hopeful that in the post-Stalin thaw, and in particular following Khrushchev's attack on Stalin at the Twentieth Party Congress in 1956, the novel would be published. However, he had taken precautions to have a copy of the novel smuggled to the West, should his optimism prove naive and misplaced.

It was possible to attack and criticise Stalin after 1956, but there were limits to this new-found 'freedom'. The letter sent to Pasternak by the editors of *Novyi mir* in 1956 indicates that in the thaw years there could be no possible criticism of the October Revolution itself:

> The spirit of your novel is the spirit of non-acceptance of the Socialist Revolution. The pathos of your novel is the pathos of asserting that the October Revolution, Civil War and the subsequent social changes that are connected with it brought nothing but suffering, and the Russian intelligentsia destroyed, either physically or morally. The system of views that emerges from the pages of the novel on the past of our country and primarily on the first decade after the October Revolution . . . tells us that the October Revolution was a mistake, and the involvement in it by that part of the intelligentsia that supported it was an irrevocable disaster, and everything that happened afterwards was evil . . . We think that we would not be wrong to say that the tale of the life and death of Doctor Zhivago in your conception is simultaneously a tale about the life and death of the Russian intelligentsia, of its path into the Revolution and through the Revolution, and of its death as a result of the Revolution.

> (Дух Вашего романа – дух неприятия социалистической революции. Пафос Вашего романа – пафос утверждения, что Октябрьская революция, гражданская война и связанные с ними последующие социальные перемены не принесли народу ничего, кроме страданий, а русскую интеллигенцию уничтожили или физически, или морально. Встающая со страниц романа система взглядов автора на прошлое нашей страны и прежде всего на ее первые десятилетия после Октябрьской революции . . . сводится к тому, что Октябрьская революция была ошибкой, участие в ней для этой части интеллигенции, которая ее поддерживала, было непоправимой бедой, а все происшедшее после нее – злом . . . Думается, что мы не ошибемся, сказав, что повесть о жизни и смерти доктора Живаго в Вашем представлении одновременно повесть о жизни и смерти русской интеллигенции, о ее путях в революцию, через революцию и о ее гибели в результате революции.)[3]

The novel was finally published in the Soviet Union in 1988, in the years of *glasnost'*. Of the novel, Angela Livingstone notes:

> Except in talent, novelty and refusal to be scared by the censor, *Doctor Zhivago* has little in common with other outstanding fictional works of the post-revolutionary period [Babel's *Red Cavalry*, Zamiatin's *We*, Platonov's *The Foundation Pit*, Bulgakov's *The Master and Margarita*]. From all these, *Zhivago* differs both in its celebratory spirit and in its attempt at a straightforward style, a new realism. The other writers mentioned are concerned with innovation in literary language or in ways of projecting the authorial voice, but Pasternak, like his hero, sought 'an originality that would be concealed under a cover of commonplace and familiar forms, a restrained, unpretentious . . . unnoticeable style that would attract no-one's attention'.[4]

Plot

Most of the action of the novel takes place within a quarter of a century, in particular the years 1903–29, although there are other brief passages that take place both before and after these dates. The action ranges from Moscow, the wartime trenches of southern Russia and Galicia and the (fictitious) towns of Iuriatin and Varykino in the Urals. We follow Iurii Andreevich Zhivago's life from childhood in the early years of the century through to the First World War, the 1917 revolutions, the Civil War and the reconstruction and NEP of the 1920s. Because the novel is very much about the interconnectedness of human life and coincidence and chance meetings make up much of the narrative, it is perhaps best to summarize the plot in some detail, mentioning the various characters who appear and reappear in the narrative at certain junctures.

The novel begins in 1903 with the funeral of Iurii's mother when he is only ten years old. She has died of consumption. We learn that his father had long ago deserted the family. Iurii is accompanied by his uncle Nikolai Vedeniapin, a former priest; they then go to Duplianka, the estate of the industrialist Kologrivov, to see Ivan Voskoboinikov, with whom Vedeniapin has business, and there Iurii becomes reacquainted with Nika Dudorov, a boy two years older than himself. As Vedeniapin and Voskoboinikov conduct their business, they observe the passage of the five o'clock express train, which has suddenly stopped nearby. As it happens the train has come to an unscheduled stop because Iurii's father, unbeknown to them all, has committed suicide by jumping from the train. He is in the company of the lawyer Komarovskii. Also on the train is the eleven-year-old Misha Gordon, whose father had pulled the emergency cord to stop the train, and Marfa Tiverzina. In about fifteen years time, Tiverzina's son will turn out to be a committed and merciless Bolshevik, and as such a threat to Zhivago and Lara. The lives of all these characters are destined to become intertwined.

In 1905 Amaliia Karlovna Guishar arrives in Moscow from the Urals with her son Rodion and sixteen-year-old daughter Larisa, or Lara. Lara studies in the same class as her friend Nadia Kologrivova, daughter of Kologrivov the industrialist, who herself is friendly with Nika Dudorov. Komarovskii helps Amaliia Karlovna get settled in Moscow and acts as her adviser. He also has an affair with her, and soon also seduces Lara. In the meantime, Pasha Antipov's father is arrested for his involvement in the strikes that are paralysing Moscow at the time, and Pasha goes to live with the railway worker Tiverzin, also a supporter of the strike and whose mother was on the train when Zhivago's father killed himself. A sense of the emerging interconnectedness of human life in the novel should by now be apparent.

Another demonstration by workers is ambushed by Cossacks, and the carnage is observed by Vedeniapin, who also sees amongst those fleeing the boy Nika Dudorov. Nika and Pasha Antipov are also involved in the later uprising in the Krasnaia Presnia district of Moscow. Iurii is now staying in Moscow with the family of Professor Gromeko; Zhivago will later marry Tonia Gromeko, the daughter, who will bear him a son and a daughter. On hearing of the affair of her daughter with Komarovskii, Amaliia Karlovna attempts suicide and is attended by Professor Gromeko, with Misha Gordon and Iurii in attendance. Misha recognizes Komarovskii as the man who led Zhivago's father to suicide on the train; Iurii sees Komarovskii and Lara speaking in hushed tones together, and immediately realises that they are having an affair. He also understands that this is the end of his childhood innocence, and the beginning of another life.

The narrative moves to 1911–12. Anna Gromeko, mother of Tonia, develops lung problems as a result of a domestic accident. The Gromekos' janitor, Markel, has a daughter, Marina, who is six years old; she will become Zhivago's last wife, and will bear him two children. Iurii is about to graduate, and Lara moves out of her mother's house and in with Nadia Kologrivova in order to escape from Komarovskii's attentions. Her brother Rodion is an officer cadet, but has gambling problems; he prevails upon her to ask Komarovskii for a loan, thereby revealing that he cares nothing for her reputation and honour, only his own. Lara and Pasha Antipov, now a student, are good friends, and, indeed, Pasha is in love with her. Lara, now desperate, decides to shoot Komarovskii if he refuses or sets conditions on the loan. This she does, at the Sventitskiis' New Year party also attended by Iurii and Tonia. She misses, and instead slightly wounds the nearby Kornakov, a prosecutor who years before had tried the striking railway workers, including Tiverzin. This is now the second time Iurii has seen Lara, without her seeing him. At the same time, Tonia's mother dies, and is buried in the same cemetery as Iurii's mother.

Komarovskii, anxious for his reputation should certain facts become known, prevents judicial proceedings against Lara, and shortly afterwards Lara and Pasha are married. On their wedding night Lara confesses all to Pasha, who wakes up a different man. They leave for the Siberian town of Iuriatin, where they live for three years, and have a daughter, Katia. It is now 1915, and Pasha suddenly volunteers for the front. Lara trains as a nurse and follows him, leaving Katia with friends in Moscow. Iurii is working in the Moscow women's hospital, but also tending the war wounded. Tonia gives birth to their son Sasha, and her screams are likened to the screams of a man being dragged out from under the wheels of a train. There is thus a link here with Zhivago's father.

Iurii is then sent to the front, where he meets his friend Misha Gordon in Galicia. The officer Galiullin reports seeing Antipov killed in action. Galiullin is the son of Gimazetdin, the janitor of the yard where Tiverzin had lived. There is also a memorable scene in Galicia where Gordon, Zhivago, Lara, Galiullin and Gimazetdin are all next to one another on the same battlefield, but are not aware of each other's presence. Gimazetdin dies a particularly horrible death as his face is blown apart by shrapnel. Zhivago is himself wounded, and is tended by Lara; he recognizes her, but she of course does not recognize him, as she has never actually seen him before. Furthermore, she does not know Galiullin, although he also recognizes her, having been a friend of her husband in childhood; Zhivago is also unaware that Galiullin knows her. However, we do get Lara's impression of Zhivago: intelligent, but hardly handsome or remarkable — pretty ordinary, in fact.

By February 1917, news of the Tsar's abdication has reached Zhivago through the letters of Dudorov and Gordon, and from stories by soldiers at the front. Zhivago's first book of poetry has also been published. Lara and Zhivago are now in close contact through work, and Tonia in her letters accuses him of having an affair with her. He, on the contrary, does not even know where her room is in the hospital. They are based in Meliuzeev, in the house of Countess Zhabrinskaia, and tended by Mademoiselle Fleury and the cook Ustin'ia. Ustin'ia shouts down the young idealist Gints at a meeting when she claims pity and compassion as Bolshevik ideals. After this, Gints is brutally murdered by a mob of mutinous soldiers. Lara soon leaves, as does Zhivago shortly afterwards.

Zhivago goes home to Moscow to be united with the son he has never seen, and finds that his uncle Vedeniapin has returned from Switzerland and has espoused the Bolshevik cause. This causes endless arguments between him and Professor Gromeko, who is now chairman of the regional *duma* (local government council). Amidst discussions and arguments, only Zhivago sees the approaching cataclysm. The Bolshevik Revolution, like the February Revolution, is not related directly, but rather news of it is brought by Vedeniapin and Gordon. Zhivago buys a newspaper in order to read about it, and, as he retires to a building to read it by the light, bumps into his half-brother Evgraf, whom he as yet does not recognize. Further coincidences occur when Zhivago is called to a house where there is a case of suspected typhus and finds Galiullin's mother on the house committee.

Zhivago is at first enthusiastic about the 'magnificent surgery' of the

Bolshevik seizure of power, although soon he has to resort to stealing firewood for heating, half the people at the hospital where he works leave and there are food shortages. The ensuing Civil War sees the Zhivago family going hungry; Zhivago himself falls ill with typhus, and in his delirium dreams of writing poetry and of a boy with Kirghiz eyes. Only later does he learn that during his illness the family was visited by Evgraf, with his Kirghiz eyes, who brought them food. Evgraf is not only a person of influence with the authorities (he can obtain rice, sugar and raisins), but is also an admirer of Iurii's poetry. It is on Evgraf's recommendation that they leave Moscow and travel to Tonia's family estate in Varykino. They leave Moscow in April 1918.

They travel to Siberia by train, together with various soldiers, workers, stockbrokers, lawyers, traders and forced labourers. The sixteen-year-old Vasia Brykin is also on board (more will be said of him later), as is Kostoed, with whom Zhivago engages in political discussion on the peasantry, their desire for freedom and the nature of reality in Russia. He also has conversations about science and Marxism with Samdeviatov, a well-educated Bolshevik who regards Marxism as a 'historical inevitability'. As they travel through Russia they come across evidence of the excesses of the dreaded commissar Strel'nikov in the form of burned-out villages. We later learn that Strel'nikov is, in fact, none other than Pavel Antipov. Zhivago also hears rumours that the Whites, under the command of Galiullin, are about to take Iuriatin. There are also natural as well as man-made hazards to overcome: it takes them three days to clear snow from the line after a storm. Zhivago then makes the acquaintance of Strel'nikov, as he wanders from the train and is caught by sentries from Strel'nikov's armoured train. Strel'nikov recognizes him as a Muscovite and, to the surprise of his men, lets him go.

The Zhivagos alight the train at Torfianaia and travel on to Varykino. The story moves forward to winter, when Iurii is making notes about life, Varykino, Samdeviatov, the seasons, art, dreams, Pushkin and Faust. The last of his notes concern the arrival of Evgraf, who again appears and disappears mysteriously, providing for Iurii's family and offering protection. Iurii goes to Iuriatin and meets Lara once more. Just as at the Sventitskiis' party, he observes her from a distance in the library, without her seeing him. In early May 1919 he calls in on her home, and relates to her the journey from Moscow and his meeting with Strel'nikov, although he does not disclose that Strel'nikov is actually her husband. For her part, she tells him that Galiullin is the commander of the Czech forces in the district, a chivalrous and decent man. Soon an affair develops between Iurii and Lara; Iurii feels guilty and decides to confess to Tonia, but, on his way home to Varykino one day, is abducted by Red partisans under the leadership of Liverii Mikulitsyn and mobilized as their doctor.

Zhivago spends more than a year with the partisans, during which time he is forced to take part in military action. In an act symbolic of his non-alignment, he shoots at a tree, but a White soldier, Sergei Rantsevich, gets in the way. Iurii nurses him back to health and allows him to escape. He notices that Rantsevich and a dead Red telegraph officer both possess copies of the 90th Psalm: another coincidence, but one which shows that both Reds and Whites believe in the same God and are nourished by the same spiritual texts. In the partisan camp he hears the confession of the killer and fearless warrior Pamfil Palykh, and we learn that it was he who killed the young Gints at Meliuzeev in February 1917: the only murder out of the many he has committed that he actually regrets. Traitors in the camp are discovered and executed, although one of them, Terentii Galuzin, survives. A horribly mutilated partisan crawls into the camp with one arm and one leg chopped off and tied to his back, and tells of horrors and atrocities in the town under the Whites. On hearing and seeing this, Palykh kills his wife and three children to save them from the same fate, then disappears from the camp. Zhivago leaves soon afterwards, on hearing that Kolchak has been defeated and that the Red Army are about to relieve them.

Zhivago returns to Iuriatin, where he hears that his family has moved back to Moscow. He goes to Lara's, finds the flat empty, falls asleep and dreams. When he wakes up, he finds himself washed and lying in bed, with Lara nearby tending him. Lara tells Iurii that Tonia has given birth to their daughter, Masha. More ominously, old Tiverzin and Antipov's father, both ardent revolutionaries from Moscow, are members of the Iuriatin military tribunal. As members of the wrong class, Lara and Iurii may be in danger, and so they decide to move to Varykino. Iurii receives a letter from Tonia to the effect that the whole family is being exiled abroad, and is travelling to Paris. It is an emotional letter, all the more so as husband and wife will never see each other again. Lara and Iurii are visited by Komarovskii, who is highly placed with the Bolsheviks. He urges them to leave and offers them his protection. Komarovskii gets drunk, and Iurii violently throws him out.

They go to Varykino, and Lara is now pregnant with Iurii's child. Komarovskii arrives once more, and this time takes Lara and Katia with him. Iurii remains, saying that he will follow, but continues writing poetry. It is winter, and wolves gather outside. Strel'nikov appears, and he and Iurii have a long conversation about Lara. It transpires that he, too, was betrayed by Terentii Galuzin. After Iurii tells him that Lara always loved and respected him, Strel'nikov shoots himself. Iurii returns to Moscow in the spring of 1922, the start of NEP, accompanied by Vasia Brykin, whom he has picked up on the way. He takes a room in the house now run by Markel, and soon moves in with his daughter, Marina.

Although in age only about forty years old, Iurii is prematurely aged by the time he dies in 1929. By that time he is exhausted, despite his new family, as the author informs us towards the end of the novel:

All that is left to tell is the brief story of the last eight or ten (sic) years of Zhivago's life, years in which he went more and more to seed, gradually losing his knowledge and skill as a doctor and a writer, emerging from his state of depression and resuming his work only to fall back, after a brief flare-up of activity, into long periods of indifference to himself and to everything in the world. During these years the heart disease, which he had himself diagnosed earlier but without any real idea of its gravity, developed to an advanced stage.

(Остается досказать немногословную повесть Юрия Андреевича, восемь или девять последних лет его жизни перед смертью, в течение которых он все больше сдавал и опускался, теряя докторские навыки и утрачивая писательские, на короткое время выходил из состояния угнетения и упадка, воодушевлялся, возвращался к деятельности, и потом, после недолгой вспышки, снова впадал в затяжное безучастие к себе самому и ко всему на свете. В эти годы сильно развилась его давняя болезнь сердца, которую он сам у себя установил уже и раньше, но о степени серьезности которой не имел представления.)[5]

He meets Dudorov and Gordon once more, and meets Evgraf again by chance, who arranges some work for him. But despite his friends and his new family, Iurii does not want to live. He has a heart attack on a crowded tram on a blisteringly hot summer's day, as Mademoiselle Fleury passes by on her way to the Swiss Embassy to arrange an exit visa. Neither of them recognizes the other. As if to conclude the cycle of coincidence and interconnection, Zhivago's body lies in a coffin in the room in which Lara and Pasha Antipov used to live.

Lara is in Moscow to arrange for Katia to enrol in an acting school or the conservatory; she has come not because she knows Zhivago is there, but to see the room she used to live in. Evgraf relates details to her of her husband's death, and they both agree to arrange Iurii's papers. However, Lara disappears, as the author informs us, probably arrested and sent to perish in one of the many women's camps of the Gulag. In the epilogue the narrative moves to 1943. Gordon and Dudorov are Red Army officers, although both have spent time in the Gulag; Tania, the daughter of Zhivago and Lara, is the laundry girl in their unit. She tells them her terrible story, of loss, hardship, the death of her younger brother Pet'ka and a life of wandering, homeless and uncared for. She does not know who her real mother and father were, but recalls a certain Komarov. Evgraf is now a general. The novel comes to an end some time after Stalin's death, with the elderly Gordon and Dudorov reflecting on Zhivago's poetry, the truth it contained, and the new post-Stalin world. The hope of immortality is a source of inner freedom, and it is thus fitting that the novel ends with Gordon and Dudorov, in the post-Stalin thaw, holding a book of Zhivago's poems and inwardly rejoicing at the prospect of freedom that these poems represent:

> To the two ageing friends sitting by the window it seemed that this freedom of the spirit was there, that on that very evening the future had become almost tangible in the streets below, and that they had themselves entered that future and would, from now on, be part of it. They felt a peaceful joy for this holy city and for the whole land and for the survivors among those who had played a part in this story and for their children, and the silent music of happiness filled them and enveloped them and spread far and wide. And it seemed that the book in their hands knew what they were feeling and gave them its support and confirmation. (pp. 463–4)

> (Состарившимся друзьям у окна казалось, что эта свобода души пришла, что именно в этот вечер будущее расположилось ощутимо внизу на улицах, что сами они вступили в это будущее и отныне в нем находятся. Счастливое, умиленное спокойствие за этот святой город и за всю землю, за доживших до этого вечера участников этой истории и их детей проникало их и охватывало неслышною музыкой счастья, разлившейся далеко кругом. И книжка в их руках как бы знала все это и давала их чувствам поддержку и подтверждение.) (p. 531)

Themes

Zhivago lives through the great cataclysms of Russian history in the first quarter of this century, but the novel is not really about these events. Rather, the novel is about life itself, for Zhivago transforms life and experience into art through the medium of poetry. It is in these verses that he achieves immortality as they are read 'five or ten years' after the War by Gordon and Dudorov, looking out on Moscow and finding hope for the kind of freedom embodied in the poet's verses. These poems are the crowning glory of Zhivago's life. They represent the crystallization of his belief in inner freedom, the unity of man and nature and the dominance of spiritual values. They are, of course, written by Pasternak, but because they are presented as Zhivago's poems, we can be sure of the basic artistic identification of the author and his hero. Further textual evidence of this is to be found in the close similarity in their biographies: both are about the same age, both live through the same experiences and both hold the same views on art, politics and religion.

The novel is set apart from the realistic tradition of much of twentieth-century Russian fiction in that it does not stress the rational sequence of cause and effect in people's lives. People remain in what they have achieved, and in what they leave behind. It is also a novel of movement, of transformation, of sudden awareness of the power and majesty of nature. Characters such as Zhivago and Antipov-Strel'nikov do not develop in the realistic sense, they experience sudden changes or transformations of outlook. The many coincidences in the novel are part of the deeper connections that bind people to their environment and to each other. Coincidence and irrationality, not causality or inevitability, make up the fabric of being.[6] The novel is about life itself, and thus the significance of the hero's name – Zhivago, derived from the Russian word 'жив': 'living, alive'. Moreover, it is about life conquering death; the novel begins with death, but ends in resurrection. Evgenii Pasternak provides first-hand evidence of the importance his father attached to the theme of life and immortality:

'There shall be no more death' – are the words inscribed by Pasternak in a bold sweeping hand on the cover of the manuscript draft of the novel's first chapters: they comprised one of the early titles proposed for it – a title which made its appearance that same year, 1946. Below them is an epigraph indicating the source from which the words were taken:

And God shall wipe away all the tears from their eyes; and there shall be no more death, neither sorrow, nor crying, neither shall there be any more pain for the former things are passed away. (Book of Revelation (of St John the Divine), XXI:4)[7]

Zhivago paraphrases this when he talks to the dying Anna Gromeko:

You have always been in others and you will remain in others. And what does it matter to you if later on it is called your memory? This will be you – the you that enters the future and becomes a part of it . . . There will be no death, says St. John, and just look at the simplicity of his argument. There will be no more death because the past is over; that's almost like saying there will be no more death because death is already done with, it's old and we are tired of it. What we need is something new, and that new thing is life eternal. (pp. 70–1)

(Человек в других людях и есть душа в человеке. Вот что вы есть, вот чем дышало, питалось, упивалось всю жизнь ваше сознание. Вашей душою, вашим бессмертием, вашей жизнью в других. И что же? В других вы были, в других вы останетесь. И какая вам разница, что потом это будет называться памятью. Это будете вы, вошедшая в состав будущего . . . Смерти не будет, говорит Иоанн Богослов, и вы послушайте простоту его аргументации. Смерти не будет потому, что прежнее прошло. Это почти как: смерти не будет, потому, что это уже видали, это старо и надоело, а теперь требуется новое, а новое есть жизнь вечная.) (pp. 68–9)

The novel, therefore, is not about war or revolution, although Pasternak does not omit details and descriptions of battles, troop movements and casualties, even the most gruesome wounds. The October Revolution, for instance, is presented not as a historical event, objectively narrated, but through Zhivago's consciousness, as he hears of it while working in the hospital. The novel's major theme is not even the development of a poet and the creation of poetry, but the over-coming of death, the affirmation of life itself and ultimate redemption.

Yet the novel is indeed about history, in its deepest and most spiritual sense. History is inside us. In an extended quotation Vedeniapin dwells on the value of Christ and the resurrection for the whole of human history, thoughts which undoubtedly belong to Pasternak himself:

As I was saying, one must be true to Christ. I'll explain. What you don't understand is that it is possible to be an atheist, it is possible not to know if God exists or why He should, and yet to believe that man does not live in a state of nature but in history, and that history as we know it now began with Christ, it was founded by Him on the Gospels. Now what is history? Its beginning is that of the centuries of systematic work devoted to the solution of the enigma of death, so that death itself may eventually be overcome. That is why people write symphonies, and why they discover mathematical infinity and electromagnetic waves. Now, you can't advance in this direction without a certain upsurge of spirit. You can't make such discoveries without spiritual equipment, and for this, everything necessary has been given us in the Gospels. What is it? Firstly, the love of one's neighbour – the supreme form of living energy. Once it fills the heart of man it has to overflow and spend itself. And secondly, the two concepts which are the main part of the make-up of modern man – without them he is inconceivable – the ideas of free personality and of life regarded as a sacrifice. Mind you, all this is still quite new. There was no history in this sense in the classical world. There you had blood and beastliness and cruelty and pock-marked Caligulas untouched by the suspicion that any man who enslaves others is inevitably second-rate. There you had the boastful dead eternity of bronze monuments and marble columns. It was not until after the coming of Christ that time and man could breathe freely. It was not until after Him that men began to live in their posterity and ceased to die in ditches like dogs – instead, they died at home, in history, at the height of the work they devoted to the conquest of death, being themselves dedicated to this aim. (p. 19)

(Вернемся к предмету разговора. Я сказал, – надо быть верным Христу. Сейчас я объясню. Вы не понимаете, что можно быть атеистом, можно не знать, есть ли Бог и для чего Он, и в то же время знать, что человек живет не в природе, а в истории, и что в нынешнем понимании она основана Христом, что Евангелие есть ее основание. А что такое история? Это установление вековых работ по последовательной разгадке смерти и ее будущему преодолению. Для этого открывают математическую бесконечность и электромагнитные волны, для этого пишут симфонии. Двигаться вперед в этом направлении нельзя без некоторого подъема. Для этих открытий требуется духовное оборудование. Данные для него содержится в Евангелии. Вот они. Это, во-первых, любовь к ближнему, этот высший вид живой энергии, переполняющей человека и требующей выхода и расточения, и затем это главные составные части современного человека, без которых он немыслим, а именно, идея свободной личности и идея жизни, как жертвы. Имейте в виду, что это до сих пор чрезвычайно ново. Истории в этом смысле не было у древних. Там было сангвиническое свинство жестоких, оспою изрытых Калигул, не подозревавших, как бездарен всякий поработитель. Там была хвастливая мертвая вечность бронзовых памятников и мраморных колонн. Века и поколенья только после Христа вздохнули свободно. Только после него началась жизнь в потомстве, и человек умирает не на улице под забором, а у себя в истории, в разгаре работ, посвященных преодолению смерти, умирает, сам посвященный этой теме.) (р. 10)

Zhivago dies 'in history', as his verses survive him. Lara dies in an unknown prison camp, and we do not even get to know the date of her death.

Elsewhere Vedeniapin's idea of history is summed up as 'another universe – a universe built by man with the help of time and memory in answer to the challenge of death' (p. 68) ('о второй вселенной, воздвигаемой человечеством в ответ на явление смерти с помощью явлений времени и памяти', р. 66). This teaching is of vital importance to Iurii's development, for Vedeniapin's new Christianity seeks a new idea of art and Iurii's poetry will be its expression.[8] It is indeed under the influence of these ideas that Misha Gordon decides to take up philosophy at university. Iurii remains free exactly because he refuses to become involved in the life around him; thus, politics are not important. Inner truth consists of sincerity, freedom and love, and it is this truth that Lara and Iurii achieve, and why Iurii's relationship with Lara is ultimately more important than those with Tonia and Marina. Their relationship is based on their inner freedom and their unity with the natural world, and it is their relationship that gives the lie to man's pretensions to rule nature and impose his will on it. Such lines are contained within one of the most important passages in the novel:

Oh, what a love it was, how free, how new, like nothing else on earth! They really thought what other people sing in songs.

It was not out of necessity that they loved each other, 'enslaved by passion', as lovers are described. They loved each other because everything around them willed it, the trees and the clouds and the sky over their heads and the earth under their feet. Perhaps their surrounding world, the strangers they met in the street, the landscapes drawn up for them to see on their walks, the rooms in which they lived or met, were even more pleased with their love than they were themselves.

Well, of course, it had been just this that had united them and had made them so akin! Never, never, not even in their moments of richest and wildest happiness, had they lost the sense of what is highest and most ravishing — joy in the whole universe, its form, its beauty, the feeling of their own belonging to it, being part of it.

This compatibility of the whole was the breath of life to them. And consequently they were unattracted to the modern fashion of coddling man, exalting him above the rest of nature and worshipping him. A sociology built on this false premise and served up as politics, struck them as pathetically home-made and amateurish beyond their comprehension. (p. 447)

(О какая это была любовь, вольная, небывалая, ни на что не похожая! Думали, как другие напевают.

Они любили друг друга не из неизбежности, не «опаленные страстью», как это ложно изображают. Они любили друг друга потому, что так хотели все кругом: земля под ними, небо над их головами, облака и деревья. Их любовь нравилась окружающим еще, может быть, больше, чем им самим. Незнакомым на улице, выстраивающимся на прогулке далям, комнатам, в которых они селились и встречались.

Ах вот что, это вот ведь и было главным, что их роднило и объединяло! Никогда, никогда, даже в минуты самого дарственного, беспамятного счастья не покидало их самое высокое и захватывающее: наслаждение общей лепкою мира, чувство отнесенности их самих ко всей картине, ощущение принадлежности к красоте всего зрелища, ко всей вселенной.

Они дышали только этой совместимостью. И потому превознесение человека над остальной природой, модное няньченье с ним и человекопоклонство их не привлекали. Начала ложной общественности, превращенной в политику, казались им жалкой домодельщиной и оставались непонятны.) (p. 513)

Towards the end of the novel, Gordon and Dudorov discuss history, and speak for Pasternak on the falseness of Stalinism and the liberating experience of the war:

I think that collectivization was both a mistake and a failure, and because that couldn't be admitted, every means of intimidation had to be used to make people forget how to think and judge for themselves, to force them to see what wasn't there, and to maintain the contrary of what their eyes told them. Hence the unexampled harshness of the Yezhov terror, and the promulgation of a constitution which was never intended to be applied, and the holding of elections not based on the principle of a free vote.

And when the war broke out, its real horrors, its real dangers, its menace of real death, were a blessing compared with the inhuman power of the lie, a relief because it broke the spell of the dead letter. (p. 453)

(Я думаю, коллективизация была ложной, неудавшейся мерою, и в ошибке нельзя было признаться. Чтобы скрыть неудачу, надо было всеми средствами устрашения отучить людей судить и думать и принудить их видеть несуществующее и доказывать обратное очевидности. Отсюда беспримерная жестокость ежовщины, обнародование не рассчитанной на применение конституции, введение выборов, не основанных на выборном начале.

И когда возгорелась война, ее реальные ужасы, реальная опасность и угроза реальной смерти были благом по сравнению с бесчеловечным владычеством выдумки, и несли облегчение, потому что ограничивали колдовскую силу мертвой буквы.) (р. 519)

After they have heard Tania's terrible story, Gordon sums up the patterns and forms of human history:

This has happened several times in the course of history. A thing which has been conceived in a lofty, ideal manner becomes coarse and material. Thus Rome came out of Greece and the Russian Revolution came out of the Russian enlightenment. Take that line of Blok's: 'We, the children of Russia's terrible years': you can see the difference of period at once. In his time, when he said it, he meant it figuratively, metaphorically. The children were not children, but the sons, the heirs of the intelligentsia, and the terrors were not terrible but apocalyptic; that's quite different. Now the figurative has become literal, children are children and the terrors are terrible. There you have the difference. (p. 463)

(Так было уже несколько раз в истории. Задуманное идеально, возвышенно, грубело, овеществлялось. Так Греция стала Римом, так русское просвещение стало русской революцией. Возьми ты это Блоковское «Мы, дети страшных лет России», и сразу увидишь различие эпох. Когда Блок говорил это, это надо было понимать в переносном смысле, фигурально. И дети были не дети, а детища, интеллигенция, и страхи были не страшны, а провиденциальны, апокалиптичны, а это разные вещи. А теперь все переносное стало буквальным, и дети – дети, и страхи страшны, вот в чем разница.) (р. 530)

The novel encompasses half a century of Russia's turbulent recent history, but demonstrates through the love of Iurii and Lara, and the poems that Iurii writes, that the important aspect of human life is not subservience to politics, ideology or external realia, but inner freedom and an active inner life founded on love and deep reciprocity. Human history, indeed, is based on the resurrection or immortality of the soul, and in the transformation of experience into art and feeling. The individual lives on after his physical death in the minds, hearts and souls of those who survive him or her, and in that individual's love and creativity.

Characterization

Although there are dozens of minor or incidental characters, the main players in the narrative are Iurii Zhivago, Lara, Antipov-Strel'nikov, Komarovskii and Evgraf. Although an unwilling participant, Iurii cannot remain a passive observer of historical events: he tends the wounded at the front in the war, witnesses revolutionary events and is forced to work with partisans in the Civil War. Nevertheless he remains true to himself, and even when he shoots a man, he then does his best to tend him and allow him to escape. Iurii remains inwardly free, and as such is a threat to the new regime, a fact perfectly understood by Komarovskii in Iuriatin:

> There exists a certain communist style, Yury Andreyevich. Few people measure up to it. But no-one flouts that way of life and thought as openly as you do. Why you have to flirt with danger, I can't imagine. You are a mockery of that whole world, an insult to it. (pp. 377–8)

> (Есть некоторый коммунистический стиль. Мало кто подходит под эту мерку. Но никто так явно не нарушает этой манеры жить и думать, как вы, Юрий Андреевич. Не понимаю, зачем гусей дразнить. Вы – насмешка над этим миром, его оскорбление.) (p. 431)

Iurii also becomes distanced from his friends Gordon and Dudorov, who try to accept and rationalize the Stalinist regime. Iurii does not explicitly condemn conformism, but rejects spiritual enslavement (and undoubtedly speaks for Pasternak himself):

> Dudorov's pious platitudes were in the spirit of the age. But it was precisely their correctness, their transparent sanctimoniousness, that exasperated Yury. Men who are not free, he thought, always idealize their bondage. So it was in the Middle Ages, and the Jesuits always played on this. Yury could not bear the political mysticism of the Soviet intelligentsia, though it was the very thing they regarded as the highest of their achievements and described in the language of the day as 'the spiritual top-flight of the age'. (p. 431)

(Добродетельные речи Иннокентия были в духе времени. Но
именно закономерность, прозрачность их ханжества взрывала
Юрия Андреевича. Несвободный человек всегда идеализирует
свою неволю. Так было в средние века, на этом всегда играли
иезуиты. Юрий Андреевич не выносил политического мистицизма
советской интеллигенции, того, что было ее высшим достижением
или как тогда бы сказали, – духовным потолком эпохи.) (pp. 493–4)

Zhivago as poet is the witness and interpreter of human life, and as a
free man can pass judgment on his time. He is thus rather akin to the
figure of Hamlet as understood by Pasternak:

From the moment the ghost appears Hamlet turns his back on himself in
order to 'do the will of him who sent me'. 'Hamlet' is not a drama about
lack of character, but a drama of duty and self-denial. When it is discovered
that reality and its outward appearance are not the same, and that they are
separated by a gulf, it is not vital that the reminder of the falseness of the
world comes in a supernatural form and that the ghost demands of Hamlet
vengeance. What is much more important is that by the will of chance
Hamlet is chosen as a judge of his time and a servant of something more
remote. 'Hamlet' is a drama of sublime destiny, of commanded exploits, of
an entrusted predestination.

(С момента появления призрака Гамлет отказывается от себя,
чтобы «творить волю пославшего его». «Гамлет» не драма
бесхарактерности, но драма долга и самоотречения. Когда
обнаруживается, что видимость и действительность не сходятся и
их разделяет пропасть, не существенно, что напоминание о
лживости мира приходит в сверхъестественной форме и что
призрак требует от Гамлета мщения. Гораздо важнее, что волею
случая Гамлет избирается в судьи своего времени и в слуги более
отдаленного. «Гамлет» – драма высокого жребия, заповеданного
подвига, вверенного предназначения.)[9]

It is thus no accident that the first of Zhivago's poems is 'Hamlet',
where the Prince of Denmark is standing on the stage, staring out at the
audience as if looking into the future, reluctant to play his part but
seeing that he must. Thus Zhivago also looks out onto his country's
history, the events of which have irrevocably shaped his own life, not
wishing to participate but realizing that he has no choice. Hamlet is sent
by his father to serve a higher cause and thus sacrifice himself: the same
is true of Jesus Christ's life on earth. Zhivago, too, accepts life as a
sacrifice: he loses his family, his friends and his home, and holds on
only to his poetic and spiritual integrity.

Because the novel consciously rejects the realistic tradition, it is no
surprise that there is little psychological motivation of the characters,

nor are there any really rounded or developed characters. There is furthermore very little actual physical description of the characters; rather, they serve as mouthpieces for the author. The case of Zhivago has already been discussed; we should add that Zhivago is a keen observer. His medical diagnoses are good, he can foresee Russia's future ills, and he can also see the causes of Russia's sickness.

The character who embodies Pasternak's own philosophy is Zhivago's uncle, Vedeniapin. Once again the name is significant, as it comes from the Russian verb ведать, meaning 'to know', but in a spiritual, intuitive sense. A former priest who defrocked himself, Vedeniapin later accepts the ideas of the Bolsheviks and returns from Switzerland in order to be part of the new world. In other words, he represents the seduction of that part of the intelligentsia, fired by humanistic ideals, who took on board the ideas of the Bolsheviks as a way of realizing the messianic transformation of Russia. We see Vedeniapin's ideas later taken up by Sima Tuntseva in Iuriatin.

Viktor Ippolitovich Komarovskii is the novel's only real 'black' character. Lara's seducer and tormentor, the cause of Zhivago *père*'s ruin and suicide, he is thoroughly demonized: he even has a friend called Satanidi. Opportunistic and calculating, he later finds accommodation with the Bolsheviks but only so that he himself can escape from Russia. Nevertheless, as we have seen, he is fascinated by Lara, is unconsciously drawn to her and takes considerable risks to save her. Before his arrival in Varykino to take Lara away, Iurii is writing a poem about St. George killing the dragon (the name 'Iurii' is a variant of 'George'). But it is Komarovskii who saves her from the wolves, both actual and metaphorical (old Tiverzin and Antipov), gathering outside.

Pasha Antipov, husband of Lara, is a radical student who becomes transformed into Strel'nikov, the pitiless commissar who wreaks terror and bloody retribution during the Civil War (he is also referred to as 'Rasstrel'nikov', derived from the verb расстрелять, to execute by firing squad). Antipov-Strel'nikov and Zhivago are linked not only through their love of the same woman, but also through their characterization. Antipov-Strel'nikov is also the direct contrast to Zhivago: his name suggests death, while Zhivago's means life. Moreover, Antipov studies Greek and Latin at university, whereas Zhivago studies medicine. In Iuriatin Antipov moves away from the humanities and towards mathematics, physics and the exact sciences, whereas Zhivago embraces lyricism and the soul in his poetry. Zhivago is sent to the front, and is forced to work with the partisans; Antipov impulsively volunteers for the front in the First World War when he feels that Lara does not love him, and then degenerates into Strel'nikov, the avenging angel of death.

Strel'nikov and Zhivago meet twice in the novel. The first time, Zhivago is hugely impressed by someone who is 'a manifestation of the will'.[10] When he has the power to have the doctor shot, Strel'nikov spares him; after the second time, in Varykino and after a long conversation with the doctor on history, the Revolution and, in particular, Lara, Strel'nikov commits suicide. Although he knows that he will never see her, he also knows that she loves him deeply. Just as on the earlier occasion when he had gone off to war, Antipov-Strel'nikov feels unworthy of her.

The dominant female character in the novel is undoubtedly Lara Guishar, wife of Antipov and lover of Zhivago. Whereas Iurii's wife Tonia is all domesticity and nest building, Lara is an image of vitality and disruption. For her lovers – Komarovskii, Antipov and Zhivago – she represents innocence and purity, life and naturalness, individuality and the capacity to transformation. All her lovers change under her spell. Komarovskii reflects on her:

> Another reason for his agitation was that he had once again experienced the irresistible attraction of this wild, desperate girl. He had always known that she was different from everyone else. There had always been something unique about her. But how deeply, painfully, irreparably had he wounded her and upset her life, and how restless and violent she was in her determination to re-shape her destiny and start afresh! (p. 90)

> (Кроме того, он снова испытал, до чего неотразима эта отчаянная, сумасшедшая девушка. Сразу было видно, что она не как все. В ней всегда было что-то необыкновенное. Однако, как чувствительно и непоправимо, повидимому, исковеркал он ее жизнь! Как она мечется, как все время восстает и бунтует, в стремлении переделать судьбу по своему и начать существовать сызнова.) (p. 92)

Rebellious and turbulent by nature, she seems destined to suffer: as she says to herself early in the novel, after being bitten by Komarovskii's dog, 'and why is it, . . . that my fate is to see everything and take it all so much to heart?' (p. 32) ('за что же мне такая участь, . . . что я все вижу и так обо всем болею?', p. 24). It should be noted, however, that Lara does not play the conventional guilty and suffering part of the seduced young girl; rather, at least to a degree, she enjoys and is excited by the affair with Komarovskii.

Lara inspires Zhivago to poetic creativity, and in his poems at the end we see the transformation of nature and human life into an epiphany. She inspires Strel'nikov to decisive action. She is herself an image of Russia, an idea best expressed in the conversation with Zhivago by her husband, as he recalls her before they were married:

Lara's effect on her lovers.

She was still a child, but already then, the alertness, the watchfulness, the disquiet of those days – it was all there, you could read it all in her face, in her eyes. Everything that made that time what it was – the tears and the insults and the hopes, the whole accumulation of revenge and pride, all of it was already in her expression and in her carriage, in that mixture in her of girlish shyness and grace and daring. You could indict the century in her name, out of her mouth. It was no trifling matter, you must agree. It was a sign, a destiny. Something nature had endowed her with, something to which she had a birthright. (p. 412)

('Она была девочкой, ребенком, а настороженную мысль, тревогу века уже можно было прочесть на ее лице, в ее глазах. Все темы времени, все его слезы и обиды, все его побуждения, вся его накопленная месть и гордость были написаны не ее лице и в ее осанке, в смеси ее девической стыдливости и ее смелой стройности. Обвинение веку модно было вынести от ее имени, ее устами. Согласитесь, ведь это не безделица. Это некоторое предназначение, отмеченность. Этим надо было обладать от природы, надо было иметь на это право.') (p. 472)

She is in love with both the violent and cruel aspect of Russia as personified by her husband, and the reflective, creative side that Zhivago represents. In an important passage Zhivago, returning to Iuriatin from the partisan camp, explicitly equates her with the joy of life itself:

A spring evening . . . the air is punctuated with scattered sounds. The voices of children playing in the streets come from varying distances as if to show that the whole expanse is alive. The expanse is Russia, his incomparable mother; famed far and wide, martyred, stubborn, extravagant, crazy, irresponsible, adored, Russia with her eternally splendid, disastrous and unpredictable gestures. Oh, how sweet it was to be alive! How good to be alive and to love life! And how he longed to thank life, thank existence itself, directly, face to face, to thank life in person.

This was exactly what Lara was. You could not communicate with life, but she was its representative, its expression, the gift of speech and hearing granted to inarticulate being. (pp. 351–2)

(Вот весенний вечер на дворе. Воздух весь размечен звуками. Голоса играющих детей разбросаны в местах разной дальности, как бы в знак того, что пространство все насквозь живое. И эта даль – Россия, его несравненная, за морями нашумевшая, знаменитая родительница, мученица, упрямица, сумасбродка, шалая, боготворимая, с вечно величественными и гибельными выходками, которых никогда нельзя предвидеть! О как сладко существовать! Как сладко жить на свете и любить жизнь! О, как всегда тянет сказать спасибо самой жизни, самому существованию, сказать это им самим в лицо!

Вот это-то и есть Лара. С ними нельзя разговаривать, а она их представительница, их выражение, дар слуха и слова, дарованный безгласным началам существования.) (pp. 401–2)

The love she and Zhivago attain is something marvellous, based not only on physical passion but on spirituality and the awareness of being an integral part of nature, of being. Together they rise above the here and now, and it is in Lara's presence that Zhivago expresses his (and Pasternak's) rejection of materialistic revolution (words which are strongly reminiscent of Vedeniapin's dismissal of the 'pock-marked Caligulas' and all those who enslave others as 'second-rate' (бездарен):

> But it turns out that those who inspired the revolution aren't at home in anything except change and turmoil: that's their native element; they aren't happy with anything that's less than on a world scale. For them, transitional periods, worlds in the making, are an end in themselves. They aren't trained for anything else, they don't know about anything except that. And do you know why there is this incessant whirl of never-ending preparations? It's because they haven't any real capacities, they are ungifted. Man is born to live, not to prepare for life. Life itself — the gift of life — is such a breathtakingly serious thing! (p. 269)

> (А выяснилось, что для вдохновителей революции суматоха перемен и перестановок единственная родная стихия, что их хлебом не корми, а подай им что-нибудь в масштабе земного шара. Построения миров, переходные периоды, это их самоцель. Ничему другому они не учились, ничего не умеют. А вы знаете, откуда суета этих вечных приготовлений? От отсутствия определенных готовых способностей, от неодаренности. Человек рождается жить, а не готовиться к жизни. И сама жизнь, явление жизни, дар жизни так захватывающе нешуточны!) (p. 307)

This is the credo of their love, their affirmation of the desire for life and freedom.[11]

Perhaps the most enigmatic character is Evgraf, Iurii's half-brother who protects him and collects his poetry to publish it as a book after his death. Evgraf is obviously connected with the secret police, and appears mysteriously and unexpectedly in various parts of the narrative to protect Iurii and guarantee the survival of his work. Similarly in the epilogue, Evgraf undertakes to look after Iurii's daughter Tania. His relationship with Iurii is an allegory of the relationship of the writer and secular authority, as Iurii himself notes:

> Perhaps in every life there has to be, besides the other characters involved in it, a secret, unknown force, a figure who is almost symbolical and who

comes unsummoned to the rescue, and perhaps in mine Yevgraf, my brother, plays the part of this hidden spring of life. (p. 261)

(Может быть, состав каждой биографии наряду со встречающимися в ней действующими лицами требует еще и участия тайной неведомой силы, лица почти символического, являющегося на помощь без зова, и роль этой благодетельной и скрытой пружины играет в моей жизни мой брат Евграф?) (p. 297)

There are several other characters who serve as 'shadows' (in Angela Livingstone's words) of these major personages. Samdeviatov, with his cool head and his ability to follow the times, is reminiscent of Komarovskii, but with his intellectual ability to rationalize politics he is also akin to Vedeniapin. Vedeniapin's ideas are also expressed by Sima Tuntseva in Iuriatin, who also sees Christ as offering man freedom. Liverii Mikulitsyn is but a slighter version of Strel'nikov as revolutionary – significantly, both he and Strel'nikov find the doctor's company interesting and enjoy talking to him. Both are surpassed in murderous capacity by Palykh. (Palykh's disfigured face recalls the face of Bacchus in Anna Gromeko's dream, and the scar-faced thief Lara sees just before leaving for Iuriatin.) The philosophical underpinning of all their actions can be found in the words of Pogorevshikh, whom Zhivago meets on the train from Meliuzeev to Moscow, and who speaks of wholesale destruction, of razing everything to the ground before the new society can be built (his name suggests destruction by fire). It remains to be said, however, that Tonia and Marina are only sketchily drawn; they are images of domesticity and serve only to bear Iurii's children. Iurii, indeed, seems to face the prospect of separation from both of them almost with indifference. Gordon and Dudorov remain similarly thinly drawn, and their statements and utterances towards the end of the novel remain indistinguishable from each other. They are there simply to perpetuate Iurii's memory.

Style and Imagery

In terms of style, the novel is often awkward in its structure and the presentation of characters or events. For instance in the early part, before any real action has occurred, there are several important philosophical passages, especially concerning Vedeniapin, but then these recede from view (as does he, when he goes abroad). Then when we reach 1905, there is much action and an overabundance of characters, but no philosophy. Curiously, Part 10 of the novel does not feature Zhivago at all, and apart from introducing the widow Galuzina this section seems to be irrelevant to the rest of the novel. There are some particularly contrived passages; see for instance, the description of Zhivago returning to Iuriatin after escaping from Liverii's camp, which is full of forced pathos in order to increase the melodramatic impact of his appearance in the town.

On the other hand, Pasternak is at pains to present characters and events from differing viewpoints and not just Zhivago's or Lara's. At various points in the narrative he shows us Lara as seen by Komarovskii, and Strel'nikov's love for his wife and child and his desire to be with them as he wages war aboard his armoured train, and we also go inside the minds of Tonia and even Sasha (Shurochka), their child when they arrive at Torfianaia. Angela Livingstone has also drawn attention to the novel's great linguistic flexibility and diversity, embracing different speech patterns, syntax and lexis of various strata of society, and even the alterations (transformation) of individual words and names as pronounced by different people.[12]

The novel contains much nature imagery, as human life and history are consistently transformed into images of the natural world and natural time. Many times in the novel characters, especially Zhivago, wonder at the beauty and magnificence of the natural world, be it the scent of lime-trees by the station in Meliuzeev or the beauty of a river the train passes over on the way to Varykino. The rowanberry occupies a particular place in the narrative, as it appears at various times; the rowanberry tree is personified when Zhivago is in the partisan camp, and the same chapter ends with Zhivago embracing the same tree and thinking of Lara as he makes his escape. When Strel'nikov-Antipov shoots himself, the spots of blood are likened to rowanberries scattered across the snow. The wolves at Varykino symbolize the dangers of the outside world, and become transformed into the dragon which Iurii (St. George) must confront.

Water imagery, in the form of waterfalls, rain, snow or storms, is prominent. Clouds and wind bring speed and change, and water, air, earth and sky are dominant motifs as they represent the real and basic foundation of life. Spring in particular is a symbol of life overcoming the death of winter, and thus of the resurrection. The novel thus abounds in metaphors and images bringing the human world close to the world of nature. Even in the first chapter, the young Iurii, weeping at the death of his mother, is led away from the grave and likened to a young wolf cub about to howl. That night, Iurii and his uncle spend the night in a monastery and a storm breaks, wakening Iurii and impressing him with its supernatural might:

Outside there was no trace of the road, the graveyard or the kitchen garden, nothing but the blizzard, the air smoking with snow. It was almost as if the snowstorm had caught sight of Yura and, conscious of its power to terrify, roared, howled and did everything possible to attract his attention, revelling in the effect it had on him. Turning over and over in the sky, length after length of whiteness unwound over the earth and shrouded it. The blizzard was alone on the earth and knew no rival. (p. 14)

(За окном не было ни дороги, ни кладбища, ни огорода. На дворе бушевала вьюга, воздух дымился снегом. Можно было подумать, будто буря заметила Юру и, сознавая, как она страшна, наслаждается производимым на него впечатлением. Она свистела и завывала и всеми способами старалась привлечь Юрино внимание. С неба оборот за оборотом бесконечными мотками падала на землю белая ткань, обвивая ее погребальными пеленами. Вьюга была одна на свете, ничто с ней не соперничала.) (p. 4)

Such personification is not limited to Iurii's consciousness. Another such terrific thunderstorm accompanies Lara's momentous decision to leave her mother's house and so escape the clutches of Komarovskii. Storms in particular occur throughout the novel at various times: after Lara leaves Meliuzeev in 1917, the storm is embodied as a force of revolution, destructive, elemental, carrying all before it. A storm also accompanies Zhivago's departure from Meliuzeev, and also accompanies his prophetic speech in Moscow afterwards on the future of Russia:

I also think that Russia is destined to become the first socialist country since the beginning of the world. When this happens it will stun us for a long time, and when we come to ourselves we shall still be only half-conscious and with half our memory gone. We'll have forgotten what came first and what followed and we won't look for the causes of the inexplicable. The new order of things will be all round us and as familiar to us as the woods on the skyline or the clouds over our heads. There will be nothing else left. (p. 167)

(Я тоже думаю, что России суждено стать первым за существование мира царством социализма. Когда это случится, оно надолго оглушит нас, и очнувшись, мы уже больше не вернем утраченной памяти. Мы забудем часть прошлого и не будем искать небывалому объяснения. Наставший порядок обступит нас с привычностью леса на горизонте или облаков над головой. Он окружит нас отовсюду. Не будет ничего другого.) (p. 185)

Similarly the October Revolution is resolved in a snowstorm, as Iurii walks the streets of Moscow and reads about the establishment of Soviet power in a newspaper.

Other examples of anthropomorphism extend to the young Nika Dudorov, who likens a tree in the yard of a house to a giant, protecting the yard from the 'scorching' sky. As Zhivago travels to Varykino he sees a house on a hill, alone and covered in snow, and likens it to a baby nestling under a blanket. Most tellingly, Lara consciously likens Iurii to the natural world as she takes her final leave of him: 'Good-bye, my big one, my dear one, my own, my pride. Good-bye, my quick, deep river, how I loved your day-long splashing, how I loved bathing in your cold, deep waves' (p. 448) ('Прощай, большой и родной мой, прощай моя гордость, прощай моя быстрая глубокая реченька, как я любила целодневный плеск твой, как я любила бросаться в твои холодные волны', p. 514). Note here, too, the equation of water with life and vitality.

As a counterpoint to nature, the railway with its apocalyptic associations is a recurring motif. The railway kills Zhivago's father, and Strel'nikov's armoured train brings destruction to the Siberian countryside. Antipov makes his momentous decision in Iuriatin to volunteer for the front when he sees a military train pass by; on his departure from Meliuzeev, Zhivago shares a compartment with the deaf Pogorevshikh, whose fanatical extremism reminds him of the equally fanatical Petr Verkhovenskii from Dostoevskii's *The Possessed* — this at a time of wholesale destruction and anarchy in Russia.

But the railway is also a symbol of dynamic movement as it brings progress and change. The journey from Moscow to Varykino begins in an April snowfall, but ends in the heat of early summer a month later, and reveals to Iurii the changes that have taken place across Russia. Moreover, when Iurii and Tonia arrive at Torfianaia, their spirits are raised and they rejoice in their changed surroundings. Komarovskii's train will take Lara away from Iurii forever. It is no accident that travel and covering distances, and not just by train, are common motifs. Iurii is mobilized by Liverii's partisans as he travels by horse from Iuriatin to Varykino, and he travels back to Moscow on foot, both journeys which change his life. In Moscow Iurii stops at a crossroads, and in the night looks out at streets that lead to the Urals and Siberia, and which point to his destiny. The multiplicity of roads, travel and journeys makes up the fabric of everyday life, and thus helps account for the coincidences and chance meetings in the novel (referred to as 'crossed fate' (судьбы скрещенья) in the poem 'Winter Night'). Finally, and conclusively, Iurii dies of a heart attack while travelling on a tram.

The Poems

Three times in the course of the novel we see Zhivago writing: twice (the first time in Varykino, and then in Moscow just before his death) he writes prose, and only when he is in Varykino the second time does he write poetry. There are twenty-five poems that comprise the novel's final chapter, and these not only express Zhivago's creative impulse but also reflect the depth of feeling between Lara and Iurii and provide an explicit Christian framework for the poet's life.

The poems can be divided into three categories: religious, seasonal and those directly concerning Iurii's life. 'Hamlet' ('Гамлет'), as has already been noted, sets the context for Zhivago's fundamental drama: unwilling to play his part, he must nevertheless accept the cup that is passed to him. Those dealing with the seasons, in particular, trace the passage of human life in tune with the seasons.[13] In 'March' ('Март'), the second poem, the seasons are personified through various symbols and metaphors, with winter seen as weak and dying and spring as healthy and life-affirming. The rural imagery and subject-matter tell of nature coming back to life after the long death of winter. 'Spring Floods' ('Весенняя распутица') continues the personification of nature in a Siberian setting, and 'White Night' ('Белая ночь') locates the place as St Petersburg in mid-Spring. This is soon followed by 'Summer in Town' ('Лето в городе'), with its concentration on heat, a storm and the trees; in 'Wind' ('Ветер') the trees that are rocked by the wind are likened to ships in a bay, and in 'Intoxication' ('Хмель') the poet seeks shelter from the bad weather amid hops and ivy. 'August' ('Август') contains motifs of death and farewell; Iurii dies at the end of August. The seasons continue: 'Indian Summer' ('Бабье лето') takes us into late summer. 'Winter Night' ('Зимняя ночь') is an important poem that contains no personification of nature, but does repeat the image of the candle burning on the table: 'The candle on the table burned/The candle burned' (p. 488) ('свеча горела на столе/ Свеча горела') (pp. 550–1), that is, the candle in Pasha's window where Lara is at that moment telling her future husband that she is in some danger, and which Iurii sees on his way to the Sventitskiis' New Year party. We actually see Iurii writing this poem, so that its inception, creation and physical manifestation are evident throughout the course of the novel.

These poems follow the passage of the seasons, and can be juxtaposed with poems that are closely identified with the Lara/Iurii plot. 'Explanation' ('Объяснение') juxtaposes a Moscow street scene with the poet's declaration of love for his beloved. Poems about the seasons and the natural world alternate with 'The Wedding Party'

('Свадьба'), 'Parting' ('Разлука') and 'Meeting' ('Свидание'), all of which can describe the metaphorical course of Iurii's relationship with Lara. Similarly, 'Autumn' ('Осень'), although it seems to belong to those relating to the seasons, is really about the intensity and pleasure of sensuous love. A special place should be reserved for 'A Fairy Tale' ('Сказка'), for it tells of the battle of a knight with a dragon and therefore recreates the legend of St. George that so occupies Iurii before Komarovskii takes Lara away from him forever.[14]

Finally, there are the religious poems. 'In Holy Week' ('На Страстной') concerns an Easter Church service, but with an emphasis on how the natural world looks in March (significantly, it follows the poem of that name). It ends, however, with lines that could serve as the epigraph of the whole novel: 'Death can be vanquished/Through the travail of the Resurrection' (p. 470) ('Смерть можно будет побороть/Усильем Воскресенья', p. 535). The last half-dozen or so poems have an alternating religious and natural theme. 'Christmas Star' ('Рождественская звезда') concerns the birth of Christ; 'Daybreak' ('Рассвет') tells of the poet's joy in hearing of an old friend, and he compares his sudden emotion to the bursting into life of the city in the early morning. This poem is followed by 'The Miracle' ('Чудо'), about Christ walking from Bethany to Jerusalem; this in its turn is followed by 'The Earth' ('Земля'), with spring personified in Moscow and its theme of human suffering and sorrow. The last four poems are all on the Biblical theme and so represent the novel's thematic culmination. 'Evil days' ('Дурные дни') concerns the last days of Christ, offers a résumé of his life and ends with a motif of resurrection; 'Mary Magdalene I' ('Магдалина I') contains the confession of Mary the prostitute, full of self-loathing and seeking salvation through Christ, whereas 'Mary Magdalene II' ('Магдалина II') expresses grief at the death of Christ but also foretells the Resurrection. 'Gethsemane' ('Гефсиманский сад'), the last poem, tells of the crucifixion where Christ implores God to end His suffering, but in words that recall 'Hamlet': 'Sweating blood, he prayed to his Father/That this cup of death should pass him by' (p. 506) ('Чтоб эта чаша смерти миновала/В поту кровавом Он молил Отца', p. 565). Then there is a change of narrative point of view, as we hear the words of Christ himself on the cross, on his death, resurrection and the beginning of human history:

> And on the third day I shall rise again,
> Like rafts down a river, like a convoy of barges,
> The centuries will float to me out of the darkness.
> And I shall judge them. (p. 507)

(Я в гроб сойду и в третий день восстану
И, как сплавляют по реке плоты,
Ко мне на суд, как баржи каравана,
Столетья поплывут из темноты) (p. 566)

Thus does Zhivago complete his journey in life, beginning as a Hamlet figure but resembling Christ in his transformation.[15] The novel ends with an affirmation of the final triumph of Christ, of the importance of the resurrection for human history and of the human need for memory, creativity and immortality.

Conclusion

Doctor Zhivago can thus be seen as one of the key texts of Russian literature in this century. Once again we see the figure of the writer at the centre of the narrative, and the role of literature and the creative impulse at a time of upheaval and chaos is gloriously affirmed. It also offers a philosophical treatise on man's true role and place in nature and in time, at a time when man's will and reason were trumpeted as his greatest achievement. It gives us a powerful picture of the destructiveness of that rationalizing force. But it also provides a breathtakingly bold portrayal of a deep, mutual love that goes against the grain of twentieth-century realism, a love which challenged the prevailing ideology and struck at the heart of modern rationalism.

Notes

1. 'Letter of Members of the Editorial Board of the Journal "Novyi mir" to B. Pasternak' ('Письмо членов редколлегии журнала «Новый мир» Б. Пастернаку'), *Novyi mir*, no. 11, 1958, p. i.
2. Evgenii Pasternak, the poet's son, notes that Pasternak began writing the novel in the winter of 1945–6. See Evgeny Pasternak, *Boris Pasternak: The Tragic Years, 1930–1960*, trans. Michael Duncan, London, 1990, p. 160.
3. *Novyi mir*, no. 11, 1958, p. iii.
4. Angela Livingstone, *Pasternak: Doctor Zhivago*, Cambridge, 1989, p. 11.
5. Boris Pasternak, *Doctor Zhivago*, trans. Max Hayward and Manya Harari, London, 1988, p. 416; *Доктор Живаго*, Milan, 1957,

p. 477. All further references are taken from these editions, with relevant page numbers incorporated into the text.

6. Pasternak himself wrote, in English, to Stephen Spender:

For this characterization of reality of the being, as a substratum, as a common background, the nineteenth century applied the incontestable doctrine of causality, the belief that the objectivity was determined and ruled by an iron chain of causes and effects, that all appearances of the moral and material world were subordinate to the law of sequels and retributions . . .

I also from my earliest years have been struck by the observation that existence was more original, extraordinary and inexplicable than any of its separate astonishing incidents and facts . . .

. . . There is an effort in the novel to represent the whole sequence of facts and beings and happenings like some moving entireness, like a developing, passing by, rolling and rushing inspiration, as if reality itself had freedom and choice and was composing itself out of numberless variants and versions.

Hence the not sufficient tracing of characters I was reproached with . . . hence the frank arbitrariness of the 'coincidences' (through this means I wanted to show the liberty of being, its verisimilitude touching, adjoining improbability.

This letter is quoted in Richard Freeborn, *The Russian Revolutionary Novel: Turgenev to Pasternak*, Cambridge, 1982, p. 212. Helen Muchnic comments that 'coincidence, which plays a major role, far from being a structural flaw, is a symbol of Pasternak's awe before the play of Fate' (Helen Muchnic, *From Gorky to Pasternak: Six Modern Russian Writers*, London, 1963, p. 348).

7. Evgeny Pasternak, *Boris Pasternak: The Tragic Years*, p. 163.

8. Richard Freeborn comments: 'Poetry as a defiance of death is the revolutionising or transforming dynamite concealed in Zhivago's life as it is concealed in the "book of impressions of life" that is to comprise his novel' (Freeborn, *The Russian Revolutionary Novel*, p. 222).

9. 'Notes on Translating Shakespeare' ('Замечания к переводам из Шекспира'), in Boris Pasternak, *Об искусстве: «Охранная грамота» и заметки о художественном творчестве* (*On Art: "Safe Conduct" and Notes on Artistic Creativity*), Moscow, 1990, p. 179.

10. Angela Livingstone remarks on the two: 'This man [Strel'nikov] is so profoundly his [Zhivago's] opposite that a psychic bond exists between them; each is the other's "other", representing that way of being which the other person's way excludes and therefore darkly calls to mind and expects to meet. Here are decision and indecision,

the outlined and the hazy, self-projection and self-effacement, violent activity and gentle creativity' (Livingstone, *Pasternak: Doctor Zhivago*, p. 77).

11. Henry Gifford remarks: 'It can be objected that Lara too exists more fully for Yury than for the reader, at any rate once her girlhood is past. Sometimes the exchanges between Yury and her sound like the colloquy of a mind with itself' (Henry Gifford, *Pasternak: A Critical Study*, Cambridge, 1977, p. 197).

12. 'Everywhere, beside the lives of the main characters, are people of many different classes, occupations, levels of education, geographical origins, involved in their own affairs and talking about them, all briefly individualised through idiosyncrasies of speech . . . A fundamental creativity, life's "uninterrupted self-renewal" that Yurii talks of to Liverii, is constantly at work in ordinary, everyday speech' (Livingstone, *Pasternak: Doctor Zhivago*, p. 97).

13. Dimitrii Obolenskii observes: 'The treatment of nature in these poems is a counterpart of Pasternak's conception of the town as a symbol of the life and destiny of modern man' (Dimitrii Obolenskii, 'The Poems of *Doctor Zhivago*', in Victor Ehrlich (ed.), *Pasternak: A Collection of Critical Essays*, Englewood Cliffs, NJ, 1978, p. 152).

14. Henry Gifford makes the point that the poems should not be seen as a direct reflection of the events of the novel: the origins of most poems 'lie not so much in particular passages of the novel, but in the length and breadth of the imaginative experience that went into its making. It would seem that no significant part of the novel has failed to achieve resurrection in the poems' (Gifford, *Pasternak: A Critical Study*, p. 203).

15. Dimitrii Obolenskii comments:

It seems likely that Pasternak's aim in *Doctor Zhivago* was not so much to portray his hero as a Christ-like figure, as to suggest that his life and death acquire their true significance when they are illuminated by the reality of Christ's sacrificial death and His Resurrection. Viewed in this light, the life and death of Yury Zhivago appear as a sacrifice, and his loss of everything he holds most dear, save only, at the end, his poetic vision and his spiritual integrity, is a freely accepted surrender of self. And this surrender is shown to be the pledge of his immortality. (Obolenskii, 'The Poems of *Doctor Zhivago*', p. 164.)

7

Alexander Solzhenitsyn (b. 1918), *Cancer Ward* (*Раковый корпус*)

Introduction and Background

Before discussion of *Cancer Ward* (published in 1968), time should be spent discussing literary politics in the Soviet Union in the 1960s, and especially the controversy surrounding Solzhenitsyn at the time. Alexander Isaevich Solzhenitsyn had spent the years 1943 to 1953 in prison and in labour camps as a result of some mild criticism of Stalin in a letter to a friend at the front which was intercepted by the NKVD, Stalin's secret police. During the thaw years of 1953–6 he was in exile in Central Asia, and after 'rehabilitation' in 1956 he returned to Russia, working initially as a mathematics and physics teacher in Riazan'. He had been writing throughout the 1950s, although without much hope of publication. His first work was published on the express authorization of Khrushchev himself; *One Day in the Life of Ivan Denisovich* (*Один день Ивана Денисовича*) appeared in the liberal monthly journal *Novyi mir* in November 1962, and immediately became a literary sensation. It was the first work of fiction that portrayed the life of the camps in detail, with highly stylized language and narration, and the very fact of its appearance in the Soviet Union less than ten years after Stalin's death made it a 'literary miracle', as Kornei Chukovskii put it at the time.[1] Further short works by Solzhenitsyn critical of Stalinism followed in 1963–6, but with the removal of Khrushchev as Party leader in 1964 the process of de-Stalinization effectively came to an end and Leonid Brezhnev's cultural freeze increasingly took hold.

It was in 1964 that Solzhenitsyn's literary troubles began, when *One Day in the Life of Ivan Denisovich* failed to win the Lenin Prize. This event marked the beginning of a concerted conservative campaign against him. Things worsened in 1965 with the KGB's confiscation of part of his archive and manuscripts at the house of a friend (although these were later returned to him). 1966 turned out to be something of a watershed, for it was the year when the writers and critics Andrei Siniavskii and Iulii Daniel' were tried and imprisoned on the basis of having published their work in the West without initial publication in the USSR. A discussion of *Cancer Ward* in the Moscow writers' organization in 1967 demonstrated that many of the leading literary bureaucrats were generally in favour of the novel's publication, but no journal would print it. In protest at the continuing censorship of his works and those of other writers, he addressed a letter to all the delegates of the Fourth Writers' Congress in May 1967, thus bringing his conflict with the authorities into the open.[2]

Such a challenge to the literary bureaucracy ensured that *Cancer Ward*, a novel he had written with the explicit intention of publication in the USSR, was not published in that country. Moreover, a copy of the manuscript was sent abroad by the KGB, to ensure publication in the West which would preclude its appearance in the Soviet Union (and thereby demonstrating, at least in the eyes of Soviet officialdom, that its author, like Siniavskii and Daniel', was anti-Soviet in outlook and aiding Western imperialists). Further persecution followed when he was expelled from the Writers' Union in 1969. In 1970 he was awarded the Nobel Prize for Literature but, like Pasternak before him, was unable to accept it in person. He was allowed to publish nothing more in the Soviet Union until 1989 and Gorbachev's policy of *glasnost'*. After the publication in the West in 1974 of *The Gulag Archipelago* (*Архипелаг Гулаг*), his three-volume history of the labour camp system and its effects on Soviet society, he was arrested and deported to West Germany. From 1976 to 1994 he lived in exile in Vermont, and returned triumphantly to his homeland in May 1994.

Solzhenitsyn's two great novels, *Cancer Ward* and *The First Circle* (*В круге первом*), were both published in the West in 1968. (The 1968 version of the latter consisted of eighty-seven chapters; in 1978 Solzhenitsyn published the full, ninety-six chapter version.) Whereas there was no possibility of publishing *The First Circle* in the Soviet Union in the 1960s because of its detailed portrait of Stalin and its searing examination of all layers of Stalinist society, *Cancer Ward* contained little that could be construed as explicitly anti-Soviet in the changed atmosphere of de-Stalinization, and can indeed be interpreted as being written in order to support the Party's reformist policies. Furthermore, *Cancer Ward* has a rich vein of imagery and symbolism and, because of its textual ambiguities, repays close and detailed analysis.

Plot, Theme and Characterization

First and foremost, the novel is a work of literature, and it contains several important cultural cross-references. The most important of these is to Tolstoi's short novel *The Death of Ivan Il'ich* (*Смерть Ивана Ильича*, 1886). Ivan Il'ich is a rich landowner who falls ill with cancer and, as he dies, takes stock of his past life and the values he has lived by, coming to scorn the corruption and superficiality of material success. In Solzhenitsyn's novel too, cancer serves as a catalyst. The proximity of death enables the author to examine the values of his characters, and to place them in an existential situation where they have to face the prospect of death. Such a situation has an added interest in that it is set in an atheistic society, without the comfort of the Christian belief in the afterlife, where death is the end of everything.

The novel takes place in the spring of 1955, covering a period of several weeks, and is set in the cancer ward of a Tashkent hospital. The plot is relatively straightforward, and largely recounts the sufferings of several characters, their relationships with each other and others, their reflections on life, history and politics, and their treatment. In particular, the narrative contrasts the worlds of Oleg Kostoglotov, a former prison camp inmate and harsh critic of all things Stalinist, and Pavel Rusanov, a secret police official who basks in the relative splendour of his material affluence and rejoices in the 'social cleansing' effected by the terror and the purges. Other characters appear in the course of the novel who represent certain aspects of these two, so that Solzhenitsyn succeeds in creating a series of 'mirrors'. Thus alongside Rusanov are the more sympathetic communists Vadim Zatsyrko and Aleksei Shulubin; alongside Kostoglotov as victims of injustice are the Kadmins.

Solzhenitsyn was himself treated for cancer in a Central Asian hospital in the mid–1950s and, given his first-hand experience of the *gulag*, we can see that there is a strong autobiographical basis to the novel. Kostoglotov indeed serves as the focus for two struggles: against cancer and death, and against political injustice and tyranny. In both struggles he succeeds in surviving, not only physically but morally. The theme of survival with honour and integrity is as important in this novel as it is elsewhere in Solzhenitsyn's writings (especially *One Day in the Life of Ivan Denisovich*).[3]

The novel can be categorized as 'epic' because it encompasses not only a wide variety of characters representing various layers of Soviet society, but also the key historical events of Soviet history. Other lesser characters in the novel include doctors, Party officials, NKVD men, scientists, former prison camp inmates and their guards, old and young, the elite and the scorned, and representatives of various nationalities such as Germans, Uzbeks, Russians, Tartars and Kazakhs. We get very much a cross-section of society, a cross-section which also includes various character types: the arrogant and the cowardly, the conscience-stricken, the repentant and the self-seeking.

Although set within the confines of a hospital, the novel is above all concerned with life outside its walls. In particular, the novel concerns itself with the crimes, injustices and plain misdemeanours of the recent Stalinist past: the exiling of whole peoples following the Second World War for alleged collaboration with the enemy, such as the Volga Germans, Kurds and Greeks; the Russo-Finnish War of 1939–40, which revealed the inefficiency and lack of preparedness of the Soviet fighting machine; the purges and terror of 1937; the Soviet Union's failure to heed the warnings of Hitler's attack in June 1941; the post-war imprisonment of Soviet citizens who had been prisoners or slave labourers of the Germans during the war; Stalin's patronage of Lysenko; the official anti-Semitism of Stalin's last years, as evinced in the *Doctor's Plot*, in which Kremlin doctors of Jewish descent were accused of sabotage and attempted murder; the execution in 1953 of Lavrentii Beria, Stalin's head of secret police and confidant; the thaw and cultural developments following it. The novel is thus concerned with the truth about Soviet history, but Solzhenitsyn is careful to provide a detailed cultural and social background: the dictates and effects of socialist realism in the arts are discussed, we are given a substantial picture of literary life in the country, and we are introduced to members of the new thriving middle class, the class that has embraced Stalinism and reaped its rewards.

One of the patients, Shulubin, advocates the concept of 'moral socialism', where 'all relationships, fundamental principles and laws flow directly from ethics, and from them *alone*' ('все отношения, основания и законы будут вытекать из нравственности – и только из нее').[4] It is not enough to assert that this is the author's sop to censorship, an effort to bypass the hardline purists in the literary establishment by affirming a viable *socialist* alternative. Moreover, even in recent statements, such as his 1990 pamphlet *How We Can Rebuild Russia* (*Как нам обустроить Россию*), for instance, he advocates a solid moral and ethical base for all legislative and executive bodies regardless of their political imprint. Shulubin impresses upon Kostoglotov the vitality of socialism and the collapse of capitalism, in line with orthodox Marxist-Leninist doctrine. Certainly, Shulubin's 'moral socialism' does not get such a sympathetic airing elsewhere in Solzhenitsyn's fiction or public statements; indeed, socialism and ideology are Solzhenitsyn's twin evils, and in his many other public statements he sees little difference between Stalinist totalitarianism and West European social democracy.

The hospital can also be seen in terms of analogy, as its secretiveness and repressive habits are reminiscent of those of the Party and the government. The senior doctor, Nizamutdin Bakhramovich, is seen by Lev Leonidovich to have become corrupted by power. Those in the hospital who show talent in bureaucracy are promoted, while those who care and show pity towards their charges are not. The hospital rounds are like a police investigation, with doctors finding out as much as possible about the patient's background, but then facts are distorted so that the patient does not get a true picture of his or her illness. The main aim of the rounds is to improve morale, just as Party information bulletins are intended to impart abstract optimism and not hard facts. Only Rusanov believes all that he is told by the doctors, just as he believes what he reads of the budget in the newspapers. Consultancies and blood transfusions are run according to 'norms' in line with the Plan. The structures within the hospital mirror those of the state: Nizamutdin Bakhramovich runs the hospital with a dictatorial severity, those beneath him are overworked and underpaid, and Lev Leonidovich, with experience of the thaw taking place in Moscow, represents the humane spirit of the emerging post-Stalin society. Old Dr. Oreshchenkov is the figure harking back to an earlier, pre-revolutionary era, as he advocates a return to private medicine and a more personal relationship between patient and doctor. This view can also be seen as an allegorical statement on the bureaucratization of society, and a call for the democratization of society. Oreshchenkov further likens the senior doctors to government functionaries.[5]

The right to treat is central to this theme in *Cancer Ward*. Kostoglotov asserts his right not to have X-ray treatment: he would like to be cured of his cancer, but not at the cost of his masculinity. For Kostoglotov, the right to refuse such treatment in tantamount to being in control of his own life. As he says to Liudmila Dontsova, the doctor administering the treatment: 'Why do you assume you have the right to decide for someone else? Don't you agree it's a terrifying right, one that rarely leads to good? You should be careful. No one's entitled to it, not even doctors' (p. 89) ('Почему вообще вы берете себе право решать за другого человека? Ведь это – страшное право, оно редко ведет к добру. Бойтесь его! Оно не дано и врачу', p. 76). She argues, on the contrary, that 'you must accept your treatment not just with faith but with *joy*! That's the only way you'll ever recover!' (pp. 91–2) ('переносить лечение но только с верой, но с радостью! Вот только тогда вы вылечитесь!', p. 78). The Party expects the population to accept its policies in the same way. Furthermore, 'Ludmila Afansevna was unshakably convinced that any damage to the body was justified if it saved life' (p. 98) ('Людмила Афанасьевна непреклонно считала, что всякий ущерб оправдан, если спасается жизнь', p. 83). The Party, too, believed that the end justified the means, that the cost could not be too high. Kostoglotov argues that 'there isn't anything in the world for which I'd agree to pay *any* price' (pp. 87–8) ('такого и на свете нет ничего, за что б я согласился платить любую цену!', p. 75).[6] Yet at the end of the novel Kostoglotov's life is saved, but because of intensive chemotherapy treatment he will become impotent. This is hinted at in several references: he wears a woman's dressing gown, and during a blood transfusion he is given a woman's blood (significantly, on March 5, the day of Stalin's death: as Stalin dies, so Kostoglotov, the survivor of the camps and representative of the people's suffering, is given new blood to live).

In *Cancer Ward*, however, Solzhenitsyn's targets are not in full view. The novel can pass as an attack on Stalin and Stalinism, in keeping with de-Stalinization, but there are hints and suggestions of the larger themes that dominate works such as *The First Circle* and, more substantially, *The Gulag Archipelago*. For instance, the symbolism of cancer as a metaphor for the illness of society can be extended into allegory. The cancer ward of the hospital contains all manner of nationalities, characters, lives, feelings and experiences, and can be seen as a cross-section, if not a microcosm of society. Cancer affects the body politic just as it does the corporeal frame, and the prison camps are its physical manifestations. Stalinism is the cancer from which the country is trying to recover, but is Stalinism the cause or merely the symptom of the illness? Did Stalin begin the spread of this cancer, or can its roots be traced back to the origins of Soviet society in the Bolshevik revolution of 1917 and Lenin himself? These questions are not openly broached in this novel, although they are investigated in full in Solzhenitsyn's other writings, but there are still some hints. There is on the wall of the cancer ward an issue of the journal *The Oncologist*, dated November 7, the date of the official celebration of the Bolshevik Revolution, thus suggesting that the real cause of the cancer lies in that Revolution.[7]

There are also suggestions that the cause of the country's recovery, and its hope for the future, lie not in other types of socialism or ideology but within the resources of Russia itself. Indeed, Solzhenitsyn in this novel, as elsewhere, is interested not so much in the fate of the Soviet Union as of Russia. For example, rumours go round the ward about a mystical folk remedy that can cure cancer: *Chaga* is a tea-like drink made from a birch tree fungus, and has been drunk for centuries by Russian peasants. The birch tree is the symbol of Russia itself and, to continue the allegory, Solzhenitsyn's veiled message is that the cancer afflicting Russia can be cured only if Russia refers back to its natural ethnic strengths. In other words, recovery comes not from a change of political leadership, or even change of ideology, but from a rediscovery and reaffirmation of traditional and age-old Russian values. In *Cancer*

Ward, these traditions are primarily cultural ones.

Those characters committed to regeneration and recovery, or who admit to errors in the past and therefore spiritually regenerate themselves, consistently quote nineteenth-century Russian writers such as Pushkin or Lev Tolstoi, while the bespectacled Rusanov, still living a blinkered existence according to official values, quotes Gor'kii, the father of Soviet literature, or extols the therapeutic value of reading Nikolai Ostrovskii. Socialist realism, that artificial and tyrannical dogma grafted onto Russian literature, is the focus of much satire in the novel. When Podduev discusses his new-found morality based on a reading of Lev Tolstoi's *What Do Men Live By* (*Чем люди живы?*), Rusanov confuses this, the great Tolstoi, with the Soviet hack Aleksei Tolstoi, before stating categorically that 'people live by their ideological principles and by the interests of their society' (p. 117) ('люди живут идейностью и общественными интересами', p. 98). Podduev replies to Rusanov that people live by their love for another, and Solzhenitsyn then unmistakeably loads Rusanov's unconsidered response with irony, at the expense of the latter and of the inhuman system he serves: '*Love*? . . . No, that's nothing to do with our sort of morality' (p. 119) ('Лю-бо-вью? Не-ет, это не наша мораль', p. 99).

Podduev is indeed a complex character, one of the few fully developed by Solzhenitsyn in the novel. When we first meet him he is thoroughly disagreeable, a self-centred boor who has no qualms about having assisted the regime in its murderous policies. His private life has been a series of betrayals and casual affairs. Yet after reading Tolstoi he is a changed man, and he becomes aware of the spiritual and moral barrenness of his past life. In the end, Podduev earns our sympathy as a lonely, embittered man who has at least, on the threshold of death, learned something about himself.

The same cannot be said of Rusanov. Rusanov's spirits are raised when he is visited by his daughter Avieta, who brings him some 'optimistic and patriotic' literature he had encouraged the others to read: works by Dmitrii Kholendro, Vsevolod Kochetov, Konstantin Simonov, Semen Babaevskii and Alexander Chakovskii, all writers who slavishly followed the socialist realist line under Stalin (and even subsequently). Avieta has published a book of verse, a feat achieved not necessarily by virtue of her talent, of which we see nothing, but more through connections and friends with influence in publishing houses, of whom we learn a lot. She yearns to join the Writers' Union, and is overawed and impressed by the writers she has met: 'They have such delightfully simple relationships with each other. They may be Stalin Prize winners, but they're all on first-name terms. They're such unconceited, straightforward people' (p. 307) ('Какие у них простые между собой отношения! Лауреаты – а друг друга по именам. И какие они сами люди не чванные, прямодушные', p. 244). She cynically dismisses her father's suggestion that she will not make the grade: 'If the worst comes to the worst I can become a children's writer. Anyone can do that' (p. 308) ('Ну, а в крайнем случае стану детским писателем, уж это-то всякому доступно', p. 244).

Avieta is continuing the narrow dogma of her father, thus symbolizing, albeit ironically, the continuity of the generations as beloved of socialist realism. She believes whole-heartedly in the positivist slogans of socialist realism, as she patronizingly explains its fundamental precept to young Dema:

> Now, my boy, . . . you must understand this. Describing something that exists is much easier than describing something that doesn't exist, even though you know it's going to exist. What we see today with the unaided human eye is not necessarily the truth. The truth is what we *must* be, what is going to happen tomorrow. Our wonderful 'tomorrow' is what writers ought to be describing today. (pp. 311–12)

> (Так вот, мальчик, пойми. Описывать то, что есть гораздо легче, чем описывать то, чего нет, но ты знаешь, что оно будет. То, что мы видим простыми глазами сегодня – это не обязательно правда. Правда – то, что должно быть, что будет завтра. Наше чудесное «завтра» и нужно описывать.) (p. 248)

Solzhenitsyn obviously takes great delight in ridiculing the self-important bombast of this proponent of socialist realism, but he also manages to give an exact and succinct description of 'the basic method employed by Soviet artistic literature and literary criticism'. In line with the conservative diehards of the thaw period, Avieta abhors the new trend in literature calling for 'sincerity', giving expression to the fears of the Stalinists in the immediate post-Stalin years:

> Sincerity can't be the chief criterion for judging a book. If an author expresses incorrect ideas or alien attitudes, the fact that he's sincere about them merely increases the harm the work does. Sincerity becomes *harmful*. Subjective sincerity can militate against a truthful representation of life. (pp. 309–10)

> (Искренность никак не может быть главным критерием книги. При неверных мыслях или чуждых настроениях только усиливая вредное действие произведения, искренность – вредна! Субъективная искренность может оказаться против правдивости показа жизни.) (p. 246)

Her words could come straight from a Soviet textbook on socialist realist theory. Significantly, many Party-minded critics voiced the same objections during the thaw of 1953–4.[8] She further lambasts the 'unknown' poet Evtushenko, a hero for many of the younger generation of the time, for his popular public readings, and regrets the post-Stalin critical demolition of such a socialist realist stalwart as Babaevskii. Avieta may be a caricature of the Stalinist writer or would-be writer – cynical and materialistic yet believing that she has a higher calling, apprehensive of change and clinging to abstract formulae – but she voices opinions and views that have often been expressed in the literary press. She is not a wholly unbelievable figure – in Solzhenitsyn's view, many so-called Soviet writers are caricatures of what a writer should be: a spiritual guide and teacher, who speaks against tyranny and oppression directly to the people.

Avieta is also a moral cripple, as brought up by her equally monstrous parents: we learn that when she was four years old, much to the amusement of her parents, she would spit in a neighbour's pans, the neighbour being the pregnant wife of a man Rusanov had sent to the camps. She therefore shares her father's fears of political change, and brings him the news of prisoners returning from the camps and the first wave of 'rehabilitations'. Her response to the news of returnees is breathtakingly fatuous, but reveals the twisted rationalizations of the oppressors about to lose their monopoly of power: 'How *can* they stir up this hell? They should spare a thought for the people who were doing a job of work for society. How are *they* going to come out of all these upheavals?' (p.302) ('Да вообще как можно ворошить этот ад, не подумав о людях, кто тогда работал. Ведь о них-то надо было подумать! Как им перенести эти внезапные перемены?', p. 240). Avieta also brings her father news that people in Moscow are now being tried for giving false testimony twenty years before, and thus causing wrongful imprisonment. Rusanov is particularly upset at the prospect of meeting Rodichev, the neighbour whom he denounced in order to claim the consequently vacated living space, for fear of being physically beaten up.

On the other hand, the figure of Avieta is counterbalanced by that of Rusanov's son Iurii, a lawyer whose intent is to determine whether a man is guilty or not, rather than follow his father's practice of indiscriminate condemnation. When Iurii expresses his doubts about the presumed guilt of a man, his father is aghast, for to him mere suspicion is tantamount to proof of guilt. Iurii represents those in the young post-Stalin generation keen to undo the injustices of their fathers, and to condemn their fathers' participation, or at least acquiescence, in the worst excesses of Stalinism. Iurii, indeed, is one of the 'respectable' characters in the novel, in the sense that he is so obviously meant to represent the 'new' mentality and the overcoming of the past. In terms acceptable to literary censorship, he thereby conforms to certain socialist realist stereotypes and contributes to the novel's ideological acceptability. Iurii's function in the novel is to demonstrate that the sins of the fathers can be corrected.

His father, however, is obviously a 'negative' character, and has no redeeming features. Rusanov is selfish and totally unscrupulous, pampered with relative material comforts and now perceiving these comforts as a right commensurate with his status: he has his own car and flat, travels by train only in first-class carriages, has a separate room reserved for him in hotels, and relaxes with his family only in the best sanatoria. He exults in the power he has over others: 'The poetic side of his work lay in holding a man in the hollow of your hand without even starting to pile on the pressure' (p. 211) ('Поэзия работы была в этом ощущении, что ты полностью держишь в руках человека, еще по сути даже на него и не надавив', p. 170). It is the exultation of the tyrant, knowing that he has the power literally of life or death over any other individual whose path he crosses.

Rusanov resolutely believes that he can vanquish all ideological enemies and solve all political arguments with a quotation from Lenin or Gor'kii, or a topical slogan. He and his family share the same morality as their friends the Shendiapins, who had their daughter's simple and rural fiancé arrested in order to avoid a marriage beneath their social station. But Rusanov and his wife sincerely believe that they love their *narod*; it is real people they cannot stand.

Rusanov first enters the ward expressing his disdain for others, and his wife openly flouts hospital regulations. He has never known fear because he has never had anything to fear, although he has struck fear into others. He was not sent to the front during the war but was evacuated from his home town before it was bombed, and has himself never been subject to judicial investigation. He is the supreme opportunist, and therefore a spiritual brother of the black marketeer Chalyi, whose friendship he courts only in order to get some tyres for his car. Yet when misfortune arises, he shows that he is cowardly and cringing, in the face of both his tumour and the prospect of being physically manhandled by returning camp inmates whom he had put away.[9] In particular, he fears being punched in the face. His fear of those returning, especially his former friends Rodichev and Guzun, whom he denounced, is expressed as part of a long interior monologue comprising almost the whole of the chapter entitled 'Justice' ('Правосудие'): 'Better to die than live in fear of every man who returned. What madness it was to let them come back! Why did they do it? They'd got used to being where they were, they were resigned to it – why let them come back here and upset people's lives?' (p. 214) ('Лучше умереть, чем бояться каждого возврата. Какое это безумие! – возвращать их! Они там привыкли, они там смирились – зачем же пускать их сюда, баламутить людям жизнь?', p. 173). Only in a dream do we see the first stirrings of conscience in Rusanov's sub-conscious. Rusanov, his wife and daughter, and the system they represent and serve are treated with the utmost contempt by Solzhenitsyn the author, and by Kostoglotov his *alter-ego*.

As has been mentioned, *Cancer Ward* was written with an eye for Soviet publication, and so the uncompromising stance of *The Gulag Archipelago* and *The First Circle* is here muted, as in *One Day in the Life of Ivan Denisovich* and the novella 'Matrena's Home' ('Матренин двор'). Yet for all this the work is arguably better in artistic terms: there is a wealth of meaning and interpretation to be gleaned from the various levels of symbolism and the novel's rich imagery, and one can see the entire work as an allegory of the post-Stalin condition. The work is tendentious and still contains an overwhelming sense of moral purpose, but it lacks the stridency and self-righteousness of those written 'for the drawer' and later in emigration. Characterization is achieved on the basis of contrast and mirror image, where characters such as Rusanov and Zatsyrko are linked through their allegiance to the Party but contrasted in terms of their morality.[10] Likewise Shulubin and Kostoglotov, once on opposite sides of the ideological divide, are now linked by their fundamental loathing of Stalinism. At the centre of the narrative is the variety of viewpoints, where each major character is seen both externally from the point of view of others, and from the inside through their own eyes. Kostoglotov of course represents the author, and we are never in doubt that his judgments carry the moral weight of the author's own views.

Cancer Ward is a novel about suffering and death, but it is also about self-awareness in the face of death, and ultimately the overcoming of death. As Kostoglotov leaves the hospital it is spring, with the onset of the thaw after the long Russian winter. The final pages concentrate on Kostoglotov's physical and mental sensations as he walks the streets, a free man after ten years. He stands next to a girl on a crowded bus, watches a man try on a shirt, eats an ice-cream, visits a zoo, boards a train. The novel ends with an assertion of the immediacy of everyday life with its joys, confusions and disappointments. But life has its price, and Kostoglotov, though a free man, cannot avail himself of any sexual freedom. The likes of Rusanov are still abroad in society, and are still a threat to freedom, and the sight of the Macaque-Rhesus monkey in the zoo, blinded because someone for no reason threw tobacco in its eyes, is a reminder that evil still exists in the world.

Style and Imagery

Truth and the nature of reality are twin themes that are prominent in the novel. These themes are expressed largely through Solzhenitsyn's emphasis on individual fields of vision and perception. Kostoglotov's gaze is dark and accusing, whereas Rusanov observes the world through his spectacles, unable to see reality as it is, and suggesting a closed, suspicious nature.[11] Vera Gangart, one of the doctors with whom Kostoglotov develops an emotional relationship, has gentle hazel eyes, and lowers her gaze when she thinks ill of someone. Shulubin, the repentant Communist, has 'unkind eyes', 'a disapproving gaze', judging people for past crimes and injustice; Rusanov, in particular, is uneasy before him. Rusanov's own son, Iurii, averts eyes from his father's gaze when talking to him, suggesting not only that he does not share his father's views, but also that he disapproves of them. Kostoglotov tells the young Dema that the best advice is 'trusting your eyes and not your ears' (p. 31) ('Глазам своим верь, а ушам не верь', p. 30).

Eyes can reveal what words are afraid to utter. The patient Sibgatov understands from the doctor Dontsova's eyes that his illness is terminal; when Kostoglotov's eyes meet those of Zoia, the young nurse he is courting, he realizes that their relationship is over. The author often intrudes into the narrative to underline a point made by his characters, as here:

When eyes gaze endlessly into each other, they acquire an entirely new quality. You see things never revealed in passing glances. The eyes seem to lose their protected coloured retina. The whole truth comes splashing out wordlessly, it cannot be contained. (p. 357)

(Когда глаза неотрывно-неотрывно смотрят друг в друга, появляется совсем новое качество: увидишь такое, что при беглом скольжении не открывается. Глаза как будто теряют защитную цветную оболочку, и всю правду выбрызгивают без слов, не могут ее удержать.) (p. 283)

The attention paid to eyes and inner fields of vision contributes to a polyphonic narrative structure. This means that at different points in the narrative we see various characters and their perception of other characters through their eyes, and the narrative is constructed around viewpoints and ideas given equal weight and in conflict with one another. We see characters both from the inside and as they are seen by others. We hear their arguments and counter-arguments put forward by others. The obvious example of ideological and moral confrontation is that of Rusanov and Kostoglotov, but there are many examples of a subjective universe presented before us: we see Vera's world from her own point of view, her life and experience; we also see the senior doctor Nizamutdin Bakhramovich first through his own eyes and then through the eyes of Lev Leonidovich, a fellow doctor. The narrative as a whole therefore represents a multi-faceted totality of experience, each of which has its own validity. For example, Vadim Zatsyrko, the honest Communist and the nearest approximation to a positive hero in the narrative, has a generous and charitable view of Kostoglotov, the hard-bitten ex-zek, and Lev Leonidovich sees Nizamutdin Bakhramovich as vain, conceited and arrogant with his status and the privileges it brings.

There is also a symbolic or even allegorical level of discourse here. The action of the narrative takes place at the onset of the thaw, with mention made of the execution of Beria, the dismissal of Malenkov and the appearance in print of iconoclastic works by literary figures such as Vladimir Pomerantsev and Evgenii Evtushenko. As the truth about Stalin's crimes is beginning to be published, the country's eyes are being opened to the truth about its past and it is slowly emerging from its former blindness. Kostoglotov interprets Tchaikovskii's Fourth Symphony in terms of a man regaining his sight after being blind. Again the author intercedes: 'If decade after decade the truth cannot be told, each person's mind begins to roam irretrievably. One's fellow countrymen become harder to understand than Martians' (p. 492) ('Если десятки лет за десятками лет не разрешать рассказывать то, как оно есть – непоправимо разблуживаются человеческие мозги и уже соотечественников понять труднее, чем марсианина', p. 385)[12]

Characters therefore communicate by gesture, conversation and movement. Characters have their own individualized movements and gestures: Vera's lips are always moving, as if she personally feels the suffering all around her; Shulubin is distinguished by his inertia, his 'motionless' eyes and 'frozen gaze'. Verbal communication is achieved through debate and argument and truth is hammered out in opposing viewpoints, sometimes violently expressed. Solzhenitsyn also stresses the unity of existence, as the human world is consistently compared to or juxtaposed with the natural world.

This narrative device is not new in Russian literature, and post–1917 Russian literature is particularly rich in narratives where animals assume human characteristics and humans are likened to animals: suffice it to mention Bulgakov's *Master and Margarita*, and the same author's *The Heart of a Dog* (*Собачье сердце*, 1925), Olesha's *Envy*, and Georgii Vladimov's *Faithful Ruslan* (*Верный Руслан*, 1975). In this novel Kostoglotov is constantly likened to a dog, and even his name has canine associations: *Kosto-glotov* means literally 'bone-swallower'. Shulubin is likened to a bird, usually an owl, Lev Leonidovich to a gorilla (both he and Kostoglotov have 'paws'), and Ordzhonikidze is 'an eagle'. Kostoglotov calls Zoia a 'little bee', and remarks that the first two letters of her name suggest 'zoo', a further reference to her physicality. A tumour is described as a 'toad' lurking in someone's body, and cancer itself is 'the crab' (as it is in the zodiac). Vera is described as a gazelle, gentle and timid, and the promiscuous young Asia is like a restive horse. The young Dema, who tries to attach himself to Asia, is 'a kitten' or 'a young suckling-pig', suggesting his youth and naivety.

Associations with animals not only reveal a character's psychological make-up or personality traits; attitudes to animals reveal a character's moral essence. Kostoglotov corresponds with some elderly friends, the Kadmins, a couple who love cats and dogs, and the old doctor Oreshchenkov treats his St. Bernard as an equal. On the other hand, the Rusanovs' dog is allowed to chase and terrorize people, and the city authorities hire huntsmen to kill stray dogs. The Kadmins' dog is shot by the authorities (significantly, through the eye). Efrem Podduev equates man and animals when he recounts the tale of Allah giving man his years of life:

The first twenty-five years you will live like a man. The second twenty-five you'll work like a horse. The third you'll yap like a dag. And for the last twenty-five people will laugh at you like they laugh at a monkey. (p. 34)

(Первые двадцать пять пет будешь жить, как человек. Вторые двадцать пять пет будешь работать, как лошадь. Третьи двадцать пять лет будешь гавкать, как собака. И еще двадцать пять над тобой, как над обезьяной, смеяться будут.) (p. 32)

Human society is likened to a zoo, where a house is described as 'a five-storeyed cage'. It is thus no accident that at the end of the novel Kostoglotov, released and apparently cured, though now sexually impotent as a result of chemotherapy, makes a visit to the zoo. Here he likens the animals he sees to people he has known. Polar bears, he reasons, find it as difficult to live during the Central Asian summer as did the zeks in the Arctic winter, the gazelle reminds him of Vera and the chimpanzee of Shulubin. The most obvious similarity between these animals and humans is that the animals are all prisoners, condemned to sit out the rest of their lives in their cages, their own prison cells. Significantly, the Russian word клетка means both 'cage' and 'cell'. Finally Kostoglotov notices the yellow eyes of the tiger, the merciless killer, and he looks with hatred at it (in *The First Circle* Stalin is perceived as having yellow eyes). The zoo's Macaque-Rhesus monkey has been blinded as a result of someone throwing tobacco in its eyes (we recall the fate of Zhuk, the Kadmins' dog). Elsewhere the author dwells on the treatment of animals by humans to make a general moral point, one which underpins his whole vision of human society: 'Nowadays we don't think much of a man's love for an animal; we laugh at people who are attached to cats. But if we stop loving animals, aren't we bound to stop loving humans too?' (p. 294) ('Любовь к животным мы теперь не ставим в людях ни в грош, а над привязанностью к кошкам даже непременно смеемся. Но разлюбив сперва животных – не неизбежно ли мы потом разлюбиваем и людей?', p. 234).

On the other hand, Soviet citizens behave like beasts: young girls such as Zoia and Asia treat sex as nothing more than a casual physical diversion, devoid of emotional commitment; camp guards refuse to see inmates as people, but treat them as animals. Spiritual values are sorely lacking in this society. Kostoglotov, as the author's mouthpiece, uses the animal world to decry the paucity of spiritual values. In debate with Rusanov, he describes and ridicules the Soviet 'philosophy of life': 'Oh, life is so good! . . . Life, I love you . . . Life is for happiness! . . . What profound sentiments. Any animal can say as much without our help, any hen, cat, or dog' (p. 152) ('Ах, как хороша жизнь! . . . Люблю тебя, жизнь! . . . Жизнь дана для счастья! . . . Что за глубина! Но это может и без нас сказать любое животное – курица, кошка, собака', p. 125). Although man and animals share the same level of material existence, and man's morality is measured by his attitude to animals and the natural world, he rises above the level of animals through his spirit and his soul.[13]

Kostoglotov questions whether man can be explained purely in terms of logic, economics or physiology, but it is Shulubin, the repentant Communist and atheist, who personifies the potential for spiritual rebirth. As he says, quoting Pushkin: 'Not all of me shall die' (p. 516) ('Не весь умру', p. 404). Before his possibly fatal operation, Shulubin shares with Kostoglotov his faith in a dimension of life beyond the corporeal: 'Sometimes I feel quite distinctly that what is inside me is not all of me. There's something else, sublime, quite indestructible, some tiny fragment of the universal spirit. Don't you feel that?' (p. 517) ('А иногда я так ясно чувствую: что во мне – это не все я. Что-то очень есть неистребимое, высокое очень! Какой-то осколочек

Мирового Духа. Вы так не чувствуете?', p. 405).

It is this spiritual insight which has enabled Shulubin to come to a fundamental reassessment of Soviet socialism as built under Stalin, and considerable space is devoted in the novel to Shulubin's views. Shulubin is a Communist and a scientist, veteran of the Revolution and Civil War, who for twenty-five years did everything possible to please the authorities in order to survive. He voted for the execution of 'enemies of the people', confessed his own 'mistakes' and accepted lower-status jobs, avoided arrest through complete moral capitulation. He did not believe in the guilt of those arrested, executed, imprisoned and exiled, but he feared for his own freedom and that of his family. The fury and scorn with which he enters into ideological debate with Rusanov and Vadim, the other Communists in the ward, reflect the pain and anger of the quarter century of moral cowardice he has been forced to live through.

Conclusion

Shulubin again quotes Pushkin in characterizing the nature of his times:

In our vile times
... Man was, whatever his element,
Either tyrant or traitor or prisoner! (p. 466)

(В наш гнусный век
На всех стихиях человек
Тиран, предатель или узник!) (p. 365)

In other words, the state has divided its citizens into the oppressors and the oppressed, between whom there are the informers, those who betray their friends, colleagues and neighbours.

Shulubin uses the sixteenth-century philosopher Francis Bacon to develop his ideas about the nature of human society. He talks to Kostoglotov about the 'idols' of the cave, the theatre and the marketplace. The 'idols' represent man's prejudices which prevent him from living a 'pure' life. The idols of the cave, for instance, are sufficient to keep the caveman happy, for he wants nothing more than to eat and have a full belly. The idols of the theatre are translated as the opinions or views of others, no matter how erroneous, to which individuals and societies slavishly adhere. The idols of the marketplace represent the values which hold communities together but which prey on individuals, such as the state's demands that everyone join in the chorus of voices shouting for the death penalty for 'traitors' and 'enemies of the people'. Each of these 'idols' can be seen to represent a certain facet of Stalinist society, and together they suggest the level to which civilization has now descended.

Solzhenitsyn has succeeded, through polyphony, metaphor and subtle characterization, in creating a picture of a society morally and spiritually sick, crisis-stricken by the physical and moral cataclysms to which it has been subjected. Kostoglotov's walk in freedom at the end of the novel, his physical sensations and joy at being alive, are rendered with simplicity and immediacy, but the tiger with Stalin's eyes at the zoo and the blinded monkey remind him, and the reader, of the evil still prevalent in the world. It is the time of the thaw, a time when there is hope for truth and justice, and when morality can once more be based on individual selflessness and spiritual beliefs.

Notes

1. Quoted in Zhores Medvedev, *Ten Years after Ivan Denisovich*, Macmillan, 1973, p. 5.
2. Original documentary materials, including the text of the letter and a transcript of the discussion in the Writers' Union in September 1967, are included as appendices in Alexander Solzhenitsyn, *The Oak and the Calf: A Memoir*, trans. Harry Willetts, London, 1980.
3. For a detailed analysis of this theme, see Diana Lewis Burgin, 'The Fate of Modern Man: An Examination of Ideas of Fate, Justice and Happiness in Solzhenitsyn's *Cancer Ward*', *Soviet Studies*, vol. 26, 1974, pp. 260–71.
4. Alexander Solzhenitsyn, *Cancer Ward*, trans. David Burg and Nicholas Bethell, Harmondsworth, 1971, p. 474; *Раковый корпус*, Paris, 1970, p. 371. All further references to the work will be taken from these editions, with page numbers incorporated directly into the text.
5. Alan J. Whitehorn also argues this:

    The doctors claim by power of their specialized knowledge the authority to institute treatment of the patient (society). Yet, in so doing, they hide the results of all diagnoses, deny any danger in the methods of treatment, and generally 'prescribe medicines about which they know little, for an organism about which they know less'. Kostoglotov's apprehension of possible doctors' mistakes and his wish for release in order to enjoy life raises the question of whether or not the doctor (Party) has the right to treat (rule) the patient (society/individual) irrespective of his wishes.

See Alan J. Whitehorn, 'What Men Live By: An Analysis of Solzhenitsyn's Writings', *Canadian Slavonic Papers*, vol. 13, 1971, p. 239. Gary Kern, however, asserts the opposite:

The surgeons are not prison guards or officials: they may mutilate bodies, lop off legs and breasts, but they are fighting a disease, their motives are humane. They are not cruel and self-serving, but self-sacrificing, overworked, kind. The patients are not social prisoners: they have been confined not by the free decisions of men but by nature. They themselves seek help in the hospital, make demands on their physicians. (Gary Kern, 'The Case of Kostoglotov', *Russian Literature Triquarterly*, vol. 11, 1975, p. 430).

6. Compare the following lines from *The Gulag Archipelago:*

And then – from all kinds of socialists, and most of all from the most modern, infallible, and intolerant Teaching, which consists of this one thing only: The result is what counts! It is important to forge a fighting Party! And to seize power! And to hold on to power! And to remove all enemies! And to conquer in pig iron and steel! And to launch rockets!

And though for this industry and for these rockets it was necessary to sacrifice the way of life, and the integrity of the family, and the spiritual health of the people, and the very soul of our fields and forests and rivers – to hell with them! The result is what counts!!!

But that is a lie! Here we have been breaking our backs for years at All-Union hard labour. Here in slow annual spirals we have been climbing up to an understanding of life – and from this height it can all be seen so clearly: It is not the result that counts! It is not the result – but *the spirit!* Not *what* – but *how!* Not what has been attained – but at what price. (Alexander Solzhenitsyn, *The Gulag Archipelago 2*, trans. Thomas P. Whitney, London, 1975, p. 591.)

7. Solzhenitsyn makes explicit the link between cancer and the camps in *The Gulag Archipelago:*

It was my fate to carry inside me a tumour the size of a large man's fist. This tumour swelled and distorted my stomach, hindered my eating and sleeping, and I was always conscious of it (though it did not constitute even one-half of one percent of my body, whereas within the country as a whole the Archipelago constituted 8 percent). But the horrifying thing was not that this tumour pressed upon and displaced adjacent organs. What was most terrifying about it was that it exuded poisons and infected the whole body.

And in this same way our whole country was infected by the poisons of the Archipelago. And whether it will ever be able to get rid of them someday, only God knows (Solzhenitsyn, *The Gulag Archipelago 2*, p. 614).

8. At the 1966 Writers' Union meeting called to discuss the novel, Solzhenitsyn pointed out that Avieta was a far from fictional figure:

> I adopted here an impermissible device – there is not in the section about Avieta a single word of my own – she uses words spoken in the last fifteen years by our most important writers and literary critics. From the point of view of eternity, there is no need for that chapter. But after all words like that were being spoken for such a long time from platforms higher than this one and to audiences bigger than this one. Is it right to forget this? Yes, it is undisguisedly a farce, but it's not mine. (Leopold Labedz (ed.), *Solzhenitsyn: A Documentary Record*, London, 1970, pp. 61–2).

9. Christopher Moody comments:

> Unlike the other patients, Rusanov's long look at his past is induced as much by the fate which awaits him if he survives as by the fear of death itself. He reviews his life not in order to attain self-awareness, but for self-justification . . . For every act of self-interest he can supply some spurious social vindication. (Christopher Moody, *Solzhenitsyn*, Edinburgh, 1973, pp. 143–4).

10. Deming Brown comments on the similarities of Vadim, Rusanov and Chalyi:

> With his cold honesty, party idealism, single-minded ambition, and devotion to the future, Vadim is the New Soviet Man whom the softer Rusanov mistakenly thinks himself to be. At the same time, Vadim, in his arrogance and spiritual blindness, is a subtle, terrifying parody of Rusanov. In Chaly, Rusanov senses a kindred spirit, a fellow crook; but Chaly is embarrassing because he is not a hypocrite like Rusanov. Vadim and Chaly are examples of Solzhenitsyn's brilliant use of foils: each character is a subtle commentary on all the others. (Deming Brown, '*Cancer Ward* and *The First Circle*', *Slavic Review*, vol. 28, 1969, p. 309).

11. Edward J. Brown suggests that Rusanov is 'existing in a tightly curtained void impenetrable even to the thought of death' (Edward J. Brown, 'Solzhenitsyn's Cast of Characters', *Major Soviet Writers: Essays in Criticism*, New York, 1973, p. 357).

12. Compare the following lines from *The Gulag Archhipelago*:

> Truth, it seems, is always bashful, easily reduced to silence by the too blatant encroachment of falsehood.
> The prolonged absence of any free exchange of information within a

country opens up a gulf of incomprehension between whole groups of the population, between millions and millions.

We simply *cease to be a single people*, for we speak, indeed, different languages. (See Alexander Solzhenitsyn, *The Gulag Archipelago 3, 1918–1956: An Experiment in Literary Investigation V–VIII*, trans. H. T. Willetts, London, *1978, p. 475.*)

13. For further discussion of the animal imagery in this work, see Gary Kern, 'The Case of Kostoglotov', *Russian Literature Triquarterly*, vol. 11, 1975, especially pp. 423–6.

8

Andrei Bitov (b. 1937), *Pushkin House* (*Пушкинский дом*)

Introduction and Background

It seems fitting, given the novel's preoccupation with literature, literary conventions and cultural history, to begin this study of *Pushkin House* at the point where the text actually ends. The author optimistically affirms his powers as a writer and his ability to continue writing: 'As you see, the author is serious about his own work. He is full of faith. There is yet SOMETHING TO BE DONE' ('Как видите, автор относится к собственной работе всерьез. Он полон веры. Ему все еще есть ЧТО ДЕЛАТЬ').[1] The deliberate use of upper case for the last two words in the Russian, invoking the famous title of a classic of nineteenth-century Russian utilitarian literature, will be discussed later.

The novel was written from 1964 to 1971, and although parts of the novel appeared separately in the Soviet Union in the 1970s, the text in its entirety was refused publication and appeared in full only in the West in 1978. It was published in the Soviet Union under Gorbachev's *glasnost'*, in 1987.[2] It is above all a novel about Russian literature, both its history and its relevance for modern Russian society, and as such is a fitting work to bring our discussion of twentieth-century Russian novels to a cumulative close.

Andrei Georgievich Bitov was born in Leningrad in 1937 and was evacuated to the Urals during the Second World War, returning to that city in 1944. He studied at the Leningrad Mining Institute from 1955 to 1962, during which time he also did his military service. His first short stories were published in 1959, and after the publication of his first collection of short stories in 1963 (*The Big Balloon, Большой шар*), became both an acclaimed and controversial writer. He continued to publish in the Soviet Union until the *Metropol'* affair. *Metropol'* was a collection of poetry, prose and social comment that appeared in Moscow in *samizdat* (illegal printing, usually done in someone's home) in 1979; it was controversial in that it had not been passed by the censor, and it included texts and writers who had in earlier years been refused permission to publish, such as Iuz Aleshkovskii, Vasilii Aksenov, Evgenii Popov and Vladimir Vysotskii. Bitov was both a contributor to and editor of the collection and, as a result of his participation, almost nothing of his appeared in print until Gorbachev's policy of *glasnost'* in the arts in 1986.

Some of the reasons why *Pushkin House* was deemed unfit for publication in Brezhnev's Soviet Union are obvious, while others are not. First and foremost, it discusses aspects of Soviet society and history – the Gulag, censorship, the repressive literary bureaucracy, virulent Russian anti-Semitism, the seeming omniscience of informers – that were impossible to discuss publicly in the 1960s and 1970s. Also, with its disjointed chronological structure, its post-modernist narrative style and semi-serious, semi-jocular deliberations on the nature of literary history and continuity and on the relationship of the written word to concrete reality, it flies in the face of traditional socialist realist style and structure. Moreover, it also insists on the continuity and interconnectedness of Russian and European cultural experience, denying the socialist realist assertion that 1917 provided a break between the 'old' and the 'new' orders. In particular, Bitov restores the place of Vladimir Nabokov in Russian literature at a time when that writer's place in Russian cultural history was denied by Soviet ideologues.[3]

Also, the novel has no recognizable beginning or end. Rather, we the reader are placed at the beginning of the narrative in the middle of a situation – a body lying in the middle of a litter-strewn floor, with the wind streaming into the room through an open window – and three hundred pages later we are back in the same situation, having seen how it developed and reached such a dramatic *dénouement*. The time seems ripe now to discuss the plot and the main characters in the novel.

Plot and Characterization

Despite the novel's length, there is very little actual plot line; similarly, there are few main characters. The focal point of the narrative is the character and development of Lev Nikolaevich Odoevtsev, and the novel follows him through his childhood and adolescence against the background of Stalinism, with mention of arrests, imprisonment and mass deportations providing the factual backdrop. As the first chapter unfolds, Bitov is at pains to describe the changing times, with the onset of the 1950s, narrow trousers and *stiliagi*.[4] There are many other aspects of Soviet urban reality mentioned in the opening pages, and these are referred to and explained in the semi-academic annotations to the text that come at the end of the book (such as popular cigarettes, new journals for young people, films about the achievements of great Russian scientists, explorers and musicians, such as Popov, Przheval'skii, Glinka and Musorgskii). As narrative time passes, Bitov/ Odoevtsev notes features of social life in the 1960s and 1970s, such as the currency reform of 1961, the ideological and cultural stand-off in the 1960s between the 'liberal' journal *Novyi mir* ('New World') and its ultra-conservative counterpart *Oktiabr'* ('October'), and the change of militia uniforms in 1970.

Social reality, however, plays no significant role in the novel's development. Rather, as a child Leva has doubts about his fatherhood, meets his grandfather who has returned from imprisonment and exile, goes into higher education, falls in and out of love with various women, and becomes a successful, occasionally brilliant, postgraduate student at the Pushkin House literary research institute. Leva's best friend and fellow-student, who also serves as his *bête noire*, is Mitishat'ev. The latter half of the novel sees Leva agreeing to spend the whole of the November celebrations, lasting three days, on special watch duty at the Pushkin House. There he is visited by Mitishat'ev, they have a duel of words and then an actual duel with the same pistols used in Pushkin's fatal duel with d'Anthès, Leva falls to the ground . . . and then the narrative returns us to the point where the novel began. Three hundred pages on from this beginning, Leva is lying on the floor clutching a pistol with blood seeping from a head wound, apparently dead. Indeed, Leva the literary character is dead, but Leva the actual person comes round, shakes himself down, and then accompanies a visiting American scholar and his wife on an excursion to places associated with Pushkin in Leningrad. The novel's preoccupation with the link between life and literature thus becomes obvious.

As for characterization, there is in fact very little. Leva is obviously the pivotal character in the novel, and his personality corresponds closely to the usual Bitov hero, as defined by Deming Brown: 'On the surface a normally functioning, creative, responsible individual, Bitov's hero is often lonely and tormented, puzzled over his own behaviour and its ethical implications.'[5] Moreover, Leva tells lies, shows weakness when he fails to help or support those in need and is easily dominated by others. His grandfather, Modest Platonovich, on the other hand, who has returned from the camps after thirty years, was once a brilliant scholar, but is now reduced to bitterness and alcoholism. Mitishat'ev, Leva's rival, is cynical and street-smart; he likes the good things in life, and can summon up women with a single phone call. He is also a violent man: he makes rabidly anti-Semitic remarks, attacks Leva for his supposedly aristocratic descent, hurls an inkwell used by the nineteenth-century writer Dmitrii Grigorovich through the window of the Pushkin House, and finally shoots Leva, calmly smoking a cheap cigarette afterwards. There are also three women in Leva's life: the fickle and superficial Faina, who does not love him and sleeps around (including with Mitishat'ev), causing him great pain; Al'bina, who is honest and sincere and loves Leva, who in turn cares little for her and eventually leaves her; and Liubasha, who is thinly sketched, but we learn that she too shares her affections with both Leva and Mitishat'ev.

Style and Theme

It may be apparent by now that there is a strong element of parody in the novel. Leva's duel with Mitishat'ev is a parody of Pushkin's fatal duel (as well as Lermontov's). Leva sits on the lion statue opposite the Bronze Horseman monument in a parody of a scene in Pushkin's epic poem *The Bronze Horseman* (*Медный всадник*). The fact that there are alternative endings parodies accepted literary practice, and Leva even has an alternative father. People tell lies to each other, or at least hide the truth: Faina's gold ring is not really gold, and Leva's family do not tell him of the existence of his grandfather, who has been in the Gulag for thirty years. Indeed, the whole novel is based on variants and alternatives, truth and actuality are not apparent as the whole of Soviet society is based on deception and artificiality.[6]

The novel has to be read as an entire unified text. It contains not only chapters relating plot developments, as we would expect, but also authorial asides, sections on 'variants and versions', footnotes and substantial annotations (almost fifty pages in the 1989 Sovremennik edition). It would be no exaggeration to say that the main feature of *Pushkin House* is its narrative style, for the unity of the novel is itself a reflection of its main theme, the unity of Russian literature. A particular feature of the book is the frequent occasions when the author introduces himself into the text in order to draw our (the reader's) attention to the fact that the text is a fiction, and that the characters, the narrative time and the action are not 'real'; that is, they exist outside of our (the reader's) time. Moreover, not only is there a clear identification of the author with his hero Leva, but there is also an increasing merging of the two. Indeed, it would be no exaggeration to say that the novel's main theme emerges through a study of its style.

Pushkin House is about Russian literature, affirming and celebrating its wholeness and continuity, and the novel's structure reflects this. There are three main sections (разделы), entitled, respectively, 'Fathers and Sons' ('Отцы и дети'), 'A Hero of Our Time' ('Герой нашего времени'), and 'The Poor Horseman' ('Бедный всадник'). These are all titles (or, in the last instance, a parody of two titles) of famous nineteenth-century Russian novels. Furthermore, individual chapters within these sections also recollect famous works of nineteenth-century writers: 'Masquerade' ('Маскарад'), the title of a poem by Lermontov; 'The Shot' ('Выстрел'), the title of a story by Pushkin; 'The Duel' ('Дуэль'), another story by Pushkin. The section 'A Hero of Our Time', like its illustrious predecessor, contains chapters named after the women in the hero's life, in this case Faina, Al'bina and Liubasha, as well as one entitled 'The Fatalist' ('Фаталист'), which, like its prototype, sees the hero test his own will, gambling with himself and winning.[7]

Moreover, the three titles have a thematic significance: 'Fathers and Sons' offers the author's own discourse on the intelligentsia, its role and its moral, psychological and intellectual make-up. In other words, it is an attempt to give Turgenev's novel a contemporary resonance. The section 'A Hero of Our Time' explores Leva's character, with particular emphasis on its spiritual and moral development – again, in the spirit of Lermontov's novel. Even the prologue is entitled 'What Is To Be Done?' ('Что делать?'), a question which is the contender for the most frequent title of a Russian book (all made famous, in their own different ways, by Lev Tolstoi, Nikolai Chernyshevskii and Alexander Herzen in the last century, and Vladimir Lenin in this). The final chapter, 'The Poor Horseman', is a play on the titles of two famous nineteenth-century works: Dostoevskii's *Poor Folk* (*Бедные люди*), and Pushkin's *The Bronze Horseman* (*Медный всадник*), and makes frequent reference to both Pushkin and Dostoevskii.

Many chapters, especially in the last two sections, begin with epigraphs from the equivalent works, sometimes several: a chapter entitled 'Devils Invisible to the Eye' ('Невидимые глазом бесы') begins with epigraphs from Pushkin's poem 'Devils' ('Бесы'), Dostoevskii's novel of the same name and Fedor Sologub's novel *The Petty Demon* (*Мелкий бес*); the chapter 'The Duel' ('Дуэль') begins with quotations from the writers Evgenii Boratynskii (1828), Pushkin (1830), Lermontov (1839), Turgenev (1862), Dostoevskii (1871), Chekhov (1891) and Sologub (1902). The hero's surname is reminiscent of that of a famous St Petersburg writer, Irina Odoevtseva, wife of the poet Georgii Ivanov, who went into emigration after the Revolution. Let us not forget, too, the name and patronymic of the main character: Lev Nikolaevich, the same as the great Tolstoi.[8]

Indeed, not only Russian literature is considered: Leva has an uncle affectionately referred to as 'Dickens', and there are further references to *Bleak House* in the novel as well as to Dumas' *The Three Musketeers*, long a favourite with Russian children, and to James Joyce, Franz Kafka and Marcel Proust, all long regarded by the Soviet authorities as European 'modernists' inimical to socialist realism, and whose works were not available in Soviet editions until the late 1980s.[9]

Thus, the novel self-consciously and often ironically refers to literature and the literary process, contriving to produce a totality of experience and history.[10] This sense of unity is made apparent in the concluding comment of Bitov/Odoevtsev on Nabokov at the end of the notes that bring the book, the text as an entity, to a close (we must recall that at the time when Bitov was engaged on the book Nabokov was still *persona non grata* in the Soviet history of Russian literature):

> One more point. Literature is a continuous and uninterrupted process. If some link is hidden, or omitted, or seems to have fallen out, this doesn't mean that the link doesn't exist, that the chain is broken – for without that link there can be no continuation. It means that we are standing right where the link is missing. This is the end, not a rupture. In order to thread the next (a new) link onto the chain, we will have to discover the lost one again, resurrect it, invent it, reconstruct it from its bones, like Cuvier. Repetitions here – the invention of the bicycle and the discovery of gunpowder – are not so much alarming as inevitable. Nabokov can't help existing in Russian literature, if only for the reason that he does exist. There's no getting away from this. We cannot subtract him, even if we don't know of his existence. Paleontology of this kind is inevitably weaker than the unknown original, but that's another matter. Nabokov is uninterrupted Russian literature, as though nothing had happened to it after his departure; fate had to take a unique zigzag to arrange, for him personally, the phenomenon of extrahistoricity. (pp. 413–14)

> (И еще вот что. Литература есть непрерывный (и непрерванный) процесс. И если какое-то звено скрыто, опущено, как бы выпало, это не значит, что его нет, что цепь порвана, – ибо без него не может быть продолжения. Значит, там мы и стоим, где нам недостает звена. Значит, здесь конец, а не обрыв. Чтобы нанизать на цепь следующее (новое) звено, придется то, упущенное, открыть заново, восстановить, придумать, реконструировать по косточке, как Кювье. Тут повторения, изобретение велосипеда и открытие пороха не так страшны, как неизбежны. Набокова не может не быть в русской литературе, потому хотя бы, что он – есть. От этого уже не денешься. Его не вычесть, даже если не знать о его существовании. Другое дело, что такого рода палеонтология слабее неизвестного оригинала. Набоков – есть непрерванная русская литература, как будто ничего не произошло с ней после его отъезда: судьбе пришлось уникально извернуться, чтобы организовать персонально для него феномен внеисторичности.) (pp. 398–9)

It is in its attitude towards Nabokov that the novel's real interest in Russian literary history lies. Bitov's novel is in many ways a rewriting of Nabokov's novel *The Gift* (*Дар*), for this novel too takes as its central theme Russian literary history. In particular, *The Gift* contains a chapter that purports to 'recreate' the biography of Nikolai Chernyshevskii, the nineteenth-century radical, but actually mingles fact with fiction. Chernyshevskii features in *Pushkin House* in the refrain 'what is to be done?' Both novels, furthermore, contain long deliberations on Russian literature, especially Pushkin; both contain elaborate word-play and literary games and both contain scenes of mock duels.

It is thus no accident that the author, in the first of several sections entitled 'The Italics Are Mine – A. B.' ('Курсив мой – А. Б.'; the title recalls a book of literary reminiscences of the same name by the *émigrée* Nina Berberova), calls the work 'a museum novel' ('роман-музей'). Furthermore, in the novel literature and morality are linked explicitly several times. Leva's grandfather, Modest Platonovich (his father's father), was an eminent and influential literary academic thirty years previously, who fell foul of the Stalinist authorities and subsequently spent thirty years in camp and exile. His son (Leva's father) had disowned him in order to survive, a not uncommon practice in those years. Furthermore, he had built his subsequent career on his criticism of his own father's work. Modest Platonovich returns to Moscow, refusing to see his son but admitting the adolescent Leva. The friends of Modest Platonovich – a young boy Leva's age (Rudik) and an older man (Koptelov) who reminds him of his uncle Dickens – offer a mirror image of Leva's own family, with himself, Dickens and his own father seemingly seen from another angle. That angle is unfettered anger and bitterness. The grandfather drunkenly harangues him on nature, progress and Russian literature in a tour-de-force of a monologue (ten pages in the Russian text):

Perhaps – and this is the most optimistic view – what's happening in the world now, not on the social surface of the processes but in their invisible depths, is a struggle, a rivalry, between human intellect and progress (God and the devil, to the old way of thinking). In that case the task of intellect is to succeed – at all costs, before the critical point (of irreversibility) when earth is destroyed by progress – to succeed in discrediting all false concepts, to be left with nothing and *suddenly* grasp the *secret*. Here a revolution takes place in consciousness – and the earth is saved. . . . The whole strength of the human spirit, in our century, has been redirected to the mere spending, voiding, unmasking, and discrediting of false concepts. All the positivism of contemporary spiritual life is negative. False concepts are wiped out and replaced by nothing. You had one stroke of luck: for thirty years (exactly while I was gone) the hunting of word and concept was forbidden, words ran wild and at the same time ceased to fear man, they wandered off – plenty of room – and they're roaming unrecognized, uncaught, unpronounced. Now, you think that '17 destroyed, devastated our previous culture. But it didn't; it canned and preserved it. What matters is the break, not the destruction. The authorities froze there untoppled, unmoving: they're all in their places, from Derzhavin to Blok – the sequel won't shake their order, because there won't be a sequel. Everything has been turned upside down, but Russia is still a land off-limits. You can't get there. Life, not as it had been but any at all, began only in '17, but there came to be a lot of it, and they put a stop to it. (pp. 63–4)

(Может быть – и это еще самый оптимистический взгляд – то, что сейчас происходит в мире, не на социальной поверхности процессов, а в невидимой глубине их содержания – есть борьба, соревнование человеческого разума и прогресса (бога и дьявола, по-старому). Тогда задача разума – успеть во что бы то ни стало, до критической точки (необратимости) разорения Земли прогрессом, развенчать все ложные понятия, остаться ни с чем и внезапно постичь тайну . . . Тут происходит революция в сознании – и земля спасена. (. . .) Вся сила человеческого духа повернулась в наш век лишь на истрачивание, отмену, разоблачение и дискредитацию ложных понятий. Весь позитивизм современной духовной жизни – негативен. Ложные понятия изничтожаются – и не заменяются ничем. Вам еще повезло – у вас лет на тридцать (как раз пока меня не было . . .) была запрещена всякая охота за словом и понятием, слова одичали и перестали бояться человека одновременно, они разбрелись – пространство большое – и бродят неузнанные, непойманные, непроизнесенные. Вот вы считаете, что семнадцатый год разрушил, разорил прежнюю культуру, а он как раз не разрушил, а законсервировал ее и сохранил. Важен обрыв, а не разрушение. И авторитеты там замерли несвергнутые, неподвижные: там все те же на том же месте, от Державина до Блока – продолжение не поколеблет их порядка, потому что продолжения не будет. Все перевернулось, а Россия осталась заповедной страной. Туда не попадешь. Жизнь, не какая была, а какая ни на есть, началась лишь с семнадцатого года, но и ее стало много, и ее остановили.) (pp. 65–6)

This passage reads like a grotesque parody of Vedeniapin's speech on Christ, immortality and history in *Doctor Zhivago*, but it reveals a bitter rationalization of twentieth-century Russian history and thought. Leva's grandfather is indeed a bitter man, and reveals his sincere sense of betrayal, humiliation and helplessness, when he tells how his family expected him on his return to be the same as he was thirty years before and were unprepared for the change, and when he got lost in his own district, as he could not remember his address. Leva eventually leaves when the insults, especially aimed at his own father, prove too much. The whole drawn-out story is told from Leva's point of view, as he perceives his grandfather and the others in the room; we see his reactions, his thoughts, his apprehension, anxiety and fears. The grandfather is further likened to Lev Tolstoi by the manner of his death: he tries to return to his place of exile, and dies on his way there. The inference is clear: the younger generation is lost and confused because of the crimes visited upon their fathers and grandfathers in their time.

Another such conversation about literature and society occurs when Leva is on duty at the institute during the November public holiday. He is visited by Mitishat'ev and his friend Gottikh (who is probably an informer), and then his own friend Blank, an elderly man who used to work at the institute and who has taken Leva under his wing. Gottikh says next to nothing, and seems to get more drunk as the evening progresses, but Mitishat'ev and Blank represent the opposing poles of temptation and good-will struggling for Leva's soul:

> Mitishatyev and Blank were contraindicated for each other. Mitishatyev killed Lyova in Blank's eyes, and Blank killed Lyova in Mitishatyev's eyes. Discreditation and exposure . . . How Lyova would extricate himself – how he would speak two languages at once, act within two opposite systems simultaneously – he hadn't a clue. (pp. 264–5)

> (Митишатьев и Бланк были противопоказаны друг другу. Митишатьев убивал Леву в глазах Бланка, и Бланк убивал Леву в глазах Митишатьева. Развенчивание и разоблачение . . . И как предстояло Леве выкрутиться, как говорить сразу на двух языках, поступать в двух противоположных системах одновременно, – Леве было невдомек.) (p. 265)

Mitishat'ev is seen as a Dostoevskian devil, either as the nihilist Petr Verkhovenskii from *The Possessed* or Ivan Karamazov's ultra-rationalist devil from *The Brothers Karamazov*.[11] Blank, on the other hand, refuses to judge people, he is the epitome of decency and honesty and always sees the best in people, even when those same people have committed base acts. He too is verbally abused by Mitishat'ev.

When they are all together, they talk especially about Pushkin, Russian literature, Pushkin's relations with his wife and the involvement of d'Anthès, the officer who was to kill Pushkin in a duel provoked by his affair with Pushkin's wife. It is worth quoting at length once, not only to get an idea of the range of subjects covered but also the author's deliberately stylized presentation (of which more later):

> They spoke as one man, one bulky man with indefinite clay features who had absorbed them all. And all their trite words were made new again by the mere fact that this clay mouth had never before pronounced them, no one before had heard them from this mouth . . . They spoke of the weather, freedom, poetry, progress, Russia, the West, the East, the Jews, the Slavophiles, the liberals, cooperative apartments, cheap boarded-up country houses, the people, drunkenness, vodka-making methods, hangover, *Oktyabr* and *Novy Mir*, God, women, Negroes, currency, authority, privilege

certificates, contraceptives, Malthus, stress, stoolies (Blank kept giving
Lyova cautionary winks behind Gottich's back), pornography, impending
change, corroborated rumors, physics, a certain movie actress, the societal
meaning of the existence of brothels, the decline of literature and the arts,
their simultaneous upsurge, the social nature of man, the fact that there was
no place to hide . . . (p. 267)

(Они говорили как один человек, как один такой громоздкий,
неопределенно-глиняных черт человек, который, вобрав в себя всех,
обновил все стертые слова тем одним, что никогда еще их не
произносил именно тот глиняный рот, что никто еще их же из того
рта не слышал . . . Они говорили о погоде, о свободе, о поэзии, о
прогрессе, о России, о Западе, о Востоке, об евреях, о славянофилах,
о либералах, о кооперативных квартирах, о дешевых заколоченных
деревенских домах, о народе, о пьянстве, о способах очистки водки,
о похмелье, об «Октябре» и «Новом мире», о Боге, о бабах, о
неграх, о валюте, о власти, о сертификатах, о противозачаточных
средствах, о Мальтусе, о стрессе, о стукачах (Бланк без конца
предостерегающе подмигивает Леве за спиной Готтиха . . .), о
порнографии, о предстоящей перемене, о подтвердившихся слухах,
о физике, об одной киноактрисе, о социальном смысле
существования публичных домов, о падении литературы и
искусств, об их одновременном взлете, об общественной природе
человека и о том, что деться – некуда . . .) (pp. 266–7)

Furthermore, the whole scene is described through Leva' eyes and, as
he gets more drunk, takes on an increasingly hallucinatory and
disjointed aspect as other characters appear and disappear. Illusion and
reality, the nineteenth and twentieth centuries, become blurred as
Mitishat'ev, ever mindful of Leva's aristocratic descent, refers to him as
a 'prince' and Gottikh as a 'count' (significantly, in the chapter entitled
'Masquerade' ('Маскарад')). Eventually Leva and Mitishat'ev leave
the institute, travel to the centre of town by tram, where Leva tries to
imitate the actions of Evgenii from Pushkin's epic poem *The Bronze
Horseman* and is pulled from on top of some marble lions by a
policeman. He runs away, and then he and Mitishat'ev have their 'duel'
back in the institute.

The above quotation is notable in another respect. The range of
subjects covered, and the almost breathless, machine-gun style in which
they are rattled off, is reminiscent of the mature style of another 'urban
prose' writer of the period, Iurii Trifonov. Trifonov too links literature
and morality, and also looks into the past for clues in order to interpret
and make sense of the present.[12] This reference to Trifonov is not
entirely fortuitous, for there is an episode that is almost an exact copy
of one that takes place in Trifonov's 1976 novella *The House on the
Embankment* (*Дом на набережной*).

In Trifonov's work, a postgraduate student at the Literary Institute in Moscow is called upon to defend publicly his supervisor, a respected professor, who is threatened with dismissal during the anti-cosmopolitan campaign of the late 1940s. Circumstances conspire to prevent him from doing so; furthermore, at a second public gathering he makes a speech attacking his supervisor, who is then dismissed. In Bitov's work, Leva is also a postgraduate student of literature and is called upon by various parties both to defend and attack a friend. He does neither, due to a combination of domestic circumstances, including his own illness. The friend is dismissed from the institute, and subsequently refuses to greet Leva in the street. During this episode Leva particularly senses the shadow of his grandfather near him, as if passing judgment on his pusillanimity. The remarkable similarity of both episodes is reinforced by their style of narration: in both cases they are told from the point of view of the protagonist, who tries to rationalize the experience and absolve himself of blame. Here, Leva pretends that this friend was not such a good friend after all. Once more we the reader get to see his fears and his reactions to events at first hand.

Trifonov's work was something of a *cause célèbre* when it appeared, and was subject to hostile attack by party-minded critics. Bitov's novel was completed in 1974, and therefore it is unlikely that he was influenced by Trifonov's novella. Nevertheless, it is striking that both Bitov and Trifonov emphasize the interconnectedness of life and the continuity of cultural history. Bitov's conscious reference to other literary works extends even to Pushkin himself. The motif of fatherhood is a strong one in the early part of the novel (we learn that the first book Leva read was Turgenev's *Fathers and Sons*), when his grandfather returns after thirty years and refuses to meet the son who had disowned him. Leva feels that his father cannot be his real father, and prefers to have as his father his uncle Dickens; indeed, as the author tells us directly, uncle Dickens may well be his real father:

And Father is again double when retribution begins, when he is crushed by his own treachery, when the image of Uncle Dickens expands and masks Father. Because, although the author may snicker at Lyova's youthful fantasy, he himself hasn't made a final decision that Uncle Dickens is not Lyova's father. Anything can happen . . . (p. 44)

(И еще раз двойной отец, когда наступает возмездие, когда он раздавлен собственным предательством, когда расширяется образ дяди Диккенса и заслоняет отца . . . Потому что хотя автор и посмеивается над Левой за юношескую игру воображения, однако и сам еще не решил окончательно, что дядя Диккенс ему не отец. Чего не бывает? . . .) (p. 45)

Such reflections on fatherhood, real and metaphorical, are reminiscent of Pushkin's novel *The Captain's Daughter* (*Капитанская дочка*). Here the issue is not so much on actual parentage but on statehood, national identity and the right to be the 'father' of the nation (the Russian Tsar is also called 'little father') set against the background of the Pugachev rising against Catherine the Great in the eighteenth century. One of the novel's epigraphs is explicit: 'So who is his father?' ('Да кто его отец?'), as the hero, Grinev, is forced to choose between the charismatic peasant leader Pugachev, representative of the crude, elemental and violent peasant mass, and his own father, who represents stability, order and tradition.

The author's deliberate intrusion into the text in the above quotation brings him to reflect further on the possibility of another family for Leva, and sure enough, he produces a possible 'variant'. Here we are introduced to Leva's wonderfully happy childhood and youth, where the family is a harmonious unit, the grandfather returns from exile with his wife and child, there is no bitterness and everyone is happy. But the author is not content with this family; the first one is more real, 'more honest'. Other 'variants' in the novel occur with reference to Leva's acquaintance with Al'bina: both times he was involved with Faina at the time, but in the first instance he met her at the flat of uncle Dickens, when she seemed to be his consort, while in the second instance, he met her at his funeral. There are also two versions of the occasion when Leva meets Mitishat'ev, Al'bina and Al'bina's husband. Thus within the novel's very structure the author 'thinks aloud' as he reflects on narrative strategies and possibilities.

The novel is not just about literary history, but also about the literary process, in other words, what it is like to be a writer in Russia in the late twentieth century. Certain materials written by the characters of the novel are incorporated into the text itself in the form of 'appendices' to each of the three sections. Thus, the first section ends with the literary legacy of uncle Dickens (whose real name is Dmitrii Ivanovich Iuvashev); this consists of various short novellas, all of which tell of his unhappiness and loneliness as well as his reflections on God. He was twenty-seven years old when he wrote them, and Leva is the same age when he reads them and copies them out. The second appendix quotes Leva's article, entitled 'Three "Prophets"' ('Три «Пророка»'), on Pushkin, Lermontov and Tiutchev. This article was actually published by Bitov under his own name in 1976 in the journal *Voprosy literatury* ('Questions of Literature'), another example of the merging of author and hero. Leva here attempts a comparative analysis of three poems, Pushkin's 'The Prophet' ('Пророк'), Lermontov's poem of the same name, and Tiutchev's 'Insanity' ('Безумие'). All three poems were written by their corresponding authors when each was twenty-seven years old, and Leva is now twenty-seven himself. Leva constructs an image of each poet from these poems: Pushkin reflects the world and is inspired and guided by God in his art, Lermontov feels self-pity and laments that God has abandoned him, and in a parody of the relationship between Mozart and Salieri, Tiutchev is jealous and resentful of Pushkin and wishes him dead. Leva sees Tiutchev as holding a metaphorical 'duel' with Pushkin, and one of his chapters is entitled 'Tiutchev as Pushkin's Killer' ('Тютчев как убийца Пушкина').

The third appendix ends with brief notes by Modest Platonovich on the meaning of words, and how meaning can be lost in time, resulting in 'dumbness'. Modest Platonovich has also suffered for his inner freedom, for it was his refusal to compromise his integrity that caused him to spend so many years in Siberia. In other words, each appendix concerns the literary legacy of the Odoevtsev family, the truth of the word and the possibility of the truth being overtaken by the lie. Ultimately, literature is about communication; the word contains the truth, which must be passed on from generation to generation.

As the novel draws to a close, so the narrative becomes increasingly self-referential. As mentioned already, the opening lines of the novel are repeated almost three hundred pages later; as Leva comes to, sentence structure and the meaning of words become turned in on themselves: 'he was coming to consciousness – consciousness was coming to him; he glances at the window – the window glances at him' (p. 315) ('он приходил в сознание, сознание приходило к нему'; 'он взглянул в окно, окно взглянуло на него', p. 313). Literary conventions become more and more meaningless and absurd; the author reveals that as the novel ends and the hero dies, so real life continues and the boundaries between real life and fiction become blurred. Indeed, life becomes a part of literature:

So, Lyova the man woke up. Lyova the literary hero perished. What comes next is Lyova's real existence, and the hero's beyond the grave. . . . Here we enter the zone of Lev Odoevtsev's life where he has ceased to be reason's creation. He has acquired reason himself and doesn't know what to apply it to; i.e., he has become almost as alive as you and I. And that is the highly fantastic working hypothesis of our further narrative – that our own life is the shady, beyond-the-grave life of literary heroes after the book is closed. (p. 317)

(Итак, Лева-человек – очнулся, Лева-литературный герой – погиб. Дальнейшее – есть реальное существование Левы и загробное – героя. (. . .) Вот мы и вступаем в полосу жизни Льва Одоевцева, когда он перестал быть созданием разума, а сам его приобрел и не знает, к чему приложить, то есть стал почти так живым, как мы с вами. И это весьма бредовая наша рабочая гипотеза для дальнейшего повествования, что наша жизнь – есть теневая, загробная жизнь литературных героев, когда закрыта книга.) (р. 316)

That is, the literary hero must die in order for the real person to live; thus does art influence life, and the writer acts as a bridge between culture and life. Indeed, the writer becomes the prime mover of human life.

The hero and the author merge, and the final pages of the narrative, where Leva travels round the city in the company of an American couple, are related as part of a dream, so that fiction, fantasy and reality all become one. In the appendix, Leva meets and talks with the author on his own writings, and those of his grandfather.

We should also point out that there are many scenes and episodes in the novel that are described by the author with great feeling and narrative power, and demonstrate Bitov's considerable abilities as a psychological novelist. For instance, the character of the meek and submissive Al'bina is vividly portrayed, and the scene when Leva parts with her is told with attention drawn to the emotions of both, as well as to seemingly insignificant but telling details, so that we get to sense her deep injury as well as Leva's growing self-disgust:

'Well, what is it,' Lyova said, exasperated. A single large drop fell on the leaf. Now again Lyova felt her *full* torment in him, heaving about in his alien soul, and he could not bear it . . . He narrowed his eyes and spoke. She was silent. Lyova could not bear the pause and talked for quite a while longer, coating the pill with an acknowledgment of her virtues such that Albina was finally frozen solid by his icy compliments. A little drop hung on her nose. 'But you're mine, *mine!*' she exclaimed desperately, and saw that he was looking at the tip of her nose, at the drop . . . She did not start dithering, did not get flustered, she wiped it off and said stonily, 'Well then, goodbye.' 'You have to understand–' Lyova began, and did not continue. 'Go.' Lyova felt a cold jab, as if from the other side of his heart, where he had never felt pain – as though his heart, like the moon, had a back side – and realized, almost with disappointment, that he had achieved his goal, it didn't *seem* over, it *was* over. (pp. 183–4)

(«Ну так что?», – сказал Лева, разозлившись. Большая одна капля упала на лист. Тут Лева опять ощутил всю ее муку в себе, мечущейся в его чуждой душе, и не вынес ее . . . Зажмурился – и сказал. Она молчала. Лева не вынес паузы и еще довольно долго говорил, обмазывая пилюлю таким признанием ее достоинств, что от этих ледяных комплиментов Альбина застыла окончательно, капелька повисла на ее носу . . . «Но ведь ты – мой, мой!» –

отчаянно воскликнула она и увидела, что смотрит он ей – на кончик носа, на каплю . . . Она не засуетилась, не смутилась, а смахнула ее и сказала каменно: «Ну что же, прощай». – «Ты пойми . . .» начал Лева и не продолжил. «Иди». Лева почувствовал какой-то холодный укол, будто с другой стороны сердца, с которой никогда не ощущал боли, будто его сердце, как Луна, имело обратную сторону, понял, почти с разочарованием, что достиг своей цели, что – не кажется, а – все.) (pp. 185–6)

Another example is when Bitov shows us Leva's growing jealousy, pain and irrational obsession, at a party when he sees Mitishat'ev and Faina together and becomes increasingly convinced (the more he drinks) that they are having an affair. Typically, the author never resolves this question. Another particularly masterful example is the dialogue between Mitishat'ev and Leva at the zoo, when they reel off all the names of classmates, whom Mitishat'ev asserts are all Jews – including, finally, Leva himself.

Conclusion

The title *Pushkin House* refers not only to the famous literary institute of that name in St Petersburg, where most of the action takes place, but also to the whole edifice of Russian literature whose foundations were laid by Pushkin. The novel thus serves as a fitting culmination to this study of the twentieth-century Russian novel, as it affirms this century's continuity with the preceding one and places the modern literary age (post-Stalin) within a definite historical and literary context.

There are many references to Russian writers and their works (those not discussed in detail in this study include Andrei Belyi, Iurii Tynianov, Ivan Bunin and Lidiia Ginzburg). The novel's self-conscious style constantly draws attention to its own status as a literary text, where the very notion of 'literature' is then questioned by its relation to the reality in which it is supposedly rooted. But it is not just the links of literature and life that are here under scrutiny: the bonds between people – lovers, family members, friends, colleagues – show the novel's preoccupation with moral and spiritual questions. The last forty or so pages of the novel take the form of Leva's own notes (thus offering a parody, given that Leva is commenting on his own novel and life, of the traditional academic edition). These notes, however, serve to provide a panorama of the literary life of Bitov/Odoevtsev's generation.

The notes relate the onset of the post-Stalin thaw, including the first republication of Dostoevskii (*Poor Folk*, in 1954), criticism of certain literary figures (not named, but recognizable by their initials and reputations as the feared literary assassins Vladimir Ermilov and Iakov

El'sberg) noted for their denunciations of fellow-writers in the later years of Stalin, the founding of the journal *Iunost'* ('Youth') in 1954 (actually a mistake: it was founded in 1955). We also learn that the fictional figure of Leva's grandfather is based on a combination of Iurii Dombrovskii and Mikhail Bakhtin, both writers of considerable bravery and integrity, and both of whom suffered persecution and imprisonment under Stalin.

There is some typically Nabokovian literary tomfoolery as well. Bitov-Odoevtsev asserts that Raskol'nikov in Dostoevskii's *Crime and Punishment* did not have it in him to kill the money-lender, but he certainly could have killed her meek sister Lizaveta. Also, he takes issue with the common notion that Dostoevskii demonstrated remarkable perspicacity in foretelling the course of twentieth-century Russian history in *The Possessed*; rather, these 'devils' were subsequently victorious in Russia exactly because Dostoevskii wrote about them. If it were not for Dostoevskii, these 'devils' would not have become famous, and no-one would have paid attention to them. In the last few pages of the notes Bitov/Odoevtsev becomes Bitov proper as he relates problems of censorship with regard to his works *The Wheel* (*Колесо*) and *Life in Windy Weather* (*Жизнь в ветреную погоду*).

Reference is also made to the author's conversation with the respected Leningrad literary scholar Lidiia Ginzburg on the juxtaposition of Lev Tolstoi and Marcel Proust and even on the nature of socialist realism from Maksim Gor'kii and Mikhail Sholokhov, and the indebtedness of such 'modern classics' as Konstantin Simonov and Solzhenitsyn to the works of Tolstoi and Gogol'. The latter topic especially demonstrates the close connection the author feels between nineteenth-century Russian literature and that of the modern age. The final image in the novel is that of the phoenix with reference to meaning. Like that fabulous bird, the word and Russian literature, like Leva the literary character, have died under Stalin but will nevertheless, like Leva the real person, rise again to resume life.

Moreover, the novel's heart is the great cultural and social rupture that occurred under Stalin, for Stalinism served to cut Russia off not only from mainstream European culture, but also from Russia's own cultural heritage. Thus three generations of a family are cut off from one another, friends and lovers tell lies to each other and, in the case of Faina's ring, all that glitters is literally not gold. The novel's celebration of nineteenth-century Russian literature is also a condemnation of the banality of the present, a parody of modern Russian society. The whole novel offers a parody of Soviet society where literature and life become blurred, as do the distinction between author and hero, past and present. The image of the duel becomes dominant, and can be extended from that between Leva and Mitishat'ev to include author and hero, and reader and writer. For, above all, *Pushkin House* challenges the reader to decode, analyse, interpret and make value judgments, to compare past and present.

Pushkin House joins a long list of works of twentieth-century Russian literature that constantly refers back to the literary heritage for inspiration and moral purpose. The novels of Nabokov are an obvious example, as is Belyi's *Petersburg* (*Петербург*), but we can mention in this respect even works published since Bitov's novel, such as those by the contemporary authors Evgenii Popov and Vladimir Sorokin.[13] The abiding impression is that Russian literature has to refer back to itself and its own lineage, bypassing the social and political conditions of the age. Identity in Russia is above all based on cultural traditions. The past, then, lives on through literature and the word. Such thoughts on the continuity of the literary process bring us back to the opening lines of this essay, perhaps a fitting way to complete this study of a novel which begins where it ends, and which ends where it begins.[14]

Notes

1. Andrei Bitov, *Pushkin House*, trans. Susan Brownsberger, London, 1990, p. 414; *Пушкинский дом, Роман*, Moscow, 1989, p. 399 (note that the word games inherent in the Russian are absent in the translation). All further references to the novel are taken from these editions, with relevant page numbers incorporated into the text.
2. Ellen Chances, *Andrei Bitov: The Ecology of Inspiration*, Cambridge, 1993, p. 202.
3. In his recent book, Deming Brown provides a succinct summary of the novel's subject-matter:

   The work is packed with overt and covert allusions to Russian literature (Dostoevsky, Tolstoy, Blok, Nabokov, etc.) and to a lesser extent to foreign literatures (Proust, Joyce, Hemingway, etc.). There are chatty little essays on cultural and moral topics, and on writing and writers in general. Bitov toys with his plot, offering hints and foreshadowings, repeating whole passages, commenting on his authorial difficulties, discussing alternative versions of episodes and developments, and inviting the reader to choose between them. The sum total of all this is a kind of literary compendium focusing on St. Petersburg and designed to make a statement, in historical perspective, about the condition of Russian culture in the 1960s.

See Deming Brown, *The Last Years of Soviet Russian Literature: Prose Fiction 1975–1991*, Cambridge, 1993, p. 51.

4. Richard Stites describes the external appearance of the *stiliagi*: 'broad-shouldered jacket, fat tie adorned with cactus or cowboys, narrow pants, and boxy shoes for the boys. The costuming, a "cool" personal style, terse speech forms, a special argot, and other symbols and codes were statements about differentness, toughness, and a vague foreignness'. He also quotes a definition of them by the satirical weekly *Krokodil* as 'rude and ignorant freaks who did weird dances and knew more about Viennese operetta than about Russian culture'. See Richard Stites, *Russian Popular Culture: Entertainment and Society since 1900*, Cambridge, 1992, pp. 124–5.

5. Brown, *The Last years of Soviet Russian Literature*, p. 46.

6. Ellen Chances tells us that a possible title for the novel was *The Lie* (*Ложь*). See Chances, *Andrei Bitov*, p. 209.

7. On the recurrence of the duel and the Bronze Horseman in the novel, see ibid., pp. 226–8.

8. Alice Stone Nakhimovsky comments: 'For all the complexity of form, however, the central problem of *Pushkin House* can be stated fairly simply: If it could be condensed into a single sentence it might be this: the disorientation of the new generation, cut off irretrievably from its cultural past' (Alice Stone Nakhimovsky, 'Looking Back at Paradise Lost: The Russian Nineteenth Century in Andrei Bitov's *Pushkin House*', *Russian Literature Triquarterly*, vol. 22, 1989, p. 196.

9. On the connections with *Bleak House*, and with Proust's *Swann in Love*, see Chances, *Andrei Bitov*, p. 226.

10. Ellen Chances notes the frequent use of circles and rings in the novel to emphasize the sense of completeness and inter-connectedness. Ibid., pp. 205–9.

11. Ellen Chances states unequivocally that 'Mitishat'ev wants to destroy Russian literature . . . . By throwing away Grigorovich's inkwell, Mitishat'ev is, symbolically, breaking the continuity of Russian literature.' Ibid., p. 235. Elsewhere the same critic quotes Bitov as saying in 1989 that 'Mitishatiev is a potential leader of a nationalist party, of Pamyat, for example' (Ellen Chances, '"In the Middle of the Contrast": Andrei Bitov and the Act of Writing in the Contemporary World', *World Literature Today*, vol. 67, no. 1, 1993, p. 66.) Alice Stone Nakhimovsky makes the point that Leva's name and patronymic link him to Prince Myshkin in Dostoevskii's *The Idiot*, and she sees Mitishat'ev as Rogozhin: 'the gentle prince and the rough, menacing commoner united in love and hatred both for each other and for a single woman' (Nakhimovsky, 'Looking Back

at Paradise Lost', p. 199).

12. For further discussion of Trifonov's exploration of the historical past, and his interweaving of past and present, see David Gillespie, *Iurii Trifonov: Unity through Time*, Cambridge, 1992.

13. See, for instance, Evgenii Popov, *The Soul of a Patriot, or Various Epistles to Ferfichkin*, trans. Robert Porter, London, 1994 (*Душа патриота, или различные послания Ферфичкину*), and Vladimir Sorokin, *Норма* ('The Norm'), Moscow, 1994. John Friedman also links Bitov's novel to Sasha Sokolov's avant-garde novel *School for Fools* (*Школа для дураков*), published abroad in 1977. See his comparative analysis, concentrating on the treatment of time and reality, entitled 'Reflections on the Text: The Distortion of Reality and Time in the Search for Truth in the Novels "Pushkin House" and "School for Fools"' ('Размышления над текстом: Искривление реальности и времени в поиске истины в романах «Пушкинский дом» и «Школа для дураков»', *22*, vol. 48, 1986, pp. 201–10.

14. Ellen Chances argues persuasively that the organizing principle of the book is 'the principle of organic chemistry', for this science studies 'connections, bonds of elements'. See Chances, *Andrei Bitov*, p. 245.

Select Bibliography

The purpose of this bibliography is to provide a guide for further reading on the novels discussed in this book. In the main, I have included titles available in English, although for some writers (Ostrovskii, Bulgakov and Bitov, for instance) some of the most relevant criticism is in Russian. These titles have also therefore been included.

General

Bethea, David, *The Shape of Apocalypse in Modern Russian Fiction*, Princeton, Princeton University Press, 1989.

Brown, Deming, *Soviet Russian Literature since Stalin*, Cambridge, Cambridge University Press, 1978.

Brown, Edward J. (ed.), *Major Soviet Writers: Essays in Criticism*, New York, Oxford University Press, 1973.

Brown, Edward J., *Russian Literature since the Revolution*, revised and enlarged edition, Cambridge, MA, Harvard University Press, 1982.

Clark, Katerina, *The Soviet Novel: History as Ritual*, Chicago, Chicago University Press, 1981 (reprinted, with a new afterword, 1985).

Cornwell, Neil, 'Through the Clouds of Soviet Literature', *The Crane Bag*, vol. 7, no. 1, 1983, pp. 17–31.

Freeborn, Richard, *The Russian Revolutionary Novel: Turgenev to Pasternak*, Cambridge, Cambridge University Press, 1982.

Garrard, John, *The Russian Novel from Pushkin to Pasternak*, New Haven, Yale University Press, 1983.

Hayward, Max, *Writers in Russia: 1917–1978*, London, Harvill, 1983.

Hingley, Ronald, *Russian Writers and Soviet Society, 1917–1978*, London, Wiedenfield and Nicolson, 1979.

Kasack, Wolfgang, *Dictionary of Russian Literature since 1917*, New York, Columbia University Press, 1988.

Maguire, Robert, *Red Virgin Soil: Soviet Literature in the 1920s*, Princeton, Princeton University Press, 1968.

Moser, Charles (ed.), *The Cambridge History of Russian Literature*, Cambridge, Cambridge University Press, 1989; revised and updated, 1992.

Muchnic, Helen, *From Gorky to Pasternak: Six Modern Russian Writers*, London, Methuen, 1963.

Slonim, Marc, *Soviet Russian Literature: Writers and Problems, 1917– 1977*, 2nd edn, New York, Oxford University Press, 1977.

Struve, Gleb, *Russian Literature under Lenin and Stalin*, New York, Routledge and Kegan Paul,1971.

Terras, Victor, *A History of Russian Literature*, New Haven, Yale University Press, 1992.

Evgenii Zamiatin

Barratt, Andrew, 'The First Entry of *We*: An Explication', in J. Andrew (ed.), *The Structural Analysis of Russian Narrative Fiction*, Keele, Keele University Press, no date, pp. 95–114.

Collins, C., *Evgenij Zamjatin: An Interpretative Study*, The Hague and Paris, Mouton, 1973.

Edwards, T. R. N., *Three Russian Writers and the Irrational: Zamyatin, Pil'nyak and Bulgakov*, Cambridge, Cambridge University Press, 1982.

Hersh, M. A., 'Zamyatin's "We": A Mathematical Model Society', *Rusistika*, vol. 8, 1993, pp. 19–26.

Hoisington, Sona S., and Imbery, Lynn, 'Zamjatin's Modernist Palette: Colors and their Function in *We*', *Slavic and East European Journal*, vol. 36, 1992, pp. 159–71.

Kern, Gary (ed.), *Zamyatin's "We": A Collection of Critical Essays*, Ann Arbor, Ardis, 1988.

Lanin, Boris, 'Images of Women in Russian Anti-utopian Literature', *Slavonic and East European Review*, vol. 71, 1993, pp. 646–55.

Myers, Alan, 'Evgenii Zamiatin in Newcastle', *Slavonic and East European Review*, vol. 68, 1990, pp. 91–9.

Myers, Alan, 'Zamiatin in Newcastle: The Green Wall and the Pink Ticket', *Slavonic and East European Review*, vol. 71, 1993, pp. 416– 27.

Richards, D. J., *Zamyatin: A Soviet Heretic*, London, Bowes and Bowes, 1962.

Russell, Robert, 'Literature and Revolution in Zamyatin's *My*', *Slavonic and East European Review*, vol. 51, 1973, pp. 36–46.

Shane, Alex M., *The Life and Works of Evgenij Zamjatin*, Berkeley and Los Angeles, University of California Press, 1968.

Isaak Babel'

Andrew, Joe, 'Babel's "My First Goose"', in J. Andrew (ed.), *The*

Structural Analysis of Russian Narrative Fiction, pp. 64–81.

Avins, Carol J., 'Kinship and Concealment in *Red Cavalry* and Babel's 1920s Diary', *Slavic Review*, vol. 53, no. 3, 1994, pp. 694–710.

Carden, Patricia, *The Art of Isaac Babel*, Ithaca, Cornell University Press, 1972.

Danow, David K., 'A Poetics of Inversion: The Non-Dialogic Aspect in Isaac Babel''s *Red Cavalry*', *Modern Language Review*, vol. 86, 1991, pp. 939–53.

Falen, J. E., *Isaac Babel, Russian Master of the Short Story*, Knoxville, University of Tennessee Press, 1974.

Ehre, Milton, *Isaac Babel*, Boston, Twayne, 1986.

Falchikov, Michael, 'Conflicts and Contrasts in Isaac Babel's *Konarmiya*', *Modern Language Review*, vol. 72, 1977, pp. 125–33.

Hallett, Richard, *Isaac Babel*, Letchworth, Bradda, 1972.

Luplow, Carol, *Isaac Babel's "Red Cavalry"*, Ann Arbor, Ardis, 1982.

Murphy, A. B., 'The Style of Isaac Babel', *Slavonic and East European Review*, vol. 44, 1966, pp. 361–80.

Sicher, Efraim, *Style and Structure in the Prose of Isaak Babel'*, Columbus, Slavica, 1985.

Scheglov, Yuri K., 'Some Themes and Archetypes in Babel's *Red Cavalry*', *Slavic Review*, vol. 53, no. 3, 1994, pp. 653–70.

Schreurs, M., *Procedures of Montage in Isaak Babel's 'Red Cavalry'*, Amsterdam, Rodopi, 1989.

Sinyavsky, Andrey, 'Isaac Babel', in E. J. Brown (ed.), *Major Soviet Writers*, pp. 301–9.

Trilling, Lionel, 'Introduction', as appendix to Isaac Babel, *Collected Stories*, trans. David McDuff, Harmondsworth, Penguin Books, 1994, pp. 339–64.

Iurii Olesha

Barratt, Andrew, *Yurii Olesha's "Envy"*, Birmingham, Birmingham Slavonic Monographs, 1981.

Beaujour, Elizabeth Klosty, *The Invisible Land: A Study of the Artistic Imagination of Iurii Olesha*, New York, Columbia University Press, 1970.

Belinkov, Arkadii, *Сдача и гибель советского интеллигента. Юрий Олеша*, Madrid, publisher not indicated, 1976.

Cornwell, Neil, 'Olesha's "Envy"', in J. Andrew (ed.), *The Structural Analysis of Russian Narrative Fiction*, pp. 115–36.

Ehre, Milton, 'Olesha's *Zavist'*: Utopia and Dystopia', *Slavic Review*, vol. 50, 1991, pp. 601–11.

Harkins, William E., 'The Theme of Sterility in Olesha's *Envy*', in

Edward J. Brown (ed.), *Major Soviet Writers*, pp. 280–94.

Nilsson, Nils Åke, 'Through the Wrong End of Binoculars: An Introduction to Jurij Olesha', in Edward J. Brown (ed.), *Major Soviet Writers*, pp. 254–79.

Peppard, Victor, *The Poetics of Yury Olesha*, Gainesville, Florida University Press, 1989.

Piper, D. G. B., 'Iurii Olesha: "Zavist'"': An Interpretation', *Slavonic and East European Review*, vol. 48, 1970, pp. 27–43.

Nikolai Ostrovskii

Anninskii, Lev, *«Как закалялась сталь» Николая Островского*, 3rd corrected edn, Moscow, Khudozhestvennaia literatura, 1988.

Günther, Hans, 'Education and Conversion: The Road to the New Man in the Totalitarian *Bildungsroman*', in H. Günther (ed.), *The Culture of the Stalin Period*, Basingstoke, Macmillan, 1990, pp. 193–209.

Mathewson, Rufus, *The Positive Hero in Russian Literature*, 2nd edn, Stanford, Stanford University Press, pp. 247–53.

Ostrovskaia, R., *Николай Островский*, Moscow, Molodaia gvardiia, 1984.

Tregub, S., *Жизнь и творчество Николая Островского*, 2nd edn, Moscow, Khudozhestvennaia literatura, 1975.

Tregub, S., *Николай Островский: Критико-биографический очерк*, Moscow, Sovetskii pisatel', 1954.

Vengrov, N., *Николай Островский*, Moscow, Izdatel'stvo Akademii Nauk, 1952.

Mikhail Bulgakov

Barratt, Andrew, *Between Two Worlds: A Critical Introduction to 'The Master and Margarita'*, Oxford, Oxford University Press, 1987.

Chudakova, Marietta, *Жизнеописание Михаила Булгакова*, Moscow, Kniga, 1988.

Curtis, J. A. E., *Bulgakov's Last Decade: The Writer as Hero*, Cambridge, Cambridge University Press, 1987.

Curtis, J. A. E., *Manuscripts Don't Burn. Mikhail Bulgakov: A Life in Letters and Diaries*, London, Bloomsbury, 1991.

Ericson, Edward E., Jr., *The Apocalyptic Vision of Mikhail Bulgakov's 'The Master and Margarita'*, Lewiston-Queenston-Lampeter, Edwin Mellon Press, 1991.

Gasparov, B. M., 'Из наблюдений над мотивной структурой романа М. А. Булгакова «Мастер и Маргарита»,' *Slavica Hierosolymitana*, vol. 3, 1978, pp. 198–251.

Select Bibliography

Ianovskaia, Lidiia, *Творческий путь Михаила Булгакова*, Moscow, Sovetskii pisatel', 1983.

Krugovoy, George, *The Gnostic Novel of Mikhail Bulgakov. Sources and Exegesis*, Lanham, University Press of America, 1991.

Losev, V., '«Рукописи не горят»', in M. Bulgakov, *Великий канцлер: Черновые редакции романа «Мастер и Маргарита»*, Moscow, Novosti, 1992, pp. 3–22.

Milne, Lesley, *Mikhail Bulgakov: A Critical Biography*, Cambridge, Cambridge University Press, 1990.

Pittman, Riitta, *The Writer's Divided Self in Bulgakov's "The Master and Margarita"*, London, Macmillan, 1991.

Proffer, Ellendea, *Bulgakov: Life and Work*, Ann Arbor, Ardis, 1984.

Stenbock-Fermor, E., 'Bulgakov's *The Master and Margarita* and Goethe's *Faust*', *Slavic and East European Journal*, vol. 13, no. 3, 1969, pp. 309–25.

Boris Pasternak

Barnes, Christopher, *Boris Pasternak: A Literary Biography. Volume I: 1890–1928*, Cambridge, Cambridge University Press, 1989.

Cornwell, Neil, *Pasternak's Novel: Perspectives on 'Doctor Zhivago'*, Keele, University of Keele Press, 1986.

Erlich, Victor (ed.), *Pasternak: A Collection of Critical Essays*, Englewood Cliffs, NJ, Prentice-Hall, 1978.

Fleishman, Lazar (ed.), *Boris Pasternak and His Times*, Berkeley, Berkeley Slavic Specialties, 1989.

Fleishman, Lazar, *Boris Pasternak: The Poet and His Politics*, Cambridge, MA, Harvard University Press, 1991.

Gifford, Henry, *Pasternak: A Critical Study*, Cambridge, Cambridge University Press, 1977.

Gladkov, Alexander, *Meetings with Pasternak: A Memoir*, London, Collins and Harvill, 1977.

Hughes, Olga R., *The Poetic World of Boris Pasternak*, Princeton, Princeton University Press, 1974.

Ivinskaya, Olga, *A Captive of Time: My Years with Pasternak*, London, Collins Harvill, 1978.

Levi, Peter, *Boris Pasternak: A Biography*, London, Hutchinson, 1991.

Livingstone, Angela, *Pasternak: Doctor Zhivago*, Cambridge, Cambridge University Press, 1989.

Loseff, Lev (ed.), *Boris Pasternak, 1890–1990*, Northfield, VA, Norwich University Press, 1991.

Pasternak, Evgenii, *Boris Pasternak: The Tragic Years, 1930–1960*, London, Collins and Harvill, 1990.

Select Bibliography

Alexander Solzhenitsyn

Brown, Deming, '*Cancer Ward* and *The First Circle*', *Slavic Review*, vol. 28, no. 2, 1969, pp. 304–13.

Brown, Edward J., 'Solzhenitsyn's Cast of Characters', in E. J. Brown (ed.), *Major Soviet Writers*, pp. 351–66.

Burgin, Diana Lewis, 'The Fate of Modern Man: An Examination of Ideas of Fate, Justice and Happiness in Solzhenitsyn's *Cancer Ward*', *Soviet Studies*, vol. 26, 1974, pp. 260–71.

Dunlop, J. *et al.* (eds), *Aleksandr Solzhenitsyn: Critical Essays and Documentary Materials*, New York, Macmillan, 1975.

Feuer, Kathryn (ed.), *Solzhenitsyn: A Collection of Critical Essays*, Englewood Cliffs, NJ, Prentice-Hall, 1976.

Kern, Gary, 'The Case of Kostoglotov', *Russian Literature Triquarterly*, vol. 11, 1975, pp. 407–34.

Koehler, Ludmila, 'Eternal Themes in Solzhenitsyn's "The Cancer Ward"', *The Russian Review*, vol. 26, 1967, pp. 53–65.

Labedz, L. (ed.), *Solzhenitsyn: A Documentary Record*, Harmondsworth, Penguin, 1970.

Lukacs, Georg, *Solzhenitsyn*, London, Merlin Press, 1969.

Moody, Christopher, *Solzhenitsyn*, Edinburgh, Oliver and Boyd, 1973.

Medvedev, Zhores, *Ten Years After Ivan Denisovich*, Basingstoke, Macmillan, 1973.

Pontuso, James F., *Solzhenitsyn's Political Thought*, Charlottesville, Virginia University Press, 1990.

Scammell, Michael, *Solzhenitsyn: A Biography*, London, Hutchinson, 1985.

Whitehorn, Alan J., 'What Men Live By: An Analysis of Solzhenitsyn's Writings', *Canadian Slavonic Papers*, vol. 13, no. 2, 1971, pp. 235–41.

Andrei Bitov

Brown, Deming, *The Last Years of Soviet Literature: Prose Fiction 1975–1991*, Cambridge, Cambridge University Press, 1993, pp. 45–53.

Chances, Ellen, *Andrei Bitov: The Ecology of Inspiration*, Cambridge, Cambridge University Press, 1993.

Chances, Ellen, '"In the Middle of the Contrast": Andrei Bitov and the Act of Writing in the Contemporary World', *World Literature Today*, vol. 67, no. 1, 1993, pp. 65–8.

Friedman, John, 'Размышления над текстом: Искривление реальности и времени в поиске истины в романах

«Пушкинский дом» и «Школа для дураков», *22*, vol. 48, 1986, pp. 201–10.

Mondry, Henrietta, '*Literaturnost'* as a Key to Andrey Bitov's *Pushkin House*', in H. Mondry (ed.), *The Waking Sphinx: South African Essays on Russian Culture*, Johannesburg, University of Witwatersrand Library, 1989, pp. 3–19.

Nakhimovsky, Alice Stone, 'Looking Back at Paradise Lost: The Russian Nineteenth Century in Andrei Bitov's *Pushkin House*', *Russian Literature Triquarterly*, vol. 22, 1989, pp. 195–204.

Index

Akhmatova, Anna 103
Aksenov, Vasilii 153
Aleshkovskii, Iuz 153
Anninskii, Lev 76, 79

Babaevskii, Semen 138, 140
Babel', Isaak 2, *24–42*, 43, 45, 104
Bacon, Francis 147
Bagritskii, Eduard 43
Bakhtin, Mikhail 167
Barratt, Andrew 9, 21, 55, 58, 59, 61, 82, 98, 99, 100, 101
Beaujour, Elizabeth 46, 60, 61
Belinskii, Vissarion 3, 5, 77
Belyi, Andrei 166, 167
Berberova, Nina 158
Beria, Lavrentii 135, 144
Bitov, Andrei 1, 4, *152–70*
Blok, Alexander 116, 168
Boratynskii, Evgenii 156
Brezhnev, Leonid 81, 132, 153
Brown, Deming 150, 154, 168, 169
Brown, Edward J. 5, 6, 150
Budennyi, Semen 24, 25, 26, 68
Bulgakov, Mikhail 3, 4, 43, 58, *81–101*, 104, 144–5
Bunin, Ivan 166
Burgin, Diana Lewis 148

Capek, Karel 58
Cervantes, Miguel de 58, 87
Chakovskii, Alexander 138
Chances, Ellen 168, 169, 170
Chekhov, Anton 82, 156
Chernyshevskii, Nikolai 3, 6, 77, 152, 156, 158
Christianity 3, 4, 18, 28, 30–32, 34, 51, 82, 83–84, 89, 91–92, 95, 112–14, 128–9, 131
Chudakova, Marietta 82
Chukovskii, Kornei 132
Clark, Katerina 63–4, 67, 78, 79
Cornwell, Neil 3, 5, 61
Curtis, Julie 98, 99, 100, 101

Daniel', Iulii 132, 133

Dickens, Charles 156
Dobroliubov, Nikolai 77
Dombrovskii, Iurii 167
Dostoevskii, Fedor 9, 11, 13, 43, 58, 88, 126, 156, 160, 166, 167, 168, 169–70
Dumas, Alexander 156

Ehre, Milton 24, 39, 40, 41, 42
El'sberg, Iakov 166–67
Ermilov, Vladimir 166
Esenin, Sergei 100
Evtushenko, Evgenii 140, 144

Freeborn, Richard 130

Garibaldi, Guiseppe 67
Gasparov, Boris 99
Gifford, Henry 131
Ginzburg, Natal'ia 166, 167
Goethe, Johann Wolfgang von 87, 88–9, 103
Gogol', Nikolai 87, 90, 167
Gor'kii, Maksim 3, 6, 24, 25, 138, 141, 167
Gorbachev, Mikhail 2, 7, 59, 82, 133, 152, 153
Grossman, Vasilii 1
Gumilev, Lev 103
Günther, Hans 76, 79
Gus', Mikhail 81

Harkins, William 60, 61
Hemingway, Ernest 168
Herzen, Alexander 156
Huxley, Aldous 9

Ianovskaia, Lidiia 82, 89, 98, 100
Il'f, Il'ia 43, 44
Ivanov, Georgii 156
Ivinskaia, Ol'ga 103

Joyce, James 156, 168
Judaism, 28–30, 34, 36

Kafka, Franz 156
Kataev, Valentin 43, 66

Index

Kern, Gary 149, 151
Kholendro, Dmitrii 138
Khrushchev, Nikita 81, 103, 132
Kochetov, Vsevolod 138
Kol'tsov, M. 64

Lakshin, Vladimir 81
Lanin, Boris 15, 22
Lenin, Vladimir 3, 29, 33, 38, 69, 73, 141, 156
Lermontov, Mikhail 155, 163–4
Livingstone, Angela 104, 123, 124, 129, 130, 131
London, Jack 7
Lunacharskii, Anatolii 101
Lysenko, Trofim 135

MacLauren, Colin 14, 22
Maiakovskii, Vladimir 100
Malenkov, Georgii 144
Medvedev, Zhores 148
Milne, Lesley 96, 100
Moody, Christopher 150

Nabokov, Vladimir 153, 157–8, 167, 168
Nakhimovsky, Alice Stone 169
Nekrasov, Nikolai 77
Nilsson, Nils Åke 55, 61

Obolenskii, Dimitrii 131
Odoevtseva, Irina 156
Olesha, Iurii 2, 43–61, 145
Ordzhonikidze, Grigorii 145
Orwell, George 9
Ostrovskii, Nikolai 1, 3, 62–80, 138

Pasternak, Boris 1, 4, 102–31, 133, 159
Pasternak, Evgenii 129, 130
Pasternak, Leonid 103
Petliura, Semen 68, 70, 73
Petrov, Evgenii 43
Pil'niak, Boris 8
Piper, D. G. B. 58, 61
Pittman, Riitta 99, 100, 101
Platonov, Andrei 1, 104
Pomerantsev, Vladimir 144
Popov, Evgenii 153, 167, 170
Pribludnyi, Ivan 100
Proust, Marcel 156, 167, 168
Pushkin, Alexander 13, 68, 87, 138, 146, 147, 154, 155–6, 158, 160, 161, 162–4

RAPP (Russian Association of Proletarian Writers) 8, 63, 90
Romain, Rolland 7

Serafimovich, Alexander 25
Shakespeare, William 13, 51, 58, 103, 118
Shentalinskii, Vitalii 25, 40
Sholokhov, Mikhail 25, 167
Simonov, Konstantin 138, 167
Siniavskii, Andrei 132, 133
Skorino, Liudmila 81
Skriabin, Alexander 14
Socialist realism 3, 4, 63–4, 138
Sokolov, Sasha 170
Sologub, Fedor 156
Solzhenitsyn, Alexander 4, 5, 102, 132–51, 167
Sorokin, Vladimir 167, 170
Stalin, Iosif, 3, 4, 6, 8, 23, 26, 43, 63, 64, 72, 77, 78, 82, 98, 103, 111, 115–16, 117, 132, 133, 135, 137, 146, 147, 148, 167
Stanislavskii, Konstantin 82
Stites, Richard 169

Taylor, Brook 22
Taylor, F. W. 14, 22
Tchaikovskii, Petr 144
Tiutchev, Fedor, 163–4
Tolstoi, Lev 134, 138, 156, 159, 167, 168
Trifonov, Iurii 92, 161–2, 170
Trotskii, Lev 25, 73
Turgenev, Ivan 155–6, 162
Tvardovskii, Alexander 81
Tynianov, Iurii 166

Vengrov, N. 77, 80
Vinogradov, Igor' 81
Vladimov, Georgii 145
Voinych, L. 72
Vrangel', Baron Petr Nikolaevich 69
Vysotskii, Vladimir 153

Wells, H. G. 7, 58
Whitehorn, Alan J. 148–9

Zamiatin, Evgenii 1, 2, 3, 7–23, 45, 102, 104
Zhdanov, Andrei 3, 6, 63